SEX, ...

44
CHAPTERS
ABOUT
4
MEN

Also by BB Easton

The Sex/Life Novels

Darkly funny. Deeply emotional. Shockingly sexy.

Skin (Knight's backstory, Book 1)

Speed (Harley's backstory, Book 2)

Star (Hans's backstory, Book 3)

Suit (Ken's backstory, Book 4)

SEX/LIFE:
44 CHAPTERS ABOUT 4 MEN

BB EASTON

FOREVER

NEW YORK   BOSTON

Copyright © 2016 by BB Easton
Excerpt from *Skin* copyright © 2016 by BB Easton

Cover design by Daniela Medina.
Cover copyright © 2021 by Hachette Book Group, Inc.

Forever
Hachette Book Group
1290 Avenue of the Americas, New York, NY 10104
read-forever.com
twitter.com/readforeverpub

Originally published as *44 Chapters About 4 Men* by BB Easton in 2016

First trade paperback edition: April 2020
Reissued as *Sex/Life: 44 Chapters About 4 Men*: June 2021

Forever is an imprint of Grand Central Publishing. The Forever name and logo are trademarks of Hachette Book Group, Inc.

The publisher is not responsible for websites (or their content) that are not owned by the publisher.

The Hachette Speakers Bureau provides a wide range of authors for speaking events. To find out more, go to www.hachettespeakersbureau.com or call (866) 376-6591.

LCCN: 2019957169

ISBN: 978-1-5387-1833-9 (trade paperback)

Lyrics to "You Never Even Called Me by My Name" used with permission from Al Bunetta d/b/a Jurisdad Music o/b/o itself and Turnpike Tom Music.

Printed in the United States of America

LSC-C

Printing 1, 2021

I was going to dedicate this book to my husband,
but seeing as how he doesn't know and must never,
ever find out that it exists, I decided to dedicate it to you,
my dear sweet reader, instead.

CONTENTS

CONTENTS

AUTHOR'S NOTE

Sex/Life: 44 Chapters About 4 Men is based on true events that have been embellished, approximated, and exaggerated for the sake of humor and/or due to the author's tendency to write while drunk and deprived of sleep. All names, places, and identifying characteristics have been altered to protect the identities of everyone involved. Should you decipher the true identity of Ms. Easton or any other character in this book, the author asks that you kindly allow her to fulfill a short list of demands in exchange for your silence.

Due to excessive profanity, vulgarity, and graphic sexual content, this book is not intended for—and should probably be completely hidden from—anyone under the age of eighteen.

INTRODUCTION

That's right, folks. If you get nothing else out of this experience at least you can tell all your friends that somebody dedicated a book to you.

And a whole memoir, at that. Not just some bullshit novella. No, sir.

It's the least I could do. After all, you are the only reason I decided to publish this embarrassingly personal pile of journal entries, emails, and smut in the first place. It's a terrible decision (in a long line of terrible decisions that you will soon read all about), but I'm doing it for *you*.

You see, I'm a school psychologist, so behavior modification is kind of my thing. Want to get your kid to stop acting like an asshole? I'm your girl. Want to figure out if little Johnny has an autism spectrum disorder or is just really, really into *Minecraft*? Let me at him. But want to know how to get your cold, distant, communication-averse partner to show you more affection? *Um...*

Fuck if I knew. In 2013 my marriage felt more like ottoman and owner than man and wife, and it was only getting worse. Until the day that changed everything—the day Kenneth Easton started reading my journal.

From there I stumbled upon a breakthrough psychological

technique so simple, so stupid, so perfect, that it transformed my introverted, number-crunching husband into a smoldering sex-panther over the course of a few months. I was so excited that I gathered up all my notes and lashed them together under the cover of night. I wanted to rain copies of this Frankenbook down, from sea to shining sea, on every poor sap slogging it out in a monotonous, long-term relationship. "There is hope!" I would cackle into the darkness as I flung copies from my stolen crop duster. "You don't have to settle for boring bullshit!"

But, rather than learn to pilot a single-engine aircraft to share my little discovery, I decided to do the next best thing. I'm going to publish it.

Sure, I could get fired, served with divorce papers, and/or assigned to mandatory parenting classes by the Department of Family and Child Services (which will be pretty hard to attend once my car gets repossessed) if anyone I know reads this thing, but my motto has always been, "Consequences shmonsequences." (Which explains most of the events in this book.)

Hopefully something you read here will help you light a fire under your own comatose partner. Hopefully you'll get a much needed break from your own life to laugh at mine for a while. But all that failing, at least you can tell your friends that BB Easton dedicated her memoir to you... which will be cool for approximately one-point-five seconds until your friends ask, "BB who?"

SEX/LIFE:
44
CHAPTERS
ABOUT
4
MEN

GLOSSARY

(*Webster's*, give me a call if you see anything you like.)

Abraised (adj.): a word that should exist but doesn't; the raw, painful quality of skin after an abrasion.

Badassery (noun): the behavior of one who is a badass—intimidating, rebellious, defiant.

Bonerversary (noun): the yearly recurrence of the date that one's male partner, who usually lies motionless for the duration of all sexual activities like a disinterested invertebrate, made love to him or her. Commemoration might or might not involve a moment of silence.

Cush (adj.): abbreviated form of *cushy*; easy and profitable.

Deceaston (adj.): combination of the words *deceased* and *in*. Example: "BB Easton is gonna make you deceaston about thirty seconds if you don't get the fuck up off her boyfriend."

Dungeony (adj.): being, resembling, or suggestive of a dungeon but not in a sexy BDSM way.

Emorection (noun): a penis that has become erect due to an emotional rather than a physical or visual stimulus.

Fanfuckingtastic (adj.): the way the words *fucking fantastic* sound when uttered by someone who's had an over-poured glass of pinot grigio.

Favoritest (adj.): a dumb way to say most favorite.

Floaty (adj.): 1. buoyant, elevated, airy. 2. carefree, content, relaxed.

Frankenbook (noun): a random pile of journal entries, emails, photos, dirty poems, and pornographic short stories that some asshole threw together and tried to pass off as a book.

Frenemies (noun): Friends? Enemies? Depends on the day and the amount of liquor involved.

Gargamelian (adj.): of or pertaining to Gargamel, villain and nemesis of the Smurfs.

Husboner (noun): a married man who *should* be sick and tired of his wife's stretched out, floppy old vagina but instead behaves like an insatiable sex machine who just snorted an eight ball of coke.

Husbot (noun): a married man who behaves more like a robot than a human being. This cyborg is typically obedient, task-oriented, introverted, rigid in his adherence to rules and routines, sexually inhibited, and averse to fun.

Judgy (adj.): 1. tending to make moral judgments based on one's own personal beliefs and experiences. 2. most females native to the southeastern United States.

Ladyfriend (noun): a female friend whom you do not wish to refer to as your girlfriend because you are culturally sensitive enough to know that African American women hate it when Caucasian women call them *girlfriend*.

Lickable/Flickable (adj.): self-explanatory.

Manfriend (noun): a male lover who is both of adult age and considerably older than his beau, causing the term *boyfriend* to seem silly and inappropriate, much like the relationship itself.

Meanius (noun): 1. a monster-genius hybrid. 2. a mean genius. 3. Insert picture of Dr. Sara Snow here.

Sausagefest (noun): a social gathering consisting primarily of people with penises.

Shivved (verb): to stab or be stabbed with a makeshift blade, referred to in prison as a shiv.

Skeezy (adj.): a sleazy person with less than honorable intentions.

Snarf (verb and proper noun): 1. to swallow or gobble up ravenously and with zero respect for table manners. 2. the name of Lion-O's slightly annoying catlike pet on *ThunderCats*.

Stabby (adj.): 1. full of sharp points or stabbing sensations. 2. a word coined by and stolen from comedic goddess Jenny Lawson.

Stalkee (noun): the person with whom a stalker is obsessed. *Duh.*

Tuberculosed (adj.): the state of being afflicted with tuberculosis.

Underworldly (adj.): of or pertaining to hell.

Unshitty (adj.): not shitty; not necessarily nice but not shitty either.

Vagrantism (noun): 1. the state or condition of being a vagrant. 2. one who wanders about idly without a permanent home or employment yet manages to afford leather pants and partially completed tattoos.

Vandalous (adj.): of or pertaining to vandalism; basically, just a way better, sexier version of the word *vandalic*.

Vulneraboner (noun): see *Emorection*.

1

The Husbot

BB's Secret Journal

August 16

Dear Journal,

This motherfucker is killing me.

Fresh out of the shower. He's so close I can smell the Irish Spring on his skin. His hair's all damp and sexy, and his beard scruff is at that perfect length—just long enough to be soft to the touch, but not so long that it hides his perfect chiseled features. And the way his undershirt clings to his biceps and stretches across the hard planes of his chest... I could look at him all night. Actually, I have been—through the corner of my eye. But that's not enough.

I want to touch him.

In the half hour since he plopped down next to me and flipped on the Braves game I've thought of a thousand and one ways to reach over and caress this man. I could lace my fingers through his, or run my knuckles along his rough, square jaw. Maybe I could be playful and walk my mint-green nails up his sculpted abs, then, once I have his attention, I could straddle his damp, clean, hard body and thrust those same fingertips into his wet hair.

But I don't do shit, because I know all it will get me is a sideways glance and a shift in the opposite direction.

My husband is a rock. Not as in, *He's so strong and supportive. I don't know what I'd do without him.* But more like, *He's so fucking cold I wonder if he still has a pulse.* Ken has never even held my hand, Journal. Not on purpose, anyway. He has had his hand held by me, while unconscious, but whenever I've tried that move during waking hours, Ken has politely endured the discomfort of human contact for…oh, say, five and a half seconds before smoothly removing his soft, limp flesh from my grasp.

Sex is pretty much the same story. Ever the gentleman, Ken will lie on his back and allow me to have my way with him while he quietly engages in minimal and obligatory petting. (Even when I try to be fun and reenact the ice cream scene from *Fifty Shades Darker.* In his defense, I do have to play the part of Christian because Ken *obviously* doesn't know his lines. And I admit, the white noise of a baby monitor isn't exactly Al Green. And for some reason we never seem to have vanilla ice cream, like in the book. We only have Cherry Garcia, which is pretty awkward to lick off, what with all the chewing required. But still. A *little* participation would be appreciated.)

Regardless of the level of theatrics involved, afterward I always kiss and cuddle Ken's lean, beautiful body, trying to squeeze a single degree of warmth from the man-shaped boulder that is my husband. All the while, I can almost hear him counting to himself—*one one thousand, two one thousand, three one thousand*—before he taps me on the ass. My cue to get the fuck off of him.

At least, that's how it seems.

Ken's problem isn't his coldness—his complete lack of need, want, or capacity for intimacy. Those attributes actually keep our marriage quite stable and drama-free. That, and the fact that the man never does *anything* wrong.

Kenneth Easton is a lawn-mowing, bill-paying, law-abiding, defensive-driving, trash-toting *husbot*—a cyborg built specifically to withstand seventy to eighty years of gale-force matrimony. I've *never* caught him looking at another woman. Hell, I've never even caught him in a lie.

No, the problem with Ken is that he's married to *me*.

Journal, before meeting Ken, I'd been contorted into at least seventy-three percent of the positions in the Kama Sutra. I'd shaved most of my head and had all my lady bits pierced before I was old enough to see an R-rated movie. I'd spent my free time being handcuffed to things by boys with more combined tattoos than a Guns N' Roses reunion concert. Ken simply can't compete.

So, why, you might be wondering, did a slutty little punk like me go and marry someone so straight-laced?

It was because of *them*. Because of the way my adrenaline spikes and my pupils dilate in a fight-or-flight-or-fuck response every time I smell the sickly sweet musk of Calvin Klein's Obsession for Men. Because of the way a pierced bottom lip makes me want to take up smoking again. Because of the way a full sleeve of tattoos makes me want to hitch a ride on a tour bus and leave everything I worked so hard to achieve in a gutter at the side of the road. Because my nerves were fucking shot by the time I met Ken, my heart was riding in on fumes, and the stability and security and sanity he offered was a soothing balm to my spent scorched soul.

Those inked-up men-children from my past might have been ferocious lovers, but they couldn't keep their dicks in their pants, their asses out of jail, or a positive balance in their bank accounts to save their lives. Ken, on the other hand, was just so...safe. Responsible. Easy. He wore Nikes and Gap T-shirts. He owned his own home. He *jogged*. His criminal record was as ink-free as his freckled skin. And, to top it all off, he had a degree in...wait for it...*accounting*.

I might have overcorrected a bit.

Don't get me wrong. I love the shit out of Kenneth Easton. He is my best friend, the father of my children, and we are actually ridiculously happy together. Or, at least, I'm happy. I am. Really. You can be bored to tears and happy at the same time, right? They call those happy tears. Happy, bored, oh-so-bored tears. Ken is pretty anhedonic and deadpan, so it's hard to tell how he's feeling. I choose to think of him as happy, too. But let's be honest. Ken may not really have feelings.

What he does have is a Captain America–style square jaw with a subtle cleft and a permanent five o'clock shadow. And enviably high cheekbones. And aqua eyes hooded with espresso-colored lashes, and sandy-brown hair that is just long enough on top to do this cute little flip thing in front. His physique is lean and muscular. His sense of humor is dry. He is brilliant, self-deprecating, and tolerant of my bullshit.

The man is at least ninety percent perfect for me, but lately, all I can think about is the less-than-or-equal-to ten percent that's missing: passion and body art. Two things I need to mourn and move on from in order to protect my lovely, monotonous marriage.

But I can't.

Tattooed bad boys are like a drug I can't quit. I devour anti-hero romance novels like they're an essential food group. My iPhone runneth over with the songs of a thousand breathy, angsty, tattooed alt-rockers, ready to fill my head at the press of a button whenever I need to escape. My DVR is brimming with mysterious vampires, renegade bikers, hedonistic rock stars, and zombie apocalypse survivors—alpha males into whose ink-covered arms I can run whenever things around here get a little too...domestic.

And do you know what I realized during my escapes to these imaginary dystopian societies and fictional underground fight rings? I *know* these men. I dated these men—the super intense skinhead turned US Marine turned motorcycle club outlaw, the ex-convict/underground hot-rod racer with the devil-may-care attitude, the sensitive guyliner-sporting heavy metal bassist...

I had them *all*, Journal. How did I not see the parallels between my fantasy men and my ex-boyfriends before? And I call myself a psychologist!

In fact, Knight, my high school boyfriend, is probably the reason I became a psychologist in the first place. Fucking psycho. I'll tell you about him tomorrow. Ken's going to bed, which means I only have about a five-minute window to get in there and pounce on him before the History Channel lulls him to sleep. Wish me luck!

2

Skeletor

BB's Secret Journal

August 17

Knight, Knight, Knight. Where do I even begin, Journal? Being Knight's girlfriend was a lot like being a kidnapping victim with Stockholm syndrome. I had no say in the matter—Knight decided I was *his*, and nobody said no to Knight. But over time, my fear of him morphed into friendship, and I actually grew to love my captor, psychopathic tendencies and all.

Knight was a skinhead. Correction: Knight was *the* skinhead— the only one in our sprawling suburban Atlanta tri-county area, to be exact. He was so incredibly angry that none of the other angry-white-male subculture groups at Peach State High School would do. The jocks were a little too gregarious. The punks, although sufficiently violent and vandalous, had a bit too much fun. The goth kids were just pussies. No, Knight's rage was so consuming that he had to choose the one subgroup whose image screamed, *I will fucking curb-stomp you and then rip off your arm and beat you with it if you so much as breathe the same air as me.*

Knight was so successful in his mission to intimidate that he remained a subgroup of one throughout high school.

I think his fury originated at birth when his dumbass disappointment of a mother named him Ronald McKnight. It was 1981, so knowing Candi, she was probably trying to impress the married stockbroker who had knocked her up by naming their lovechild after the most famous Republican she could think of. I guess—after years of being treated like a punching bag by Candi's revolving door of abusive, alcoholic, probably married boyfriends; being treated like a burden by a woman who preferred the company of douche bags to her own son; and having to endure Ronald McDonald jokes every time he left the house—somewhere along the way, Ronald became Knight, and Knight became a holy fucking terror.

Knight had the boyish good looks and perma-scowl of Eminem—fair skin, a quarter-inch of buzzed platinum-blond hair, and practically clear eyebrows and eyelashes. Knight's ghostly colorless appearance was violently punctuated, however, by two piercing arctic-blue eyes.

Knight's physique was scrawny but cut. Like a street fighter. He took weight-training classes religiously (Seriously? Fucking public schools can't find anything better to teach kids?), and once hustled three hundred dollars out of the football team by bench-pressing three hundred pounds—over twice his body weight at the time.

Whenever Knight told the story, he would always muse, "It's not the size of the dog in the fight. It's the size of the fight in the dog."

And let me tell you, there was a whole lotta fight in Ronald McKnight—or as everyone at Peach State High called him (never, *ever* to his face), Skeletor.

What was even more interesting than Knight being the *only* skinhead in town was that he wasn't actually a racist. I never once heard him tout any Aryan pride bullshit or saw him sport any of the typical Nazi regalia. Swastikas and iron crosses were suspiciously absent from his personal effects.

Ever the psychologist, even then, I became so fascinated by his lack of fascist iconography that I actually got up the nerve to ask him about it once.

Instead of thrusting his right arm into the air and launching into a *Sieg Heil*, Knight quickly glanced up and down the hallway to make sure no one was listening. Then, he leaned in so close that I could feel his serpentine breath on my neck and whispered, "I'm not really a racist. I just hate everybody."

And I believed him. That motherfucker hated *everybody*.

Or so I thought.

There were five billion people on the planet in 1996. Ronald "Knight" McKnight hated four billion nine hundred ninety-nine million nine hundred ninety-nine thousand nine hundred ninety-nine of them. He hated his parents. He loathed his friends. He intentionally intimidated strangers. But, for some clandestine reason, Knight decided that he liked me. And being the only human the scariest boy in the universe liked was a heady thing.

When I first met Ronald McKnight I was a waifish, doe-eyed, freckle-faced freshman with a shoulder-length mop of wavy reddish-blonde hair and a devastating crush on the King of the Punks, Lance Hightower. I'd been cutting my hair shorter and shorter, adding more and more safety pins to my hoodie and backpack, and inching my way closer and closer to Lance at the elite punk-goth-druggie lunch table, which he'd presided over since the first day of school. (As it turned out, Lance was completely and hopelessly gay, something I wish I had known before shaving most of my hair off and getting multiple body piercings in my increasingly extreme efforts to get him to make out with me.)

Knight, who was a sophomore at the time, had landed at our lunch table by default. With no other skinheads to hang out with, the punks kind of adopted him as their pet rattlesnake. Day after day, he would sit there with his brow furrowed and his head down, gripping his fork hard enough to bend the metal and muttering the occasional "Go fuck yourself" whenever anyone dared to address him.

One balmy day in mid-September, I happened to overhear some upperclassman at our lunch table say to her spiky-haired pierced boyfriend that it was Skeletor's birthday. (I don't know how anyone would have known unless Knight had just thrown it out as proof that his life had somehow gotten even worse. I imagine it would have sounded something like, "I can't fucking believe my fucking whore mom stole all my cigarettes and went out of town with her faggot husband on my fucking birthday. Hey, what the fuck are you looking at, asshole?") So, naturally, I bought him a chicken sandwich while I was going through the lunch line.

Bouncing over to our table and sporting a big grin (I should explain that I have always been disgustingly hyper and enthusiastic, and I would have made an excellent cheerleader if I weren't both anti-establishment and clumsy), I thrust it into Knight's face and chirped, "Happy birthday!"

In return, Knight lifted his ever-scowling head and pinned me with what felt like two searing blue laser scopes. I stood, in a breathless state of suspended animation, realizing a moment too late that I might have just poked the rattlesnake.

As I braced myself for a barrage of expletives, I watched Knight's perma-scowl melt and slide off right before my eyes instead.

His brow, which had been tightly furrowed, smoothed and lifted in surprise. His glacial eyes widened, and his lips parted in a soul-baring silent gasp. It was a heartbreaking expression of gratitude and disbelief. It was as if the boy we called Skeletor had never received a gift in his life. I could almost hear his armor clatter to the floor as I peered into the face of someone vulnerable, aching, and alone.

I couldn't speak. Couldn't remember how air worked. Once my lungs began to burn, I finally tore my eyes away from his and sucked in a deep breath, pretending to admire my new white Doc Martens (yet another purchase made in the name of seducing Lance Hightower), but it was too late. In those few seconds I had seen it all. A lifetime of pain, a longing for significance, and a tidal wave of love waiting to crash down on the first person brave enough, or stupid enough, to wade in.

I'd expected him to recover his armor and return to his brooding—after all, it was just a dumb sandwich—but much to my surprise and mortification Knight stood up, pointed directly at me, and shouted to everyone at our table, "This is why BB is the only fucking person on this planet that I can fucking stand! None of you motherfuckers gave me shit for my birthday!" Making sure to give each and every terrified zit-faced misfit a murderous glare, he finally finished with, "I fucking hate all of you!"

Skeletor had a flair for the dramatic.

Too stunned to react, I watched helplessly as he slunk back

into his seat with the smug, lazy grace of a just-fed lion, obviously satisfied with the scene he'd just caused and the shocked silence that had fallen over the cafeteria. I was the only one standing, and all eyes were now on me, including Knight's, which were regarding me with a broad, rapacious Cheshire Cat kind of grin.

Suddenly, I wanted my money back.

You see, Journal, all I'd *thought* I was buying was a chicken sandwich and maybe, if I were lucky, a spot on the good side of the guy voted Most Likely to Kill Us All with a Two-by-Four Full of Rusty Nails. That's it.

I did not like Knight. I did not want to be friends with Knight (assuming that were even possible). He was scary and angry, and all I'd wanted was for him to like me enough *not* to scream at *or* murder me. Who knew that a stupid dollar fifty would buy me the singular obsessive, undying devotion of the town's only skinhead?

As I stood there, my big blinking green eyes caught in the crosshairs of Knight's savage blue stare—it became clear that he was going to make me his whether I liked it or not.

And in the beginning, I definitely liked it not.

3

Frenemies

BB's Secret Journal

August 24

Colton was the only guy I'd ever kissed before high school. He was a devilishly handsome spiky-haired little bad boy I dated in eighth grade. And by dated, I mean that we talked on the phone, held hands at school, toilet-papered a house together, and made out *once*. Colton reminded me of a male fairy—not like in a gay way, but in a pointy-eared, wild-haired, wicked-gleam-in-his-eye kind of way.

Wait. Shit. I might be thinking of Peter Pan.

Yes, Colton totally reminded me of Peter Pan, in a sexy, mischievous King-of-the-Lost-Boys kind of way.

Colton lived, off and on, with his bedraggled, sad single mom, Peggy, who worked, like, four jobs. Peg was skinny as a rail with scraggly long dishwater-blonde hair and could still fit into her entire skintight, high-waisted stonewashed wardrobe from 1983. Her long shaky fingers were never without an equally long Virginia Slim between them, and her voice was so hoarse that it sounded as if she'd probably gone for days at a time without speaking to anyone.

Peggy had former eighties hair-band groupie written all over her, so for all I know, Colton's dad was one of the founding members of Whitesnake. Whoever his dad was, his place in Las Vegas had to be a hell of a lot better than Peggy's shithole. That's probably why Colton never stuck around for more than a few months at a time.

During Colton's last stint at Peggy's place, he and his mom kind of adopted Knight—in part because they felt bad about how shitty his home life was, but also, I suspected, because Knight had a car.

Then, per his usual, Colton up and boarded a Greyhound back to Las Vegas just two months into our sophomore year, leaving Peggy all alone again. Since she needed a son and Knight needed a new mom, he just kept going over there every day after school, as if Colton had never left.

It was kind of sweet really. Knight would let Peggy's geriatric German shepherd out and patch up all the rotten, mildewed concave places on the house while she was off working one of her forty-seven part-time jobs. He never asked for anything in return, but what he got...was a key to the house.

It was badass—not the house, obviously. The house was a dilapidated piece of shit. But Knight had the place all to himself and would actually let us hang out there after school. Peg kept the fridge stocked with Pabst Blue Ribbon, we could smoke inside, and she had cable. It was a teenage utopia.

Every afternoon, the entire punk-rock lunch table crew would head over to Peggy's, cram ourselves into her itchy shapeless

1970s couches (me vying for a spot next to Lance), crack open some beers, and scream at the top of our lungs at whatever stripper grandma or little-person biker gang or kung fu hillbilly pimp happened to be on *Jerry Springer* that afternoon. All the while flicking Camel butts at the already overflowing ashtrays.

Knight usually spent the first hour or so letting the dog out and patching the place up, which gave me just enough time to get a good buzz on and work up a nice little flirt with the owner of whichever lap I was sitting on—not that it mattered. As soon as Knight finished his rounds, he'd flop into Peggy's tobacco-colored steel-wool-upholstered recliner with a PBR in hand and pin whichever poor fucker I was talking to with a glare so murderous that he'd be out the door before my bony ass even hit the ground.

This routine continued for weeks until, one day, I realized that it was just Knight and me. I knew the crowd had been dwindling, but I hadn't realized just how much. I always rode with Knight to Peggy's house because (A) I was fifteen and had no car, and (B) whenever anyone else had offered me a ride, Knight would immediately twist their arm behind their back and smash their face into the hood of the nearest car until they took it back.

I couldn't even ride the bus home because I *technically* didn't live in that school district.

By November of my sophomore year, Knight had single-handedly made himself my only means of after-school transportation without me even noticing it.

Every day after the final bell, whether I liked it or not, I would be sucked into the crowd of eager teenagers fleeing the building, twirled and tossed along like a spindly leaf in a stream, and deposited onto the front lawn, right at Knight's feet. Leaning against the flagpole with his arms crossed, he looked like something out of the skinhead version of *The Outsiders*—tight white T-shirt, classic Levi's 501s held up with a pair of thin red braces, black steel-toed combat boots, and a felonious gleam in his eye. The only things missing were a pack of cigarettes rolled up in his sleeve—and, of course, hair.

Even though there was something unmistakably sexy about his iconic style, self-confidence, and potential for violence, I still wasn't attracted to Knight—mostly due to my subconscious awareness that he might possibly kill me—but I had to admit, I liked the attention. Knowing that the entire school saw this modern-day Brando waiting for me, day in and day out, made me feel like I was a little bit of a badass, too.

I had always just been this quirky, perky, artsy chick who had crazy hair and dressed like Gwen Stefani. I was somebody that everyone knew—because I stuck out like a sore thumb with my bright red or orange or purple waves, glittery eye shadow, and leopard-print velour stretch pants tucked into white Dr. Martens—but I was nobody of any real consequence.

But now... now I was *untouchable*.

I was also slowly becoming Knight's *precious*. His attention to me was so focused that I felt like an ant sizzling under a magnifying glass whenever he looked at me. It was as if he were memorizing the exact size, shape, and location of every freckle and zit on my virginal face. God, it made me squirm. I never had a problem making eye contact with people until I met Knight.

Sixteen years later, I still catch myself talking to people's shirts.

At first, I was pretty freaked out about hanging out with

Knight alone, but I had no idea how to avoid it. With no bus, no car, no one brave enough to risk the wrath of "Skeletor the Skinhead" by offering me a ride, and both my parents at work (okay, one of my parents at work and one of my parents sleeping off a hangover), he had successfully made himself my only option.

And I went along with it because, well, I didn't know what else to do. I had never interacted with someone so angry, or aggressive, or powerful before. My parents were peace-loving hippie potheads, for Christ's sake. Nobody ever raised their voices or hands in anger at my house. Hell, most of the time, my parents couldn't even raise their eyelids all the way.

So I tried to play it cool. That's what you do around big, scary, unpredictable creatures that could kill you, right? You stay calm. You don't make any sudden movements. So I went with Knight to Peggy's house every day to keep him happy, and basically, I did everything I could think of to keep him strictly in the friend zone.

And you know what, Journal? It worked.

There, at Peggy's house, without anyone else around, in the idle hours we spent drinking and smoking and watching daytime TV after school, I actually became friends with Ronald McKnight.

When we were alone, Knight morphed into a completely different person. He was sweet and candid and chivalrous. He would carry my backpack and open my beers and light all my cigarettes, like a *gentleman*. He would catch me off guard and tickle me until I cried. And once, after I complained about what a bitch it was to break in a new pair of boots, Knight pulled my feet into his lap, deftly removed the forty-pound steel-and-leather monstrosities I was wearing, and rubbed my feet with his big, callused hands while we talked.

It was during these unusually intimate moments that I could sometimes get Knight to open up. I learned about the stepdad he hated, the parade of abusive boyfriends who came before him, the anger he harbored toward his mother, and the secret longing he had to see his real father. To a psychologist in the making, the intensity of those conversations was intoxicating. Not only was I fascinated by the never-ending layers of armor this freckle-faced boy wore to protect himself, but I also got high on the fact that I was the only person on planet Earth who got to see what was underneath.

The whole time I thought I was breaking down Knight's walls, but in reality he was the one chipping away at mine. Making me feel special. Giving me the illusion of safety.

Then, he pounced.

4

Props

BB's Secret Journal

Dear Journal,

On one unusually warm December afternoon, I found myself at Peggy's house, engaged in a particularly aggressive tickle fight with Knight. Well, it'd started as a tickle fight, but every time I wriggled away, that fucking ghost ninja would chase and recapture me. I made it from the couch to the floor, from the floor to the other side of the coffee table, from the other side of the coffee table to the recliner, and from the recliner to the patch of floor in front of Peggy's 1950s era wood-paneled television set. With each successive recapture, my efforts to escape would become a little more forceful, a little more panicked. I went from tickling my way free to twisting my arm free to shoving him away and scrambling across the floor on all fours, but it only seemed to excite him more.

By the time Knight finally had me pinned on my back in front of the TV, it was clear that what had started as a flirty, fun, exhilarating little chase had quickly devolved into a full contact game of cat and mouse. And now, the game was over. Other than my heaving chest and pounding heart, I was completely immobilized, ensnared by both Knight's glacial stare and his impossibly strong arms, which were straining and pulsing against the taut sleeves of his T-shirt. It was in that moment that I realized just how stupid and reckless I'd been.

Knight and I weren't friends. We were predator and prey. He'd been hunting me for over a year, and my dumb ass just fell right into his trap.

Without releasing me from his grip or gaze, Knight slowly lowered himself onto me, making his intention clear, and I surrendered. Adrenaline exploded through my body as I braced myself for something aggressive and potentially bloody to happen. Leaving my body to fend for itself, my consciousness floated up to the nicotine-stained popcorn ceiling above to watch the entire scene unfold through splayed fingers.

But rather than devouring me, Knight placed a single, lingering kiss on my lips. The shock of his tenderness reeled my consciousness back in, like the snap of a stretched rubber band, and suddenly, I was alight with sensation—the potent scent of dryer sheets and musky cologne filling my lungs, warm lips on my lips, a hard chest on my chest, forceful arms pinning my scrawnier ones to my sides, and the taste of Winterfresh gum emerging, somehow, through the tangled flavors of PBR and cigarettes.

When he finally withdrew from that gentle peck, in yet another unexpected gesture, Knight rested his forehead on mine and released a long pained breath. I felt his grip on my tiny biceps release as well. Callused hands slid down my arms, all the way to my balled little fists, which he slid up and over my head with no resistance. His movements were so controlled and his breathing so deliberate that it was as if he were calling on every ounce of self-control he had to keep from tearing me to pieces.

Oh, yes, we were definitely predator and prey.

I was sure he could feel my pulse vibrating in the air, radiating off of me like sound waves from a bass drum, as I lay there, suspended in thrilling trepidation. Once he regained his composure, Knight kissed me again.

I didn't move, couldn't breathe. Instead, all my resources had been redirected to my brain, which was struggling to form a coherent thought, once Knight's tongue began swirling around my own in hypnotizing unhurried circles.

Once he released his grip on my wrists and gave my bottom lip one final appreciative suck, all the thoughts I couldn't quite seem to form during our encounter came rushing into my mind at once. I didn't know where to begin. I had only been kissed by two other boys, one of whom used to live in this house, in my fifteen years on the planet and never, *ever* had it been like that. That was *hot*. That was—

Oh, fuck . . . what was that?

Still sprawled on the ground underneath an emotionally unstable bodybuilding skinhead, two notions finally wriggled themselves free from the tangles of my mind. One: Ronald McKnight was in love with me, and two: I was never going to escape.

Part of me loved how sparklingly special Knight made me feel and how passionate he was about me and even, to some extent, how domineering and intimidating and exciting he was. But the other much bigger part of me was scared shitless and really, really wanted this whole thing to just be our little secret.

Even though Knight had never hurt me, I'd seen him hurt plenty of other people, and sometimes for no reason at all. What the fuck would he do if I rejected him? I wasn't about to end up in some *Silence of the Lambs*–style well under Peggy's house. No, rejecting him was definitely out.

I also couldn't be seen romantically with him in public. Sure, I knew that Knight wasn't the fascist, racist monster he led people to believe, but nobody else did. What would my friends think? My BFF, Juliet, was half-black and half-Japanese, for Christ's sake!

What a clusterfuck. This could not get out. This would not get out.

———

My little secret lasted all of about three days. As it turned out, Knight wanted to shout that shit from a mountaintop. He'd walk me *everywhere*, kiss me good-bye before every class, sit with his arm around me at lunch, and shoot icicle daggers from his eyes at any guy who so much as turned his head in my direction.

Shit, shit, shit. Somehow, I had become Skeletor the pet rattlesnake's *girlfriend*.

He'd write me love letters with disturbingly graphic illustrations during almost every class and bring me random gifts—a baggie full of Goldfish, a dandelion he'd picked on the way to school, a severed head—each morning.

For a guy whose entire reputation had been built on the image of being unapproachable and potentially lethal, Knight was amazingly unfazed by the attention he was drawing. He couldn't have given less of a fuck who saw him carrying on like a damn fool, picking flowers and doodling flaming hearts all over his notebooks. I had just settled into a back-row desk in my last period class to discreetly unwrap and read yet another intricately folded piece of paper from Knight when three words immediately jumped out from his hasty, psychotic I-have-your-daughter-now-give-me-my-money–style handwriting. He had scrawled something to the effect of:

DEAR BB,
I CAN'T FUCKING WAIT UNTIL THIS AFTERNOON. I HAVE SOMETHING PLANNED THAT I'VE BEEN THINKING ABOUT SINCE THE FIRST TIME I SAW YOU. PLEASE DON'T WORRY. I KNOW YOU PROBABLY THINK I'M JUST GOING TO USE YOU FOR SEX, BUT I'M NOT.
      I LOVE YOU.
                                    KNIGHT

All my virginal fifteen-year-old brain could comprehend were the words *worry*, *sex*, and *love*.
Ohmygod.
I had to clutch the sides of the desk to keep from falling out of it.
Knight wanted to have sex. With me. In a few *hours*. And, if the tiny stick-person illustrations scrawled on the back of Knight's note were any indication, it was going to involve props.

5

Condiments Are for Hot Dogs, Not Wieners

BB's Secret Journal

August 25, continued

I'd worn a skirt to school that day. I never *ever* wear skirts, Journal, but I had just gotten some brand new mid-calf, steel-toed Grinders and I needed my future husband, Lance Hightower, to see them in all their laced-up leathery glory. They weighed a ton and cost more, but I thought that maybe, just maybe, if I could prove to Lance that I wasn't just another Doc Martens–wearing poser, he would finally realize that we were, in fact, soul mates, and then he'd whisk me away from the clutches of Ronald McKnight. Lance was six foot three and filled out in all the right places, so on paper, at least, it seemed like it would be a fair fight.

Unfortunately, my plan backfired.

In reality, Lance was far less interested in bucking up to Knight than he was in bucking *under* him, if you know what I mean.

So, rather than securing the bad boy of my dreams and my freedom from "Skeletor the Skinhead," the only thing I managed to accomplish with those two-hundred-dollar boots and that short plaid skirt fastened on the side with safety pins was pouring gasoline on Knight's already raging libido and crumbling self-control.

In the few weeks up to that point, our little make-out sessions at Peggy's house had graduated into Knight going down on me any chance he got. No shit, Journal. I had been the star of the cunnilingus after-school special, and it had been pretty fucking phenomenal. It turned out that Knight loved eating pussy almost as much as he loved, um...well, he didn't really love anything, except for me, if you could believe the angry all-caps scribble that was ticking like a time bomb in my pocket.

And not once during that time had Knight made me think that he expected anything in return, which was good because that was exactly what he'd been getting. Although I hadn't even seen it yet, I was scared shitless of the one-eyed monster living inside Knight's jeans. Every time we made out, that thing would swell so much that it would manage to escape the waistband of his impossibly tight 501s, extend up into his fitted T-shirt, and crawl halfway up his washboard abs before all was said and done. I had zero experience with peni, but I was great with visual-spatial reasoning, and there was no way that D was going to fit in my V.

Just as I'd expected, when the final bell rang, Knight was waiting for me outside. I saw him before he saw me, and I watched his expression morph from murderous to salacious the instant our eyes locked. His mouth kicked up on one side in an appreciative, hungry sneer as his eyes slid down the length of my body at a glacial pace, sending chills down my spine along with them. The next thing I knew, hard arms were around my waist, a hard mouth was seeking entrance to my own, and a particularly hard and frighteningly large bulge was being pressed into my belly.

Oh my God, oh my God, oh my God, oh my God, oh my God...

Adrenaline exploded through my bloodstream. My pulse sounded like a raging river in my ears, and the only thing I could hear over the white noise was my consciousness screaming, *Fight or flight! Fight or flight!*

The noise fell away, however, when Knight whispered in my ear, "Did you read my note?"

I swallowed hard and nodded slowly.

Please don't ask me if I love you back. Please don't make me talk about it.

Let's just get this over with.

Knight pulled away just enough so that we were eye to eye— warm earthy green to glacial blue. The paralysis was so strong whenever he looked at me like that that I couldn't even blink. Breathing required conscious effort.

"I meant it."

Gulp.

Before I could formulate a response that wouldn't get me dismembered, Knight stripped me of my backpack and slung it over his shoulder. While Knight carrying my stuff was nothing new, on that particular day, it felt more like he was using it as collateral.

With one arm draped possessively around my shoulders Knight steered me all the way to the grassy area just behind the student parking lot where the ten-foot-tall monster truck he'd pieced together from scrap parts was lurched up onto a massive boulder, looming over the Civics and Tercels below (as if our classmates were even capable of being more intimidated by him).

Every day, Knight would escort me to that mobile monument of testosterone, and every day, I'd watch with pleading eyes as, one by one, the kids whom I'd laughed and passed notes with just hours before cast their gaze downward and turned away.

I couldn't blame them. Knight had made it abundantly clear—I was *his*, and looking at what was his the wrong way could be hazardous to a person's health. But on that particular day, I stared at them extra hard as Knight dragged me past, sending out frantic, telepathic messages like, *Help!* and *Somebody call 9-1-1!* and *I'm too young to die!*

Knight's pornographic declaration of love burned a hole in my pocket and my mind as we drove in an awkward silence to Peggy's house.

We'd crossed Peggy's splintering rotten threshold a hundred times before, but on that eerily warm December day, the last day before winter break, I knew going in that part of me was never going to come back out.

Knight disappeared into the kitchen for a split second while I loitered on the four-by-four patch of parquet that Peggy liked to call *the foi-yay*. Just beyond it was the living room, home to all things brown and itchy, and beyond that was the entrance to the kitchen where I could hear Knight banging around.

Instead of grabbing a beer and settling into Peggy's Brillo Pad of a couch, per my usual, I simply stood, petrified, on the parquet, not knowing where to go or what to do. Before I could formulate an escape plan, Knight reemerged from the kitchen, looking all too pleased with himself. He stalked toward me in bare feet—*when did he take his boots off?*—grabbed my hand without saying a word, and led me up the sagging, squeaking stairs to Colton's old bedroom.

I'd only been up there once before, but it was exactly the way I remembered it—sparsely furnished, impersonal, and sad. Colton had never stayed long enough to decorate, and Peggy was either too depressed or absent to bother. The tiny wooden furniture looked as though it'd come out of a 1950s era dollhouse and been glazed with carcinogens.

Knight dropped my hand once we reached our destination and turned to face me. "Do you trust me?"

Fuck no!

I swallowed hard, straightened my posture, and forced myself to meet his gaze. "I want to."

Holding Knight's stare was never easy, but at that moment, it felt like I was peering down both barrels of a shotgun. I had been hunted, separated from the herd, groomed. And now, here I was, serving myself up to him like a prize fucking heifer.

Knight lowered those cobalt crosshairs from my face and sent them coursing over the length of my trembling body. His mouth and fingers soon followed, deftly taking with them the safety pins from my skirt, which soon became a tartan heap on the matted carpet. Resigning myself to my fate, I took a deep breath and slipped off my Siouxsie and the Banshees T-shirt and (heavily) padded bra, adding them to the growing pile of clothes on the floor.

Knight's mouth roved leisurely back up my torso, stopping to pluck and nip at each tight pearl-pink nipple he encountered along the way. My hands found their way to his velveteen scalp, as usual. I couldn't help myself. Knight's head was the softest thing I'd ever felt, and lately, I'd seemed to be finding excuses to touch it more and more.

How could someone whom my eyes found to be so terrifying also feel like cashmere to my fingertips, taste like spearmint on my tongue, and smell like freshly laundered cotton and warm musk? When I took my head and eyes out of the equation, the rest of my senses would come alive whenever we touched.

By the time I finally tasted Knight's wintery breath, he'd worked me into such a wanton lather of need that I'd forgotten I still had on my underwear. That is, until I felt his thick fingers slip between my hips and the thin strip of cotton covering them. Instead of sliding them down my thighs and continuing his unhurried seduction, however, Knight set the tone for what was to come by grasping both sides of my purple panties and stretching them to their breaking point. I released a tiny gasp of surprise, which was immediately followed by a much louder one when he then brought my shredded panties to his mouth and slowly ran his tongue over an embarrassingly large wet spot.

Knight made unwavering eye contact with me as he savored the proof of my desire, desire I hadn't even admitted to myself that I was feeling, and then reclaimed my mouth with his own. Only this time, when he kissed me, he tasted like sex, and I was shocked to discover that I fucking loved it.

Still fully clothed, Knight guided me to sit on the edge of Colton's bed. I watched in confusion as he began taking items out of his pockets and placing them on the dusty nightstand beside us—a lighter, a pack of cigarettes, his keys, a pack of gum. From his back pockets, he removed his wallet and then a pair of handcuffs, followed by *another* pair of handcuffs.

The fuck?

Flashing me a wicked grin as the second set of steel bracelets hit the table, Knight reached behind his back once more. (Those tight Levis were like a clown car of sin.) He retrieved a clear plastic bear filled with honey from his waistband.

I don't know if it was the thought of what he was about to do with those implements or the shocked expression on my face, but for the first time since we'd met, I saw Knight smile. Sure, I'd witnessed the corners of his mouth curl upward on more than one occasion, but it was always more of a sneer, smirk, or snarl. This was dazzling. His usually frosty eyes crinkled warmly at the edges, and his lips parted, revealing teeth so perfect that he could have been the spokesmodel for Winterfresh gum (especially considering how much of it he gnawed through a day). Combined with all those freckles, that smile gave me a peek at the seventeen-year-old boy hiding under Knight's armor. And he was actually really cute.

While I sat and contemplated this strange new attraction I was developing to someone whom, moments ago, I'd considered to be more my captor than my boyfriend, Knight tore off his plain white T-shirt and 501s with the grace of a jungle cat. Without his shirt, I could now see the head of his angry, massive erection protruding at least two inches above the top of his boxers, the elastic waistband straining to keep the heavy weapon holstered against his abdomen.

My brief, uneventful life flashed before my eyes. *So, this is how it all ends*, I thought. *Bludgeoned to death by a skinhead's penis in my ex-boyfriend's childhood bedroom. And I never even got to meet Billy Idol.*

Taking his first weapon of choice—the stainless steel

handcuffs—in one hand, Knight guided me onto my back on the center of the bed. Blanketing me with his hard body, he expertly spread my legs apart with his own. His carefree smile had already been replaced by something wicked, predatory. Knight made searing eye contact with me until our puffy, swollen lips reconnected. Instinctively, my hands sought his warm, fuzzy head as he began to drag his *other* head through my saturated folds.

I could feel his self-control begin to falter. Knight drove his hands into my super short platinum-blonde hair (recently bleached and hacked off in yet another fruitless attempt to seduce Lance Hightower) and tugged hard. The force pulled my head back, exposing my neck and causing my body to arch into his unyielding chest. (Lance *who?*)

Knight buried his face into the hollow of my collarbone and hissed, "God, I want you."

God, I wanted him right back. I might not have wanted to be seen with him in public or admit to anyone that we were together, but in that forgotten little room on the outskirts of town, I could pretend that everyone else and all their opinions simply didn't exist. And Knight felt safe enough to lay his armor down and be the vulnerable, affectionate—albeit kinky— fuzzy-headed boy that no one else got to see but me. The boy who smelled nice, tasted nice, and made me feel really, really nice. There was no more denying it. I was in that room because I wanted to be.

Once I was practically foaming at the mouth, Knight left me panting to secure both my wrists to Colton's bedposts, using the handcuffs I'd already forgotten he had. Although my spindly pale legs were free, the weight of my new steel-toed Grinders kept them secured to the foot of the bed almost as well as the steely bracelets around my wrists. The rest of my boyish fifteen-year-old figure was now splayed out and on display like the sacrificial virgin that I was. Unsullied, but not for long.

Within the next few minutes, that body would have its innocence ripped away in a torrent of pain and blood and honey. Within a few weeks, it would undergo an onslaught of hormonal changes from the birth control pills I would ask my doctor to prescribe. And within a few months, it would have decorative metal hoops and barbells shoved through each and every erogenous zone. I was on the cusp of a rapid transformation from girl to deviant sex goddess—I just didn't know it yet.

What I did know was that I was finally ready to accept Knight—into my life and into my body—exactly the way he was. For some reason his broken soul had chosen me to love, and he was doing it fearlessly. He should have been afraid I would reject him, like his parents, like the rest of the world. He shouldn't have been able to open up, but he did, my brave Knight. He saw something in me worthy of his trust, of his love, and I knew he would fight to the death to protect it. He had also recently made a hobby out of giving me convulsion-inducing pleasure, which was a plus.

Sure, Knight was angry and antisocial and intimidating and violent, but at that moment, he was also drizzling my throat, breasts, abdomen, and beyond with honey and feasting upon me as if I were his last meal. Violent *schmiolent*. This motherfucker was a *lover*.

By the time he made his way down to my newly shaved mound (I'd gotten self-conscious and shaved it all off after Knight went down on me for the first time), I was practically thrashing against my restraints from the exquisite torture. I wanted nothing more than to grab his ears and hump his face, but the tease persisted, and I was helpless to stop it. Knight licked and sucked the sticky sugar from my oversensitive clit, occasionally retreating to softly blow on it or flick it with the tip of his tongue. He was clearly enjoying himself and probably took even greater pleasure in the fact that I was whittling Colton's bedposts down to toothpicks with my restraints in response.

Finally taking pity on me, Knight slid his rough, callused hands up my thighs, spread me apart with his thick thumbs, and lashed me with that honey-coated tongue until my legs shook. Within seconds I shattered into a mosaic of moans and curse words and spasms and darkness. My arms involuntarily yanked at my shackles as I tried to pull my knees to my chest, doing anything to stop the flood of immaculate sensations threatening to drown me.

While I concentrated on calming the pulsing waves of pleasure between my legs, Knight stealthily slid off his boxers, slipped a condom out of his wallet, and stretched it almost to its breaking point over his very neglected, very angry-looking cock. Once I was physically able to spread my legs again, Knight positioned himself at the opening of my still throbbing orifice.

Although he should have had a smug, self-satisfied look on his face from the brutal orgasm he'd just inflicted upon me, Knight looked positively severe, worried even. "Are you ready?"

The trepidation in his eyes told me all I needed to know. My fearless Knight was scared, scared for me and of himself. It was time to acknowledge the elephant-sized penis in the room. Knight was about to hurt me worse than I'd ever been hurt by another person. And it wouldn't be the last time.

No sooner had I solemnly nodded my consent than I could feel my insides being sliced to ribbons. I grasped the handcuffs firmly with both fists and sucked in a pained breath through my clenched teeth as I fought back the tears welling up behind my tightly shut eyelids.

Don't cry out. Don't cry out. You can do this, BB. You're a bad-ass. Just go to your happy place and wait it out.

The only problem was, despite the fact that I was experiencing what reverse childbirth must feel like, I was already in my happy place. I was being worshipped by the devil himself, and I never wanted it to end.

Happily, my torture was over rather quickly, thanks to the months-long case of blue balls I'd given Knight leading up to that moment. Once it was over and he withdrew what felt like a chainsaw from my mutilated vagina, Knight wrapped his arms around me and buried his face between the pillow and my cheek. I didn't know if he was seeking comfort for what he'd done or offering it, but his arms felt like giant bandages putting me back together. I wanted to run my fingers over his fuzzy head but was met with immediate resistance and the sound of metal scraping wood when I tried to move my arms.

Knight's head shot up at the sound, and his face immediately contorted into a crumpled mixture of remorse and concern when he registered where it was coming from. "Fuck, BB! Your wrists!"

He leaped up and grabbed his key ring off the nightstand, pausing only to discard the condom into the trash can in Colton's room where it would no doubt remain for the next ten to twenty years. After freeing my hands, Knight pulled me into his lap, wrapped his arms around me, and focused his laser-like attention onto my abraded red wrists, repeatedly rubbing, sucking, and kissing them between apologies.

"I'm so sorry, Punk. I'm so fucking sorry. I didn't want to hurt you. I mean, I knew parts of it were going to hurt, but I tried so hard to make it good for you. Are you okay? Please tell me you're okay. It would fucking kill me if I broke the only thing I ever loved."

Between each kiss, Knight searched my face from under his worried arched brows. Although he had just put me through three and a half minutes of excruciating pain, I felt powerful and shiny and new, like a phoenix rising from the ashes of my decimated hymen. What didn't kill me *had* made me stronger, strong enough to have the only skinhead in the tri-county area eating out of the palm of my hand. *And elsewhere.*

Oh, I was better than okay. I was positively high.

"Let's do it again."

6

Enter the Evil Professor

BB's Secret Journal

August 29

Dear Journal,

There's a small chance that I might get disappeared soon, so I need you to know what happened in case the feds come snooping around.

I could write out the whole juicy story here, but I pretty much already did that in an email to my BFF, Sara, so I'm just going to copy and paste it in for the sake of time. And also to prove that what I'm about to do was all *her* idea.

FYI, Dr. Sara Snow is pure evil. I know I shouldn't listen to her, but I can't help it. She just has this power over me. She once picked up three hitchhikers in bumblebee costumes in the middle of the night, and made me sit on one of their laps because that was the only way we could all fit into her sub-compact Volkswagen. Sara once got us shamed out of a live sex show in New Orleans for heckling the performers but insisted that neither one of us was leaving until she had completely finished the three-dollar can of Natural Ice they made her buy on the way in. Sara once referred to the head of a child she was evaluating as "Star Trek–esque." She's a bad influence.

Up until three years ago we were colleagues in the same school system (from which Sara was trying to get us both fired), and it was magnificent. Then she had to go and get all Sheryl Sandberg on me and take a job as a psychology professor at some fancy research university on the other side of the country. She's so fucking smart she could probably cure cancer if she wasn't also crazy with a capital K and backward Z.

So don't blame me too harshly for what you're about to read, Journal. Just do what I do and blame Dr. Sara Snow.

FROM: BB EASTON

TO: SARA SNOW

DATE: THURSDAY, AUGUST 29, 9:36 P.M.

SUBJECT: SHIT. JUST. GOT. REAL.

> So . . . Ken read my fucking journal.
> I'm getting divorced.
> I'm getting poisoned or divorced.
> Just thought you should know.

FROM: SARA SNOW

TO: BB EASTON

DATE: THURSDAY, AUGUST 29, 9:41 P.M.

SUBJECT: RE: SHIT. JUST. GOT. REAL.

> No way. That doesn't sound like Ken. How do you know?

Sara Snow, PhD
Associate Professor, Department of Psychology, (name
of university deleted)

FROM: BB EASTON

TO: SARA SNOW

DATE: THURSDAY, AUGUST 29, 9:47 P.M.

SUBJECT: RE: SHIT. JUST. GOT. REAL.

Dude, I know because when I was coming downstairs
a few nights ago after putting the kids to bed I heard
him slam my fucking laptop shut. That's how I know.
By the time I got to the bottom of the stairs and
rounded the corner into the living room he was shoving
my computer across the coffee table looking guilty
as shit.

He read my fucking journal, Sara. You have no idea
what's in there. It's so, so graphic. After reading that
shit, he could probably pick Knight's giant cock out
of a lineup. I haven't slept in like three days because I
know the second I close my eyes Ken is going to go,
"Shh, shh, shh," and smother me with a pillow.

Tell me what to do. Please!

FROM: SARA SNOW

TO: BB EASTON

DATE: THURSDAY, AUGUST 29, 10:01 P.M.

SUBJECT: RE: SHIT. JUST. GOT. REAL.

For starters, you should check your browser history. If whatever he read in your journal was that bad then he probably used your computer to secure a safe house while he was at it. I'm going to save this email just in case you come up missing.

P.S. Why the hell didn't you password-protect your journal?

Sara Snow, PhD
Associate Professor, Department of Psychology, (name of university deleted)

FROM: BB EASTON
TO: SARA SNOW
DATE: THURSDAY, AUGUST 29, 10:13 P.M.
SUBJECT: RE: SHIT. JUST. GOT. REAL.

I know! I'm an idiot! I just honestly didn't think it was necessary. Ken never pays attention to anything I'm working on. I don't even think he knows that all the photos and paintings hanging in this house are mine. Plus, he's trying to watch all five seasons of The Wire and manage, like, four fantasy football leagues simultaneously right now. Who knew that fucker would pay enough attention to my covert typing to get suspicious?

I'm freaking out, Sara. It's like he's icing me or playing fucking mind games or something. Instead of dousing my computer with gasoline and piss, which would have been justified, he took me on a date. What the fuck is that?!?! Like, got a sitter, picked a restaurant, AND preordered movie tickets! I assumed he was going to serve me with papers at dinner since it was all so formal and out of character, but it was actually a really nice date. He didn't even make his usual complaint about the fact that he "could have purchased an entire vineyard" for the price of my one glass of pinot g either.

Oh! OH! Then, after dinner, when I backed Ken into our bedroom so that I could say thanks by riding his lifeless body for a few minutes, he actually stopped me and asked if I wanted to try anything new. NEW! (As in, new to him, obviously. For a sex act to be new to me it would require a stolen college mascot uniform, twelve yards of rappelling cable, a handful of gerbils, and thirty CCs of vampire blood.) And it was really good, Sara! The TV wasn't even on or anything!

And get this shit! The next day Ken tells me that he's booked another sitter for next month so that we can go see David Koechner at The Punchline. Who is this man??? (Ken, not David Koechner. I know who he is, and he's fucking hilarious.)

Maybe he's going to off me at The Punchline? It is in a super sketchy neighborhood...

FROM: SARA SNOW

TO: BB EASTON

DATE: THURSDAY, AUGUST 29, 10:35 P.M.

SUBJECT: RE: SHIT. JUST. GOT. REAL.

Ken's not icing you. He's responding to your intervention, B. Now that he's read your journal and knows how bored you are, he's making the appropriate adjustments. And the best part is that you didn't even have to talk about it. It's actually a beautiful design. I think you just discovered the holy fucking grail of marital behavior modification techniques!

Here's what you do. Now that you know he's reading your journal, you need to start planting really exaggerated stories in there so that you can milk this shit for all it's worth. Write specifically about whatever it is you want him to change, and make it as juicy as possible.

And I'M going to do a longitudinal study on the outcome so that I can go on Good Morning America and tell Robin Roberts how women across the country can save their marriages through Subliminal Spousal Bibliotherapy. (We'll call it SSB for short.) Bitch, you're going to get me tenure and an Audi R8 with this thing!

Sara Snow, PhD
Associate Professor, Department of Psychology, (name of university deleted)

FROM: BB EASTON

TO: SARA SNOW

DATE: THURSDAY, AUGUST 29, 10:48 P.M.

SUBJECT: RE: SHIT. JUST. GOT. REAL.

You.

Evil.

Fucking.

Genius.

I'm in. And I already have a list of target behaviors for progress monitoring:

1. The initiation of hot, steamy, passionate hair-pulling sex
2. The giving of compliments
3. The bestowment of a nickname
4. And the procurement of a motherfucking heart tattoo with my name on it

For data collection purposes, you can just set the baseline at zero in all four categories. Yes, zero—as in, Ken has never done any of those things. The way I see it, we have nowhere to go but up. I'll keep you abreast of my progress. (Pun intended!)

Also, you have to promise to tell George Stephanopoulos hi for me when you go on GMA. I've always liked him. I think it's because he reminds me of Michael J. Fox. Maybe don't tell him I said that. Or do?

7

The Notorious K.E.N.

BB's Secret Journal

August 30

Dear Journal,

After consulting with the devil on my shoulder, I've decided to embark on a morally bankrupt psychological experiment with the hopes of transforming Ken into someone warm and affectionate whose love for me is so immense that he *needs* a tattoo of my name and/or likeness just so that he can better broadcast his feelings for me to the world. So, pack your bags and bring a flashlight, Journal, because from now on, you'll be hiding in a dark hole in the back of my hard drive under the title Baby Shower Diaper Cake Instructions.

Don't take it personally, Little Guy. It's for your own good. I need a place to take notes on Ken's progress without him catching wind of what I'm up to, and no man will ever come snooping around a file called Baby Shower Diaper Cake Instructions, located inside a folder called...wait for it...Cute Stuff I Found on Pinterest.

Oh, and don't get jealous, but in your old spot, I'm going to start planting a glossily exaggerated Lifetime movie version of you under the filename Super Private Journal That Ken Is Never, Never Allowed to Read Ever where I will plant completely fabricated stories about my ex-boyfriends designed to inspire Ken to up his fucking game. And no, that filename isn't too obvious. Blatant reverse psychology is the only way to get shit done when you're dealing with a man—or a toddler.

Don't you read my journal again, Ken. Don't you do it. Oh . . . you'd better not.

It'll work. Trust me.

Aw, look at you, Journal. You're starting to feel bad for Ken, aren't you? That's adorable, but your sympathy is completely wasted on him. The man does not have feelings. I'm not entirely convinced that he even has nerve endings. I promise, you have absolutely nothing to worry about. Ken is a soulless gangsta, and he'll be just fine.

8

Call Me Crazy

BB's Secret Journal

August 31

Dear Journal,

I can feel you judging me. You don't have to say it. You have disapproval written all over you, like a Meat Is Murder sticker on a MacBook Air. Look at you, all smug in your ivory fucking tower.

You don't know what it's like out here in the trenches, trying to make a marriage work day in and day out. Fifty percent of these things fail, you know. Perhaps, if I gave you a little more background, a little perspective, you'd see that I'm not a monster. I'm just a frustrated wife trying to maximize the potential of her very beautiful, very cold husband. Then, maybe you could cool it with the silent treatment.

For starters, did you know that Ken has someone else's initials carved into his arm? Yep, that's right. When he was sixteen, some girl who banged him, like, twice decided to stop banging him, and he fucking carved her initials into his arm.

Now, when I was sixteen, I already had both nipples and my

clit pierced, so I'm no stranger to self-mutilation, but still. When this bastard dies, after spending, like, a thousand years being my life partner, his body is going to go into the ground with someone else's initials on it. I just want some representation on there, too, goddamn it. Preferably somewhere both visible and brazenly unprofessional.

So, you see, Journal, it's not just that I'm some self-centered only child who wants my husband to tattoo my name on his body. It's that I want my name on his body bigger and bolder than *her* name. It's a totally different thing.

You're already well acquainted with Ken's low libido and comatose performance in the bedroom, based on my first few entries, so we'll move on to the third behavior I hope to target with this little experiment, which is getting Ken to compliment me. I realize that also sounds rather petty and shallow, but if you only knew, Journal. This motherfucker has *never* complimented me without coercion—ever.

I'm sure you're wondering, how is that possible? Surely, that's an exaggeration.

Oh, it's not. Ken is stubborn as shit. Ever since the first time I pouted about his refusal to compliment me way back when we were dating, it has turned into a power struggle of epic proportions. Every four to six months (and usually about three to five days before my period is due), I bring it to his attention, and every four to six months he just rolls his eyes at me as if I'm being some needy succubus.

Take his annual company Christmas party for example. Every year, when I emerge from the bathroom after spending two hours primping for this black-tie bullshit that he knows I get anxious about, do you know what he says when he looks up from the couch?

You guessed it. Nothing.

Do you know what his face says? *Oh God, you're going to expect me to compliment you now, aren't you? Well, fuck that noise. I'm just gonna go back to watching this riveting bayou thrift store gold mine show now and pretend like you're not there.*

Shit. Why are you still there? I'm not even looking at you. Oh no, don't put your hands on your hips!

Fuck! Now you're pissed. If I club myself unconscious with this remote, can we just skip this conversation and go straight to the hospital? I don't even care that we'll miss the silent auction. Like I need another iPad. Am I right?

About two and a half minutes into this ridiculous stalemate, the crickets are so loud that it's like *they're* trying to compliment me just to cut the tension.

Inevitably, I let out a huff and hiss through my teeth, "I'm going to go back into the bathroom, and we're going to try this again. Only this time, when I come out here, you *are* going to say, 'You look nice,' and I'm *not* going to stab your dick with my stiletto."

Listen, Journal, I'm a psychologist, not a mind reader. If Ken doesn't tell me I'm pretty or that I'm a good mom or that I cook a mean bowl of cereal, how can I assume that he's thinking it? I can't. Ergo, I walk around every day under the assumption that my husband thinks I'm a homely asshole. So whenever one of the extras in the movie of my life happens to throw an errant compliment my way, I respond like a drowning drunken coed who's just been tossed a human flotation device. I cry and flail and smother that bitch.

For instance, a few months ago, I was at the grocery store feeling extraordinarily unsexy as I used my misshapen post-childbirth body to shove my three-year-old son and infant daughter around in one of those obnoxious shopping carts with the plastic race car bolted to the front that's as long as a city block and impossible to maneuver without clearing all the endcap displays when yet another mauling occurred. In an attempt to avoid being seen by any real humans, I heaved the five-hundred-pound yellow-and-red monstrosity through the self-checkout lane, flinging nursing pads and nipple cream across the scanner and in the general direction of the plastic bag carousel as quickly as my water-retaining fingers could handle. Snatching my receipt from the printer, I dug in my heels and heaved that behemoth toward the exit.

In the midst of my attempt to escape unseen, a male employee, who was easily ten years younger than me, stopped me dead in my tracks by asking with all sincerity, "Did you get your discount?"

Both annoyed that my getaway had been foiled and confused by his remark, I furrowed my brow and glared at the poor little shit, waiting for him to continue.

Dropping his professional act, the kid beamed, "We're giving fifty percent off to all the beautiful ladies today!"

Tears pricked my eyes. As if I hadn't knocked over enough in that store already, I leaped onto that twenty-year-old hard enough to send us both careening into a gigantic tower of water cooler jugs.

Thank God they held fast or else Ken would have had to watch them pulling my lifeless body out of the blue plastic rubble on the evening news above a caption reading, *This just in. Devoted mother of two and Kroger employee killed today in water cooler avalanche. Cause determined to be husband's selfish withholding of compliments.*

People could have *died*, Journal, all because of Ken's refusal to say nice things to me.

That brings me to my fourth and final marital goal—getting Ken to bestow upon me an adorable, personalized nickname. My husband has never referred to me by any name other than my full, legal name. Hey! You know what? Ken did call me Crazy once. Does that count as a pet name?

It was the middle of the night, and I'd accidentally woken him up while cursing and banging around in our master bathroom during a full-blown OCD flare-up.[1]

Ken stumbled into the bathroom, squinting into what must have felt like a supernova of light, to find me standing one-legged on the counter, dangling from a scalding hot metal wall sconce by my fingertips, while I swung a broom handle in the general direction of every shadow on the ceiling that vaguely resembled a cobweb.

I should have been embarrassed by my late-night manic cleaning frenzy, but all I remember feeling was a fuzzy, girlish giddiness when Ken sleepily raised one corner of his perfect mouth into an amused little smirk and asked, "Whatcha doing, Crazy?"

It was the closest I ever came to getting a pet name out of Ken, but since he wasn't fully conscious when he'd said it, I

---

[1] That's a gross exaggeration. I don't really have OCD. People with OCD have actual reasons for the things they do, like the irrational belief that they will contract herpes of the eyeball if they don't flip each and every light switch fourteen and a half times before they leave the house. There is nothing in the entire American Psychological Association's *Diagnostic and Statistical Manual* that describes my shit. I have three degrees in psychology, and I still don't know what's wrong with me, other than the fact that I'm a bad psychologist, obviously.

don't think I'm actually allowed to accept it. It would be like nickname rape or something. No, Crazy isn't going to work. I want a proper pet name—something personalized. Something that refers to my most endearing qualities, like Freckles, or Pink Taco.

Besides, if somebody at Ken's office saw him sporting a sacred heart tattoo on his forearm with the word Crazy inked inside, the last thought they would have is, *Damn, that guy must really love his wife. She's one lucky gal.* It would be more like, *Man, I knew Ken was an asshole. He's so quiet and good-looking. He had to be either a serial killer or an asshole. Glad I was right about the asshole thing. Now I can stop carrying that can of Mace around in my pocket. That shit makes me look like I have a perma-chub.*

9

Lady and the Tramp

BB's Secret Journal

September 7

Dear Journal,

I've been thinking about my list of target behaviors again, and I've realized that my need for a nickname goes back to my parents. (Doesn't everything?) Growing up, they *never* called me by any of my actual names. Instead, I was always Pumpkin or Cookie or Scooter or—their personal favorite—BB. My mom started calling me "Bee-Bee" when I was an infant just because it sounded cute, like *Shnookums* or *Chubberlupagus*, but my dad turned it into BB, like my initials, because he secretly wished he'd had a boy. (It seemed like the captain of the football team always had a name like TJ or JR back then.) I don't think I even knew my name was actually Brooke until I started school.

I had a great childhood—no siblings to challenge my authority—just me and a couple of stoned grown-ups who showered me with affection, attention, and nicknames. So, naturally, by the infallible laws of classical conditioning, I grew to associate nicknames with love. Even now, decades later, throw a sweetheart or honey my way, and I'll instantly assume, *This person adores me and would clearly give me a kidney if needed.*

Stupid brain.

Although I've obviously grown attached to BB, my favorite moniker by far was the one Harley, my boyfriend after Knight, gave me—Lady. I was sixteen, and it just sounded so grown-up and sexy. It wasn't generic, like baby, nor did it sound like something my parents might coo into the phone when they picked it up after ten o'clock, knowing good and goddamn well that I was talking to a boy.

Lady was statuesque. Strong. Feminine. Classy.

I was, in reality, none of those things.

When I met Harley, I had braces, weighed ninety-five pounds—including my steel-toed combat boots—and had a mostly shaved head. A charitable classmate introduced me to him after I'd been cheated on, humiliated, and repeatedly screamed at in front of the whole school by Knight.

Now, I know what you're thinking. *Knight, the angry skinhead guy, turned out to be a shitty boyfriend? No way! Fuck, I did not see that coming!*

Yeah, well, as it turned out, tidal waves eventually recede. And when they do, everything that was momentarily upended and twirled about is left smashed and soiled, miles from where it began.

As notorious and well known as Knight was, Harley James was a legend. He was the original Peach State High School bad boy. No one had ever actually seen him since he'd dropped out while my crew was still in middle school, but rumor had it that he'd been squatting in an abandoned house in Atlanta with a band of gutter punks or otherwise engaged in some form of romanticized vagrantism. I now know that such a lifestyle is actually referred to as homelessness, but at the time, Harley James was a punk-rock god and thus the *perfect* rebound.

A girl in my social studies class gave me his number after seeing how distraught I was over my very public and very scary now-everyone-thinks-I-might-wind-up-butchered-and-mounted-to-the-hood-of-Knight's-truck-like-some-fucked-up-pirate-ship-figurehead breakup.

Unbeknownst to me, Knight had started taking steroids a few months earlier and had morphed into the goddamn Incredible Hulk. Only, unlike Bruce Banner, he stayed giant and irrational *all the time*. Yeah, picture an already bloodthirsty *Romper Stomper*–looking motherfucker and then add fifty pounds of muscles and rabies. He was terrifying, and after the spectacular drama that ensued at Trevor Walcott's Halloween party, I was in need of a new boyfriend, stat.

I saw my life flash before my eyes that night. I'd developed a serious crush on Trevor, a new kid at school who'd been allowed to throw a massive Halloween party by his single mother. She was trying to make up for leaving his father and moving Trevor to a new school in the middle of the year by contributing to the delinquency of a shit-ton of teenagers. Trevor was smoldering hot in a guyliner, black hair, black fingernails, bedroom-plastered-with-*The Crow*-and-Nine Inch Nails-posters, tells-you-he-takes-lithium-for-depression-and-cutting-behaviors-the-first-time-you-meet-him kind of way. *Ooh, dark and tortured.*

I had every intention of fucking the shit out of him at his party that night. The only problem was that I was technically still dating Knight and was afraid that parts of me might wind up in his basement freezer if I tried to break up with him.

In a stroke of genius, I realized that the solution to all my problems would be to drop off a break-up note with Knight's mom on my way to the party, thus absolving me from any retribution should Knight find out that I'd banged Trevor on his bathroom floor that night. We would literally have been broken up for *hours* by the time I got around to discovering lithium's unfortunate sexual side effects.

Looky there, Skeletor. Your mom even has it in writing.

I should have been a fucking lawyer, because that shit was airtight.

Well, Knight's mom must have delivered the message telepathically because I hadn't been at the party long enough to finish whatever watered-down filth was in my Solo cup before I heard the unmistakable roar of Knight's monster truck building in the distance.

Fuck me.

The phrase *fight-or-flight* should be amended to include *freeze*, because when my temporal lobe registered the low growl of that particular F-150 my ass froze like Bambi's idiot mother...right before her head got blown off.

Ronald McKnight—'roided up archfiend from hell—was coming for me, and all I could do was silently scream at myself from inside my paralyzed body.

Run! Hide! You're gonna die, you stupid bitch! None of these anemic emo kids can save you! Abort! Abort!

But my steel-toed boots felt more like lead...and my slutty tiger costume began to feel more and more like a sick, ironic joke. Who was I kidding? I was no predator. I was a defenseless, doe-eyed little fawn who was about to become roadkill.

All I could do was stand there in Trevor's driveway, clutching my shiny red plastic cup, and wait for it—frozen like a deer in headlights before the headlights had even arrived.

Maybe he won't kill me in front of all these witnesses. Maybe he'll just almost kill me. Maybe he'll just almost kill me...

It happened so fast that when I replay the events in my head, it comes out looking like a series of still photos, like a cartoon playing in slow motion.

Knight's monster truck screeched into Trevor's teenager-filled cul-de-sac like a fucking bat out of hell. The passenger door swung open before the roaring monstrosity had even come to a complete stop, and Angel Alvarez, the skank he'd been cheating on me with, flew out toward me, screaming my name and flailing her arms, as if she were on fire.

My heart slammed repeatedly into my rib cage as if to say, *Stay here and die if you want, but I'm getting the fuck out!*

My mind oscillated between fear over my imminent death and confusion about why Angel was about to destroy *me* when she was obviously fucking *my* boyfriend. My body became rigid and tense, bracing for impact, as Angel's red eyes and bared teeth closed in on me. And then my eyes widened with shock as she toppled over the curb and face-planted her seething contorted mug right at my feet, which were still rooted firmly to the driveway.

Before my stupid deer brain could register the fact that I was still standing and in one piece, Angel's shrieking, kicking, thrashing body rose before me and began moving backward, suspended in midair, as if someone had pressed the Rewind button on my worst nightmare.

The fuck?!

It wasn't until my dilated pupils registered the silhouette of a formidable figure shoving her writhing body back into the truck that I realized that Knight had scooped her crazy Daisy Dukes–clad ass up off the driveway before she had a chance to lunge at me again. He was now putting those steroids to good use as he wrestled that syphilitic she-devil back into his eight-foot-high monster truck cab.

As they peeled away, it slowly began to dawn on me that I was not going to die. Trying to pretend like I hadn't just pissed my pants, I dramatically chucked my plastic cup onto the ground—once I'd regained the use of my arms—and shouted after them, "What the fuck was that, Angel?"

I'll tell you what that was, Journal. That was divine intervention. Angel Alvarez was a solid buck fifty of Red-Bull-and-crystal-meth-fueled trailer-park scrapper. I wouldn't have stood a chance. I would have been liquefied on impact had I not been blessed with a guardian angel who wasn't above tripping a bitch, not even a bitch named Angel.

After that little incident, I decided I needed to hook up with someone who could shoot lasers out of his fucking eyes. I had hoped it would be Trevor, but considering that he wasn't even able to shoot semen out of his penis when we fooled around in his hall bathroom that night (fucking lithium), I was in need of a new plan, stat.

That plan came together the following week when a girl in my social studies class, who had heard about my near-death experience at Trevor's party, decided to play matchmaker. Sizing up my partially shaved head, combat boots, and desperation, she told me that Harley James, *the* Harley James, was staying at his mom's place for a while. (*Oh, transient! How mysterious!*) And his mom's place just happened to be in her neighborhood.

She plopped his mom's number on my desk with a sad smile. At the time, I thought the forlorn look was her way of expressing pity over my current situation. I now know it was guilt over introducing me to the complete and utter disappointment that was Harley James.

That night, I tapped each digit on my cordless phone with shaking hands. Sitting in the middle of my bed, I clutched my knees to my chest with my free arm and took deep breaths as my other hand clutched the ringing receiver, trying hard to channel someone older, someone cooler, someone who didn't have fucking braces.

Oh my God, I'm a child calling a grown man from my bedroom in my parents' house, hoping he'll accept sex in exchange for protection from my steroid-secreting psychotic Cujo of an ex-boyfriend.

Right as I was about to slam the phone down and hyperventilate into an empty Camel Lights carton, I heard his voice. Despite being deep and rough, Harley's tone was disarmingly relaxed and warm.

I now know that he was probably just stoned out of his mind, but it was still a welcome contrast to Knight's sharpness and intensity.

Harley's slow, raspy cadence sounded like an old, familiar gravel road. I could almost hear the playful smile on his face and see the empty space on his lap where I would curl up and let him shield me from danger with his giant manly arms.

Knight's post-breakup rage had been so apocalyptic that my mother had actually let me stay home from school for three days after a particularly psychotic screaming episode he'd initiated outside of my Spanish class.

This *man*, Harley, was exactly what I needed. In my mind, he was a fifteen-foot-tall Minotaur with devil horns, who breathed napalm and could beat the shit out of Knight with nothing more than his giant, veiny cock, but now that I had him on the phone, he sounded like gritty, crystallized, slow pouring honey. *Mmm...*

Despite, or maybe because of, Harley's deep, unhurried drawl, my stomach was doing somersaults, and my skin was flushed in pink blotches from head to toe. What was happening to me? I was positively giddy. I felt excited but at ease, wanted but not hunted, and flirty without fear.

I hadn't realized until then how hypervigilant I had become with Knight. Recently, whenever he and I had been together, I'd found myself subconsciously scanning my surroundings for makeshift weapons and mapping out potential escape routes. It was like being in a relationship with a tranquilized velociraptor—or, you know, a skinhead who had recently started taking hard-core steroids.

Thank God Harley couldn't see me because I was all goofy grin and blushing cheeks and twiddling fingers and suppressed squeals.

After I nervously agreed to meet him for coffee that weekend (*Coffee! How grown-up!*) and stumbled through my awkward good-bye, Harley delivered the final blow.

I bit my lip, trying to hold in all the excited girlie noises, until he said his farewell. I was hoping he'd be quick about it because

I could feel the giggles percolating up behind my clenched jaw, but there was nothing quick about Harley James.

I waited for what felt like hours, listening to what I imagined was a self-confident I've-got-her-now smile on the other end, before Harley finally crooned in that sexy gruff voice of his, "Night, night, Lady."

Swoon!

As soon as I heard the click on the other end of the receiver, I immediately devolved into a giggling, writhing, convulsing puddle of hormones. Harley fucking James—bad-boy legend, winged mythical griffin of sex and rebellion—had called me Lady!

Lady!

Of course, in true bad-boy style, my knight in shining bondage pants[2] turned out to be a drug-dependent slack-jawed loser who lived in his mother's basement and couldn't manage to sit through a tattoo from start to finish, let alone a GED exam. But since *that* story isn't going to make Ken do anything other than get tested for hepatitis C, *this* is what I planted for his reading pleasure instead...

---

[2] In case you're wondering what the hell bondage pants are, they're ridiculous polyester plaid nightmares with loops and straps and zippers all over. They aren't actually used for bondage. They are more of a sexual impediment than anything, but in the late 1990s, nothing got me wet faster than seeing a gorgeous guy with his legs tethered to one another.

10

Ken, Meet Fantasy Harley

Super Private Journal That Ken Is Never, Never Allowed to Read Ever

"Harley, I can't. Not tonight."

"Pleeeease? I *promise* I'll have you home by curfew this time. I fucking pinkie swear. I'll even grab some beers from work and pick up dinner on my way home. Just come over. Pretty please?"

Besides being a locally infamous bad boy, Harley was a tattooed, twenty-two-year-old mechanic. To a seventeen-year-old high school senior in the late 1990s, that was basically the equivalent of dating Jordan Catalano.

"Harley, I can't. I have to finish addressing my graduation invitations tonight, or my mom is going to fucking murder me. She's been asking me to do it for weeks, but I keep blowing it off to hang out with you."

Harley grumbled into the phone.

I was usually easier to sway than this, and I could tell he was getting flustered. Harley James wasn't used to having to convince girls to make bad choices, but I was one fuck-up away from losing my car—a punishment worse than death to a seventeen-year-old girl living in a suburban town with no public transportation.

Harley had the blond-haired, blue-eyed baby face of James Dean with the body of a guy who'd done a little time for grand theft auto, hit the weights hard while he was in the clink, then decorated all his newly swollen muscles with flames and hot-rod tattoos once he'd gotten out. While he might have looked hard from the neck down—pun not intended—Harley was playful and flirty and fun to the core. Unfortunately, he was *so* carefree that he didn't take anything seriously, including my curfew or my parents' threats. Harley was the devil in a Sunday hat.

"So, bring your invitations with you and do 'em over here. I'll even take those big ole boots off and rub your feet while you work."

Mmm...

Just as he'd known it would, my mind started wandering down a rabbit hole of other things we could do with my boots off. I guess Harley was getting tired of me pretending like I wasn't going to give him what he wanted, because before I could even snap out of my daydream and slurp the drool back into my mouth, he unleashed his secret weapon.

"I miss you, Lady."

Boom. There it was. *Asshole.*

Even though I'd seen Harley almost every night for weeks, I had to admit, I missed him, too. He was just so light and airy. Compared to the brooding mood swings I'd tolerated, endured, and at times barely survived when I was with Knight, Harley made me feel like I was swimming in powdery-blue cotton candy. He smiled. He laughed. He made me laugh. When I spoke, he'd gaze at me like I had little butterflies and sunbeams dancing around my head. Knight used to look at me intensely, too, but it was more like a salivating jungle cat watching a gazelle. Harley, on the other hand, looked at me like I was the fucking *Mona Lisa* with pride and joy and disbelief that I was actually his.

I sighed into the phone and acquiesced, "Fine. But you're licking the stamps."

"Oh, I'll be licking a lot more than stamps."

⚬⚬⚬

Three hours later, I was sprawled out on Harley's living room floor, addressing my invitations safely behind the virtuous cover of my makeshift chastity wall. Chinese food cartons, empty Camel Lights boxes, crushed PBR cans, throw pillows, D-grade horror movie cases, calligraphy pens, and tiny towers of completed invitations divided Harley's living room down the middle, separating me from the oh-so-tempting mountain of muscle car–covered muscles who had been eye-fucking me from the couch all night.

When we'd met, Harley was renting a little bungalow from his uncle, who had pretty much let him decorate it however he wanted. So, basically, it was dripping with neon signs he'd stolen from the liquor store where he used to work and not much else. It was a blank canvas that I couldn't wait to get my hands all over. I didn't know if Harley actually wanted my help with decorating or if he was just humoring me, but anything I wanted for the place, he'd buy. After a few months, he even asked me to paint a mural on his bedroom wall. I'd been painting for years and could probably have done at least a decent job with whatever he commissioned.

When I asked him what he wanted, he just said, "Us," with that full-lipped smile I couldn't get enough of.

Knowing Harley's taste, I spray-painted a web of letters, his name and mine, in an aggressive sharp-angled font that took up the entire wall above the black leather headboard that I'd picked out weeks prior. I'd chosen colors that resembled the hues in his flame tattoos—reds, oranges, yellows, and electric blue. Every time I saw it, my stomach fluttered as I remembered the squealing, tickling spray-paint fight that had ensued before we'd completely devolved into a rolling rainbow-hued pair of bodies undulating on the tarp-covered carpet.

When he could tell that I was almost finished with my invitations, Harley surreptitiously slinked over and began thumbing through my done pile. "Damn, Lady. This shit looks seriously professional. Why are you still in school? You should just move in with me and do this for a living." Harley beamed like it was obviously the best idea anyone had ever come up with.

I blushed and kept working, trying to pretend like I wasn't swooning over everything that had just come out of his mouth. "Uh, thanks for the offer, but calligraphy pays shit, Harley."

He laughed and ran his fingers over the scrollwork on one of the (thankfully dry) envelopes. "Where did you learn to write like this?"

"My mom's an art teacher. She taught me calligraphy when I was just a kid so that I could help her address our Christmas cards." I gestured to the scattered piles of white all around us. "Now I'm her bitch."

Harley poked me in the ribs with the corner of the envelope he'd been admiring. "No, you're my bitch," he said with a huge twinkly-eyed grin.

Being this close to him, feeling the heat coming off his body and the warmth oozing from his every word, was making it really hard for me to concentrate. I needed to finish and go home. Finish and go home. If I didn't leave in the next fifteen minutes, my ass was going to be car-less and stranded in suburbia for the next month.

While I furiously tried to get through my final pile and ignore Harley's electric presence just inches away, he carefully picked up envelope after envelope, studying them intensely and handling each one with care.

After a few minutes, he mused, "You really have a thing for letters, don't you? Like on my wall, I said you could do anything you wanted, and you did letters."

It was so perceptive, so sweet. He just opened his eyes, got still for a moment, and saw *me*. Who knew Harley "Fun and Games" James could be so insightful?

That little observation earned him my undivided attention. I looked up and replied, "I guess so, yeah. I like to write, and I kind of feel like, by using different fonts and designs, I can make what I'm trying to say more beautiful."

Locking his playful robin's egg blue eyes on my hunter greens, he quipped, "Unless it's your name. There's no way to make *you* any more beautiful."

Gah, Harley! You're making me blush!

No one had ever complimented me as sincerely or as often as Harley. I didn't even know how to respond. Everything he said was so perfect and personalized. He complimented the things he knew I was insecure about or secretly proud of. No generic you're-so-hot bullshit. Every acknowledgment seemed to be the perfect shape and size to fill whatever void I was feeling at the time. Only, at that particular moment, the only void I could feel was the one throbbing between my legs.

Our close proximity on the floor was really starting to cloud my judgment. If he had just stayed on the couch with the chastity wall of garbage between us, like I'd begged, maybe I would have actually finished my invitations.

Instead, I decided to fight flirty with flirty. "We'll see about that. Give me your hand."

Harley gave up his right hand with an arched brow and an achingly coy little smile. I stroked the back of his hand with my thumb while I went to work, penning my best Old English across his knuckles. When I finally released him, he turned his fist around, so he could admire the word *LADY* I'd scrawled upon it. His expression went from curious to elated to mischievous in an instant. He briefly opened his fist before closing it again, this time gripping a handful of my shirt in it as he pulled me up and onto his lap.

Harley leaned in, so close that the silver hoop barely containing his big, fat, beautiful bottom lip grazed my parted mouth. "I'm never washing this hand again," he teased. With every syllable the deep rumble of Harley's voice vibrated against my mouth and traveled all the way down to the steel barbell piercing in my clit, making it thrum like a fucking tuning fork between my legs. I'd only had it a few months and it was still incredibly sensitive.

Without realizing it I hummed out loud in response.

"Mmm?" Harley replied, mocking the noise I'd just made. "You like to hum, Lady?" He ran the silver hoop slowly across my bottom lip, humming in a low growl that had my nipple piercings singing as well. "So do I."

I prayed for him to kiss me. To stop teasing me and crash those perfect, pouty lips into mine, but Harley James loved to play.

And I was his favorite toy.

Palming my mostly shaved head with the hand that read *LADY*, Harley pulled my head back slightly, breaking our almost-kiss and exposing my neck. The coolness of his lip ring mixed with the heat of his breath as he dragged his growling mouth down my throat. His tongue flicked at the base of my neck, then traced the edge of my collarbone, stopping only to skip over the thin strap of my tank top. Suddenly, I felt teeth sink into my shoulder as Harley's firm hands grabbed my thighs and spread them apart so that I was now straddling him on the couch. Closing his lips around the bite, Harley sucked on my freckled shoulder, humming against my flesh as he palmed my ass with both hands and guided my body up and down the length of his massive, almost impossibly hard shaft.

Harley's mouth left my skin with an exaggerated pop. I took that opportunity to yank my tank top off and unclasp my bra as quickly as possible. I *should* have been rushing to get my ass out the door and home before curfew, but in that moment my only priority was making sure that my nipples got the same attention that my shoulder had just gotten.

My enthusiasm made Harley chuckle. "Looks like somebody wants a hummer," he teased as I tore my own clothes off.

"Don't you have to have a dick to get a hummer?" I quipped back, chunking my bra to the floor as if it were on fire.

"Not the way I do it."

Harley's bright blue eyes were aflame as they traveled down my body. He knew exactly what I wanted, but was making me wait. Making me lose my cool. Toying with me.

Fucker.

Impatient and horny as hell, I threaded my fingers into his soft blond hair and kissed the shit out of him. My pelvis pressed against his cock and mimicked the movement of my tongue swirling around his, earning me another one of Harley's deep, pussy-vibrating moans. Without warning he broke the kiss and pulled away, giving me a cute, chastising look for not playing by his rules.

Harley wrapped his rough, permanently oil-stained mechanic's hands around my smooth, spotless rib cage and hoisted me up so that my left nipple was lined up with his mouth. "Perfect little tits," he whispered, almost to himself, then hummed quietly as he ran the seam of his lips across my ultra-sensitive pink flesh, his lip ring clinking and pulling against my nipple ring with every pass.

My clit throbbed. My panties were soaked. I needed some kind of relief, but Harley had me suspended above him so that there was nothing for me to grind against.

A whimper escaped my lips as I ran my nails along Harley's scalp to the back of his head and gently pressed his face into my breast. With a chuckle, Harley finally pulled my left nipple into his mouth and rubbed the pad of his thumb in slow circles over my right.

My head rolled back when he switched sides and captured my right nipple ring with his teeth. Keeping one hand firmly around my waist, Harley made sure I couldn't plop back down on his lap and find my release. *Asshole.*

"If I let go, do you promise to stay just like this?"

I looked down at him and shook my head *no.*

"What if I promise to do the same thing to your pussy?" His eyes twinkled up at me.

"Pinkie swear?"

Harley held up the pinkie with the *Y* on it and smiled. I let go of his head with one hand and linked my little finger with his. As we'd done a thousand times before, Harley and I locked eyes and leaned in, kissing each other's pinkie in unison before letting go.

It was what we did. We played like kids and fucked like maniacs. I craved spending time with Harley because, even though he was five years older than me and no stranger to our local correctional facility, he reminded me that I was still a teenager. At school I worked my ass off to graduate early with honors. At work I worked my ass off to pay for basic necessities like gas and cigarettes and tiger-striped velour leggings. But with Harley I just...laughed. And came. And laughed some more.

Harley expertly peeled my tight black jeans and panties off in seconds flat before returning me to my previous upright straddle position. Grabbing my ass with both hands, Harley suddenly lifted me so high I had to grab the sides of his head to keep my balance. Placing my shins on his shoulders and my knees on the back of the couch, Harley maneuvered me so that my aching, wet pussy was an inch from his mouth. Flashing me a look that said he was up to no good, Harley bit down on the end of the steel barbell between my legs, then wrapped his lips around my clit and hummed.

A few flicks of his tongue mixed with the vibration of his low moans had me writhing against his face, teetering on the edge of orgasm. *So this is a hummer,* I thought. *Holy shit.*

Just as I was about to explode, Harley stood, causing me to react and clutch his beautiful blond head even tighter, holding on for dear life.

Harley held on tight to my ass, keeping me upright, and chuckled into my vag as he kicked over the remnants of my chastity wall and splayed me out on my back in the middle of the living room floor, never taking his face away from my core. As he continued to lick and nip and suck and *hum* just lightly enough to prolong my torture, Harley began to unfasten the buckle on his studded leather belt. *Thank fucking God*, I thought as I clawed at his T-shirt, wrestling it over his head just as he got his fly open.

I practically pulled Harley's face up to mine by his ears. I was beyond done being teased and needed him inside me like I needed my next breath. As I lifted my head to taste myself on his mouth I lifted my hips to meet his hot, welcome length.

Evidently, Harley was done playing games too. Hovering over me, veins bulging out of the tattooed forearms he braced himself on, almost all traces of his playful persona were gone. Harley's eyes darkened to navy pools as the tip of his cock slid through my slippery folds, seeking entrance. In one swift thrust Harley filled me to bursting, growling into my mouth and clutching the back of my neck as my inner walls struggled to accommodate him.

Harley stayed buried inside me, grinding his pelvis against mine as he whispered into my ear. "So did you like your hummer?"

"Mmmmm…" I hummed appreciatively, unable to form words. The fullness was overwhelming in the best possible way.

"Mmmmm?" he answered back. I could feel his smile against my cheek.

Capturing Harley's earlobe between my lips I hummed, "Mm hmm," then rolled him onto his back and finally claimed his mouth like I'd been dying to since the moment he told me he was never going to wash his hand again.

Not one to relinquish the upper hand so easily, Harley grabbed my hips with both hands and thrust into me from underneath. The moan that escaped his mouth reverberated down to my swollen, sensitive flesh, causing my insides to contract in torrents of pleasure. I bit down on his shoulder to stifle my scream as Harley ignored my orgasm and continued thrusting—prolonging my ecstasy until his cock swelled and jerked inside me.

I woke up, adrift on a scattered sea of envelopes, sore and sated. Two thick and thoroughly tattooed arms were clamped down around my waist, the only things keeping me from floating away on a foggy cloud of pheromones and bliss. That is, until I realized that the ridiculous Jamaican accent coming from the TV belonged to the one and only Miss Cleo.[3]

I wriggled out of Harley's embrace and darted around the room, gathering my belongings and snatching and swatting at the square pieces of paper that were stuck all over my naked body. Where each envelope had been, an intricately penned name or address was left behind, in mirror image, on my skin.

I felt like I was that guy in the movie *Memento*. He couldn't form new memories, so he had all his most pertinent information tattooed on his body backward, so he could bring himself

---

[3] Miss Cleo's psychic hotline infomercials were ubiquitous with late-night TV in the '90s, and they never, ever came on before midnight. As soon as I heard *that* voice, I knew, even without the "free psychic readin'," that I was totally fucked.

up to speed every morning when he looked in the mirror. Only, my particular affliction wasn't that I couldn't remember—it was that I just wouldn't fucking learn.

I was livid. This was exactly what I'd known was going to happen if I came over because it was exactly what had happened every time I came over. Harley would wait until it was almost time for me to leave, and then he'd get all flirty. If that didn't work, he would go straight for pouty—wrinkling his brow, puffing out his big, fat bottom lip, and blinking his beautiful blue puppy-dog eyes at me—until I was riding his cock.

I had to roll Harley's massive, snoring body over to snatch up the last of my invitations, but that easygoing motherfucker just snorted and curled up around one of the skull throw pillows I'd made during my decorating frenzy like it was a teddy bear.

He really was just a big kid.

I took one long last look at Harley's sleeping baby face, pompadour of sunny-blond sex hair, and inked-up muscles clutching my pillow, and I choked back a sob. This man was trouble with a capital *rubble*. Even though he'd said he wanted the best for me and supported my plans, in just a few months, I'd let my obsession with this modern-day rebel without a cause destroy my perfect 4.0 GPA and ruin my relationship with my parents. Now, I'd let him come between me and my freedom.

With the sting of unshed tears in my eyes and the grip of a vise around my chest, I took one last mental picture of the cuddly sex machine at my feet, turned on my unlaced boot heel, and drove the ever-loving shit out of my beloved Mustang one last time before turning the keys over to my seething father, who was waiting for me on the front porch when I got home. Neither of us said a word during the exchange.

The next morning, I suffered through my first three classes in silence. My whole body ached from the night before, primarily from sleeping on the floor, and my eyes were puffy from crying myself back to sleep once I'd gotten home. A few patches of carpet burn had made themselves known throughout the day as well.

None of it held a candle, however, to the agony I was feeling over having to leave Harley. He had been my daily source of fun, flattery, and affection for the last six months. Leaving him behind to trudge into the dark waters of adulthood alone felt terrifying. But how would I ever become a successful college-educated grown-up when my boyfriend was the world's worst influence, his sexy wink and wicked grin undermining all my attempts to be responsible?

I was in such a fog of despair that I almost walked straight into him as I made my way to the smokers' corner of the parking lot during my lunch break.

Harley caught me in his big arms and hugged me like he hadn't seen me in days. It was a shock to my already fragile psyche to see him so out of context. I didn't exactly hug him back, but I let those warm arms squeeze a little of the frost out of my heart before I craned my neck to look at his worried face.

"What are you doing here? You got kicked out, remember? If anybody sees you here, they'll call the fucking cops!"

I could feel the stares from all around. It wasn't every day that a dangerous-looking man covered in tattoos and sporting a black beanie sauntered onto campus and snatched up a female student, especially one who'd been expelled four years prior and was practically worshipped by every kid rebellious enough to smoke at school.

"I had to see you and make sure you were okay."

Harley looked like hell—well, sexy as hell—but he did need a shave, was wearing the clothes I'd peeled off of him the night before, and his usually baby-blue eyes were pink-rimmed and at half-mast.

"Did they take your car?"

I simply nodded and turned my attention to the ground, willing my eyes to dry up, before I chanced another glance up at him.

"I'm so fucking sorry, baby." Harley held my head to his chest and splayed his fingers over my buzzed, bleached hair.

"When I woke up and you were gone, I went fucking nuts. I just had this feeling like . . . like I was never gonna see you again. I wanted to come get you so bad, but I knew I would just make things worse if I showed up at your parents' house in the middle of the night. I thought I was going to lose my shit."

Harley planted a kiss on the top of my head and pulled me even closer. At first, I thought he was trying to comfort me, but it might have been the other way around. Harley's usually playful demeanor was gone, replaced by something uncharacteristically urgent and austere. Hearing the sincerity in his voice made my heart constrict, and in that moment, I realized that I'd been blaming the wrong person. Harley was a grown man who could do and who happily did whatever he wanted. He didn't have a curfew. I did. And I was the fuck-up here.

I kept my face snuggled into his chest, into his musky T-shirt that smelled like gasoline fumes and cigarettes. He smelled like a car guy, my car guy.

"It's not your fault, Harley. This shit is on me," I said.

Harley took half a step away and held me by my upper arms so that I was forced to look at him. What I saw was heartbreaking. His beautiful, mischievous face had been transformed into something I barely recognized—the dull bloodshot scowl of a man who'd been up all night, drinking and thinking, both to excess. Even his carefree blond pompadour had disappeared, shoved under a black woolen beanie that matched the circles under his eyes almost as well as it matched the atmosphere between us.

"No, it's on me. All my life, I've just done what I wanted when I wanted and said, *Fuck the consequences.* I wanted you to stay with me, so I did whatever it took to make that happen, even after I'd promised that I would get you home on time." Harley's tone was rough and his volume was climbing.

"I just fucked your whole life up because my house feels empty and wrong when you're not in it." Harley shoved his hands in his pockets, breaking physical contact with me, then tilted his head back and shouted, "Fuuuuck!" into the sky.

I scanned the parking lot to make sure the authorities hadn't been alerted, then took a step forward and resumed our embrace. Breathing harder now, Harley reluctantly pulled his hands from his pockets, but instead of hugging me back he cupped my face in his palms and tilted it up toward his.

Harley continued in a gruff whisper, "You have no idea how sorry I am. I feel like a complete piece of shit, and I don't know what to do to make it right. You have to let me make this right, baby."

Harley's brow was furrowed, and those bloodshot blue eyes bore right into my soul. He was nervously tonguing the silver hoop piercing that wrapped around the center of his big, beautiful bottom lip, and I wanted nothing more than to kiss his fear away. Seeing the pain etched on his face hurt worse than the truckload of despair I'd been hauling around since last night.

Who was I kidding? Car or no car, I couldn't stay away from this man for a day, let alone forever.

And as if on cue, Harley, sensing that I was on the precipice of making yet another bad decision, decided to give me one last little push.

"I want this to be forever, Lady."

Jesus. Okay, okay. You're forgiven. Can we go back to being happy now?

Trying to lighten the mood and pretend as though I hadn't just broken up with him in my mind a few hours earlier, I popped two cigarettes into my mouth, lit them both, and smiled as I handed one to Harley. "Is this another proposal? You haven't asked me yet this week, you know," I mused.

Harley had been asking me to marry him almost daily for the last two or three months, ever since the day he'd found a gaudy gold Claddagh ring on the sidewalk outside my work. He'd been coming to see me on my lunch break when he spotted it, so naturally, as soon as he'd walked in, Harley dropped to one knee, thrust that little piece of shit into the air, and proposed to me right in front of my boss and all the good patrons of Pier 1 Imports. It was the first of at least three dozen humiliating public proposals.

While having to repeatedly reject Harley in front of our friends, coworkers, and strangers had started off horribly embarrassing and awkward, over time, it'd become a running joke between us. I was just too damn young, and he was just too damn carefree for either of us to take marriage seriously. But I had to admit, seeing Harley James, legendary bad boy with the face of an angel and the body of an ex-con, on bended knee was really starting to grow on me.

Harley turned a gleaming impish eye on me and brought his right hand to his chin, as if he were mulling over a quick parking lot proposal.

He's back! My playful Harley! Yes!

As he rubbed his oh-so-sexy stubble and scanned the audience of pimply-faced teenagers watching his every move, my eyes were immediately drawn to the four letters I had etched on his knuckles the night before.

Giddily, I squealed, "You really didn't wash your hand!" and reached for it reflexively.

When my thumb slid across the unexpectedly slippery *A* and *D*, I glanced down, searching for the source of the slime, and gasped. The skin around each letter was an angry pink color, and the entire surface was slick with what looked like Vaseline.

Oh.

My.

Fucking.

God.

11

Inception-Style, Muthafucka!

BB's Secret Journal

September 13

Dear Journal,

My first Super Private Journal That Ken Is Never, Never Allowed to Read Ever entry was perfection, Journal! Perfection! I covered all four objectives—an adorable pet name, compliments, spontaneous floor sex, and a surprise personalized tattoo somewhere visible and brazenly unprofessional. Check, check, check, and *check*!

None of it was true, of course. Well, *some* of it was true. Harley did have tattoos. He did have a shock of blond hair, pretty puppy-dog eyes, and a big ol' pouty pierced bottom lip. He did ask me to marry him all the time with a shitty little piece-of-shit ring he'd found on the ground. And he did call me Lady.

Swoon.

So, the Subliminal Spousal Bibliotherapy seeds have been

planted, and evidently, they have already taken root. Just last night Ken and I went to this little bar in Athens to see a local rock legend we really love named Butch Walker. While we were milling around waiting for the show to start, I got bored and decided to test the waters a little bit. Ken and I had the following conversation.

Me: So, Butch posted a photo of his new tattoo on Facebook yesterday, and it's pretty badass. He got this Sailor Jerry–style anchor on the back of his hand with his dad's name going across it in a banner. It looks so good.

Ken: I'll bet he got it next door. That place is open twenty-four hours and always looks busy.

Me: Oh, yeah? Maybe we should stop by there after the show.

Ken: You looking to get some new ink?

Me: No, but you are.

Ken: Oh, am I?

Me: Yep. You're gonna get a heart with my name on it.

Ken: And where am I going to get it?

Me: Somewhere highly visible—like your neck probably. Or the back of your hand, like Butch. YES! Oh my God, that would look SO good! You have to, Ken! A heart with my name in a banner across it right on the back of your hand! It would be soooo romantic!

Ken: What about on my forearm?

Me: Why? So, you can hide it? Like you hide your love?

Ken: Um, no. Because I like forearm tattoos. But if I did get one, it would be a compass rose, not a heart.

Me: Would it still have my name on it?

Ken: Nope.

Me: WHY NOT?!?! I gave you two beautiful children and all of my best years, motherfucker!

Ken: Exactly. I don't want the name of some old lady with two kids on my arm.

Needless to say, the tattoo objective is going to take some more work. So, while we're waiting to see if I can covertly manipulate my husband into making some poor and very permanent choices, how about I tell you the real story behind one of my own very poor choices, Harley James?

12

More Like, Billy I-*Don't*

BB's Secret Journal

September 20

I lurched my new (only in the sense that it was new to me—the damn thing was almost old enough to vote) black Mustang hatchback onto the curb and willed myself to let go of the steering wheel.

I'd only had my license for three months. My heart was pounding, and my mouth was so dry that my braces were starting to stick to the inside of my lips. Those were also new.

In fact, everything about me was new. In the two or so years since I'd started high school I had gone from an innocent little fourteen-year-old girl who could count the number of times she'd been kissed on one finger to a thoroughly fucked rock vixen with a mostly shaved head, bleach-blonde bangs, kohl-caked eyes, and a shiny steel barbell shoved through each and every one of her erogenous zones.

I ran my hands up and down the perforated leather of the steering wheel and took one last steadying drag from my cigarette before flicking it out the window with my thumb and middle finger.

Oh, I bet that looked badass. I hope Harley saw me flick my cigarette just now—or not. That would mean that he's home and that I'm going to meet him—right now. Oh my God. Maybe he's going to stand me up. But how could he? On the phone, he said he doesn't have a car.

Seriously, Journal, I was nauseatingly nervous about meeting a twenty-two-year-old guy who lived in his mom's basement and didn't have a car…while sitting inside *my car*. That's like Beyoncé worrying about whether or not she's going to impress Lil' Kim. That's like Tom Brady being anxious about going to his twenty-year high school reunion. That's like…well, you get the point.

Buying myself a little more time, I smeared some piña colada–flavored Bonne Bell Lip Smackers on my pout in the rearview mirror (to prevent that embarrassing braces-lip-snag-thing from happening) and tried to psych myself up for the long walk to Harley's front door.

Of course he'll like you. You look smoking hot! Your black eyeliner is smudged to perfection. You're wearing your signature tiger-striped velour stretch pants and black Dropkick Murphys tank top. The straps of your new red Wonderbra give a nice pop of color. And your shit-kicking black steel-toed Grinders will let him know that you're a worthy lay. And that cigarette flick? Forget about it! He'll love you! Unless your braces are a turn-off…oh God!

Pulling myself away from the mirror, I took a deep breath and opened the car door. As I stepped out into the sunshine my consciousness floated away like a balloon tethered to the top of my head. I watched from somewhere high above my body as my legs—swathed in animal-print velour—lifted, stepped, and fell alternately of their own accord toward Harley's benign-looking brown split-level. As the tiny figure below me continued to advance, now mechanically ascending the stairs to Harley's front door, my consciousness began hyperventilating into an invisible paper bag.

Oh, shit, I'm freaking out. I'm freaking out, and he's going to know. What if he watched me primping in my car? What if he knows this bra is padded? What if he doesn't know this bra is padded and we fool around? Oh no! He's a grown man! He doesn't want to fuck a child, especially not one who also looks like a little boy. Oh my God! Breathe, BB, breathe. You're a badass. You're a badass...

I watched with detached wonderment as a black fingernail shakily extended from my body and rang the doorbell. Before returning it to my side, I studied it idly, thinking surely there had to be more to meeting Harley James than this. A secret knock or handshake or something. But when I looked up from my cogitation, there, standing before me, was someone even more unapproachable than the mythical creature I'd come to see.

It was Billy Idol.

Billy fucking Idol just answered the door to Harley's mom's run-down, '70s-style doo-doo–brown tri-level house. With his messy blond pompadour, mischievous baby-blue eyes, and over-full lips pulled to the side in a self-confident smirk, Harley was a dead ringer for my beloved Billy. The familiarity instantly put me at ease.

The rest of him, however, did something else to me entirely. Harley's broad shoulders stretched the well-worn fabric of his faded black Misfits T-shirt almost to its breaking point, and his long, muscular legs were wrapped in a pair of hip-hugging red-and-black plaid bondage pants, like a Christmas gift that I would definitely not be able to wait until December 25th to open.

God, he was perfect.

Until he smiled.

In an instant my balloon of consciousness popped and came crashing back down to earth, bitch-slapped out of its reverie, by the worst teeth I had ever seen.

Fuck, they were bad. You could have parked a double-wide between those discolored front tusks, and the rest of them looked like they were engaged in fisticuffs, scrambling over each other in a desperate attempt to leap from that hellhole—pun fully intended—and finally put an end to their suffering.

They were horrifying, Journal. Horrifying. These teeth would have made Steve Buscemi blow chunks.

Oh well, he was still a legend and a damn fine one at that—with his mouth closed. As long as he kept his trap shut or semi-shut most of the time, I was thoroughly prepared to overlook this one flaw.

After all, who was I to judge? Still in braces, I wasn't completely rid of my own gap yet.

Besides, you don't see people *not* having sex with Woody Harrelson or Madonna because of a little gap, do you? Fuck no! Because they're famous, and so was Harley James, at least locally.

But then, he began to speak…

Goddamn it!

Harley was a fucking snaggletoothed moron!

I mean, I knew going in that he'd dropped out of school and was transient and all, but I'd thought it was because he was a hardened criminal, not because he had the IQ and processing speed of a three-toed sloth on barbiturates.

Ugh.

At least he was nice to look at, especially from the nose up and the neck down, and he was super warm and friendly (which was kind of unfortunate because it caused him to smile a lot, with his teeth), and his voice was every bit as slow and deep and gritty as I remembered from our phone conversation...

Hmm...

Ever the optimist, I went out for coffee with Harley anyway. If I could just get Knight to see us together while the lower half of Harley's face was hidden behind a coffee mug, it wouldn't matter that he had bad teeth and half a brain. Knight would know that I was under the protection of *the* Harley James—a gorgeous, grown-ass man who breathed napalm and ate bullies like him for breakfast. At least, that was his reputation, and for my purposes, Harley's rep was all that mattered.

I don't know if it was because my expectations for the afternoon had been so severely lowered or because Knight had literally become a stalker on steroids since our breakup, but about an hour into my date with Harley, I realized that I was actually kind of digging the guy. While he looked like he'd just stepped out of a Sex Pistols video and had a voice that sounded like it was coming through the static-laden speaker in the bulletproof visitation window at the state pen, Harley's vibe was laid-back, affable—happy, even. Having been raised by two affectionate, pot-smoking, Woodstock-era hippies, Harley's calm contentedness was strikingly familiar.

This feels nice. This feels right. This man would never hurt me. This man would cherish and protect me. This man is also probably dumb enough to throw down with Ronald fucking McKnight, if need be. Yep, this one might do after all.

Stupid, stupid brain.

As it turned out, Harley's familiar vibe had nothing to do with his spirit and everything to do with the fact that, like my parents, he was just stoned all the time. In fact, I think Harley was physically incapable of being sober. He'd smoked, snorted, and swallowed so many drugs by the time I got to him that I could have probably removed my nail polish with his blood and gotten a contact high from the fumes. In my defense, I honestly didn't know he was on drugs for the first few months of our relationship. Like I said, my parents were always stoned, too, so his half-open eyelids and inability to tell analog time was nothing new. I just blamed it on his low IQ.

Then, one day, after we'd been dating for, like, three months, Harley settled his glassy eyes on my face and casually stated, "Man, I think this is the first time I've ever seen you when I was sober."

Before I could process the significance of that statement, Harley burst out laughing, throwing his head back and wiping tears from his eyes.

It took him a moment to regain his composure before he was able to choke out, "Holy shit! I totally fucking forgot I smoked a shit-ton of weed with Mark before you came over! Bah-ha-ha-ha-ha-ha!"

And that was when I realized that Harley had never *not* been high.

In the name of protecting myself from Knight (or possibly just making him jealous), I focused solely on Harley's positive qualities. He actually was really cute, discolored Chiclet teeth aside. He had the long, lean body, wardrobe, and drug habit of a legitimate punk rocker, but none of the emotional baggage. Although his rep made him sound like a hardened criminal, to me Harley was just fun, flirty, fresh air. He made me smile, he made me come, and he was old enough to buy me cigarettes and alcohol. At sixteen, what more could I have asked for?

I didn't care about Harley's lack of education, intellect, or future. I shrugged at his lack of a car. And I'd even accepted that his living situation involved '70s-era wood-paneling, mildew, and two grown men sleeping in side-by-side twin beds.

When I first began dating Harley, he was sharing his mother's one-room daylight basement with Davidson, his younger brother, who worked at the local Army-Navy surplus store. Davidson housed an impressive cache of homemade pipe bombs, sawed-off shotguns, big Dirty Harry–style handguns, live hand grenades, and night-vision goggles in their closet. He even had what I considered at the time to be a smallish block of C4 but later learned was actually a crazy go-straight-to-Guantanamo Bay-with-a-bag-over-your-head shitload of C4. (Evidently, it's really concentrated, like wasabi.)

After discovering Davidson's stockpile of death, their mom (who was on husband number eight and looked exactly like what you'd expect a woman who'd named her sons Harley and Davidson to look like) decided that it was time to separate her increasingly criminal sons. Even though Davidson was the arms dealer of the pair, Harley was older and less employed, so he was exiled into a corner of the garage that his stepdad had hastily drywalled off and run an extension cord out to.

It reminded me of how people typically regard a litter of puppies. They're cute and cuddly but completely incapable of following basic social mores, like not pissing on the floor, so you keep them warmish and dryish in the garage and visit them when they get loud enough to remind you that they exist.

Harley did have a TV out there, so there was that.

But the one thing I *never* accepted, never failed to be humiliated by, never wanted to acknowledge or admit existed was Harley's tattoos. Oh my fucking God, the tattoos. Journal, you know I love ink on a man, but these tattoos were an embarrassment to us all. Every time I caught a glimpse of one of Harley's biceps, I wanted to weep. I don't even know where to begin. I can still feel the heat rising to my cheeks from just thinking about those crimes against art. I have an actual visceral reaction to their repugnance. That's how bad these tattoos were—*are*.

Deep breath . . . okay, here goes.

13

Knock, Knock. Who's There? Ding-Dong.

BB's Secret Journal

September 21

Dear Journal,

Of all the godawful things I've confessed so far, these tats make me feel the dirtiest, and they weren't even on my body. I guess technically they were *on* my body sometimes. (Get it?)

In my defense, I didn't even know that Harley had tattoos until the first time he parked his wienermobile in my garage. (I say wienermobile because that thing was *almost* as big as the famous Oscar Mayer hot-dog car. Almost.)

After my first run-in with that ten-pound trouser snake, I began calling Harley "Ding-Dong." He was flattered because he thought it was in reference to his penis size. *Bless his heart.*

I had ripped his clothes off in the darkness of his basement abode, so it wasn't until we were done fooling around and I'd turned on the harsh fluorescent lights that I noticed an odd little word etched on Harley's chest. It was on his left pectoral muscle but a little too high to be over his heart, like somewhere between his heart and his collarbone. The tat was so faint that it could have been written with pencil or administered in jail. Jailhouse tats always seem to have that telltale sketchy appearance. (Sketchy in both senses of the word.)

I squinted and slinked closer, trying to covertly make out what it said, while Ding-Dong concentrated on shimmying back into his leather pants, oblivious to my scrutiny. Once I was about five feet away, I was able to make out a three-letter word scrawled in a bizarre block outline—*ARM*.

That's it. Just *ARM*. On his chest. It said fucking *arm* on his chest, Journal.

Arm…arm…

Surely, there was a pun or a play on words there somewhere. People don't just ask other people to permanently label one of their body parts with the name of another body part, right?

Searching for some explanation, my brain instantly began tearing through every image, phrase, pun, anagram, song, and associated word in my entire catalog of experiences. I had nothin'.

Once Ding-Dong managed to wrestle his anaconda back into his skintight pants, I asked him about it, then immediately wished I hadn't.

A little too happily, Harley explained, "Oh, that? Well, it was gonna say *168 FARM STREET BOYS*, but the guy who was doing it skipped town before he could finish." He shrugged and began searching around for his shirt, surprisingly devoid of embarrassment.

I had so many follow-up questions after that statement that I didn't know where to begin.

So, does this mean that you're gang-affiliated? Did the guy skip town fifteen minutes into your tattoo, like, out of the bathroom window, because that piece should have taken forty-five to fifty minutes, tops? Oh, wait, is skipped town *a euphemism for* got shivved? *And why did he start with the middle of the middle word in the phrase? Was he dysgraphic?*

Sensing my confusion, Ding-Dong continued as he shoved his bare toes into his unlaced boots. "When I was living in Atlanta, I was in a crew called the One Sixty-Eight Farm Street Boys. We all lived in this shitty fucking house, and that was the address—one sixty-eight Farm Street." Smiling to himself, as if reminiscing about the good old days, he wistfully added, "They called me Scabie James."

Okay, I only had one follow-up question to that little gem. I tried to sound as non-judgy as possible when I sputtered, "Why did they call you Scabie James?"

"Oh, because I had scabies. That place was really fucking nasty."

#$%@&@$#%!

No words. My brain had no words. Just electromagnetic pulses of prickly creeped-out no-feelings and alarm bells and flashing arrows pointing me in the direction of the exit. I'd just had sex with a guy who not only used to—at least I hoped it was past tense—have scabies, but was proud of the motherfucking nickname!

Before I could snatch up the rest of my clothes and do the sprint of shame across his mother's front yard, Ding-Dong turned to pick up his studded belt. And I saw his right arm.

At first glance, it looked like any other generic tribal tattoo— a solid black design that forked and ended in sharp points. I almost dismissed it and continued to make my escape until I noticed how simple it was. Usually, tribal designs were some-what intricate and took up a decent amount of space. This thing just had three points and no twists or turns at all. It really just looked like a thick, pointy poorly drawn letter Y—as in, *why did my mom have to huff all that paint thinner while she was pregnant?*

I had to ask, again trying to mask my horror, as I pointed to his right shoulder, "Tell me about this one."

He smiled his sweet, innocent there-is-absolutely-nothing-to-be-humiliated-about smile again and said, "Oh, that's my tribal piece."

I snorted. I couldn't help it. Choking down the percolating hysterics was agony. *Agony!*

As I bit my lip and tried in vain to suppress my giggles, Ding-Dong absentmindedly went about collecting the rest of his clothes, continuing, "Yeah, it's not totally done, but I ran out of money before it was finished, and you know…whatever."

It's not totally done?? It's not halfway done! It's a fucking Y, you knuckle-dragging mouth-breather!

That was it. The mood had sufficiently been demolished, and I was in need of a turpentine douche, stat.

I politely made my exit and enjoyed the view as Ding-Dong walked me out to my car. From the back, he was all leather pants, studded belt, no shirt, just-fucked messy blond hair…

Mmm…what was I so upset about again?

Oh, yes, scabies and brain damage.

But…but he was so cute and sweet and *hung*.

I decided that maybe, as long as he continued to wear shirts with some regularity, these tats could just join the long list of Shit About Harley I'm Overlooking for the Sake of Making Knight Both Jealous and Afraid to Murder Me.

Nobody has to know about the tats, I thought. *I can pretend like they don't exist*, I thought.

That was before I saw the one on his head.

—◆—

Although I knew Harley also had a tattoo of some asinine sci-fi I-wasn't-listening-when-he-told-me-but-I-think-it-involved-a-spaceship thing on the top of his head, I thought it was a nonissue since the entire piece was buried under that oh-so adorable shock of rockabilly blond hair. The operant word in that sentence being *was*. It *was* buried—up until the day he was scheduled to meet my parents.

Before my parents ever met Harley, they hated him. I had already been busted a couple of times for lying to them about where I was spending the night. (Obviously, I had been curled up with Harley in his twin-size bed in his mother's garage.) So, I'd lost my driving privileges for a month.

During one particular bout of punishment, I decided having Harley over for dinner would make my parents more sympathetic to my cause? That question mark was intentional. I have no idea what I was thinking. It must have been the contact high I'd gotten from swapping body fluids with Harley so often.

Since Ding-Dong didn't have a car at the time and my car had been confiscated, I volunteered my parents to take me to pick him up in my mom's Band-Aid–colored Ford Taurus station wagon. I was unflappable, cavalier even, from the backseat of that rolling eyesore of festering tension. When we pulled up in front of Harley's mom's place, I was actually giddy. I'd been grounded for a week, and I was dying to see my sexy Billy Idol look-alike (while his mouth was closed and shirt was on, at least) come barreling down the stairs of his mom's rickety termite-infested front porch and into my waiting arms.

My mom honked the horn.

Real classy, Mom.

When Harley emerged, my giddiness was replaced by something else. Confusion? Disappointment? He looked different. Something was very wrong. It wasn't until he'd confidently stridden all the way across the driveway and pulled open the car door that my brain finally acknowledged what was going on.

Harley had shaved his head…completely bald…right before meeting my parents.

And…there it went. My consciousness bolted like a caged animal the moment Harley stepped into the car. It clung to the roof and watched upside down through the back windshield as he slid over to me, beaming from ear to ear, and gave my rigid, abandoned body a nuzzle.

From my vantage point above the car, I could see everything. Where Harley's adorably soft blond pompadour used to be, there was instead a crudely drawn image the size of a fucking dinner plate. It depicted a bird's-eye view of Harley's brain, as if his skull had been removed like the lid of a cookie jar. The center of his brain appeared to be hollowed out into a spaceship-style cockpit, and there, in the center, manning the craft, was a tiny fucking penis.

A tiny fucking circumcised penis with little dick arms and a look of determination on his little dick face was jostling joysticks around inside Ding-Dong's pickled brain. My parents were minutes away from finding out that their sixteen-year-old *only* child was dating a grown man with no job and no car and no brain cells and bad teeth and oh, by the way, he also has a fucking penis tattooed on his head.

Luckily, the empty shell of a body that I'd deserted in the backseat was incapable of forming coherent speech patterns, let alone demanding an explanation, because unlike the *ARM* tat,

I figured out the euphemism Harley had been going for with this piece immediately, and quite frankly, the backseat of your mother's station wagon is the last place you want to hear your adult boyfriend explain, *I think with my cock! Get it?*

The shock and dissociation I experienced after seeing that little phallus were so profound that I barely remember anything from the moment we picked Harley up to the moment we dropped him back off.

The only images I've been able to mine from that evening are of my mother lurking behind Ding-Dong like a shadow while he and I ate our Domino's pizza at the kitchen table. As he snarfed down his fifth slice of pepperoni, completely unaware of her presence, my mom made direct, searing eye contact with me over the top of his tattooed head. Raising one scarily pissed-off eyebrow, she slowly and blatantly shifted her gaze down to Ding-Dong's exposed scalp, drawing her mouth into a tight line of disgust. It was terrifying.

My mom doesn't do pissed off, Journal. She's usually too stoned to feel her face, let alone her feelings, so this little demonstration was frighteningly out of character.

Once he was out of the car and we were on our way back home, I braced myself for my mother's wrath. Sure, she was a hippie pacifist to the core and barely even raised her voice in anger, but I'd never exactly brought home a grown man with a penis tattooed on his head and zero high school diplomas before either.

All bets were off.

After riding in suffocating silence for a few miles, my natural tendency toward optimism took over, and I began to think, *Maybe she's just going to give me the silent treatment! Maybe she's not actually going to kill me!*

Then, her hand shot out in my direction.

Mommy, no!

Only, instead of smacking me in the mouth she simply reached past my tense, waifish body and opened the glove box. I watched through splayed fingers as her hand disappeared under a pile of miscellaneous bullshit for just a moment and emerged holding not a Glock, but a mundane-looking Altoids tin.

Driving with one eye on me, one knee on the steering wheel, and both hands firmly wrapped around the Altoids tin as if it held the antidote to her daughter's idiocy, my long-suffering mother pried open the lid and pulled out one pristinely rolled joint and a tiny pink lighter.

God bless her.

She puffed in silence the rest of the way home, which took for-fucking-ever, what with her driving ten miles under the speed limit and stopping at every yellow light, yield sign, and shiny object along the way. When we *finally* pulled into the driveway, her nerves appeared to have been restored to their typical Woodstock levels of tranquility, whereas mine had been utterly *annihilated*.

Just as I was about to open my door and sprint to safety, my mom took a deep, self-composing breath, pinned me with a glassy-eyed stare, and slurred, "Pumpkin, I hope you're using protection with that man. He looks like he's been to prison, and with that wiener on his head he was probably somebody's bitch. I don't want you getting the big C."

I'm pretty sure the big C is cancer, but I didn't have the heart to correct her. As my mother erupted into a giggle fit, I smiled and realized that that woman would probably help me bury a body. Especially one with a certain tattoo on his head.

14

My Tail Fell Off Again

BB's Secret Journal

September 27

Dear Journal,

Ding-Dong had three stupid tattoos when we started dating, three imbecilic tattoos that I'd learned to at least pretend to ignore. He had four when we finally broke up. (And by "broke up" I mean, I just stopped answering the phone when he called. Literally. Ding-Dong was so stoned and low-functioning and car-less that I was able to break up with him by attrition.) That fourth tattoo was the straw that broke the Camel Light, but we'll get to that in a minute.

Ding-Dong never grew his hair back out after that mortifying night at my parents' house, which was a huge blow to my libido. I mean, it's one thing to date a loser who looks like a punk rock James Dean (with his mouth shut, at least). It is another thing entirely to date a loser who has a tattoo on his head of a penis driving his brain.

I didn't break up with him right away, though. By the time he'd shaved his head we'd been together for several months and

I'd actually really grown to like the guy. He was just so much damn fun to be around. He was spontaneous and affectionate, and he really did ask me to marry him every day. But the biggest carrot on a stick for me was the fact that Harley was going to get a picture of me tattooed on his body.

I knew it was wrong, Journal—allowing a man to get your likeness permanently carved into his skin, all the while knowing your relationship had about a six-month shelf life. But I didn't really regard Ding-Dong as a real person with real feelings at the time—or now, to be honest. I might have had more of a conscience about it if he'd said he wanted to get my full name and Social Security number emblazoned across his forehead, but what he was going for was more of a cartoon-style version of me, so I figured he could just pass it off as a generic slutty anime pixie when we broke up.

See, Journal? I'm practically Mother Teresa.

For weeks, Ding-Dong had me drawing sketches for him. It was so exciting! He pored over every detail. I'd never seen him so interested in anything. I must have drawn him twenty-five designs. He wanted sad clown BB, sugar skull BB, Bettie Page BB, bionic angel BB, and even gutter-punk BB brandishing a pair of brass knuckles and a baseball bat. I couldn't wait to see which one he picked! My fragile little teenage ego was soaring. This man loved me *and* my art enough to put both of them on his body forever.

Holy shit!

Ding-Dong was actually working at the time (I know, right?) at some auto body shop a good half an hour from his house, so more often than not, I would wind up being his ride home because…no car. (How a guy with no car gets a job working on cars is still beyond me.) I would come home from school, anxiously pick at my dinner, lie to my parents about where I was going, and then dash back out the door to go take his sorry ass home.

Then, one day, when I called Ding-Dong to see if he needed me to pick him up from work, he snickered and told me I could come get him from the Terminus City tattoo parlor instead.

Oh my God! He's doing it! He's actually doing it!

My heart and my Mustang seemed to defy gravity as I sped over to Terminus City. It was like Christmas morning! I was giddy and impatient and effervescent. *This* is why I was still with Ding-Dong. He was just so dumb and carefree and fun.

When I shoved open the tattoo parlor door, I used so much force that the little silver bell above it swung all the way up into the drop-tile ceiling, sending a chunk of plaster flying. The guy behind the desk casually arched his pierced eyebrows and gazed over at the ripped red vinyl cushion of one of the cheap aluminum waiting area chairs where the dislodged piece of ceiling now rested.

"You lookin' for the dude with the pecker on his head?"

I beamed and bounced and nodded.

Captain Cheerful shoved a black-tipped thumb adorned with a heavy silver ring, not unlike the ones dangling from every convex place on his face, in the direction of an open door behind him. "He's back there."

The tattoo parlor looked like it was probably once a tanning salon. It consisted of a front lobby that bottlenecked into a long hallway with doors lining both sides. As I galloped down the hallway, I saw that only one door was open, and there was a god-awful buzzing sound coming out of it.

Bingo!

I burst into the tiny room and found a shirtless Ding-Dong lounging in what looked like a semi-reclined dentist's chair, placid as a Hindu cow, while a hulking man sitting on his left side stabbed him repeatedly with tiny, buzzing needles.

I remember thinking that Ding-Dong was a colossal badass for not even flinching when, in retrospect, he had probably just taken a fistful of Vicodin and washed it down with a bottle of Listerine.

He gave me a slow, sleepy-eyed smile and announced, "There's the pretty Lady," as he unfolded his arms and waited for my hug.

I tried to dial down the gusto to match the somber, humming, Zen-like atmosphere in that little space. After tiptoe-prancing over to Ding-Dong's right side to give him a quick hug, I wriggled loose and gingerly slinked around to the other side of his chair where a serious (and seriously scary-looking) tattoo artist was stooped between me and what I came to see.

Out of my way, asshole!

Having to stifle my excitement was making me feel like a human teakettle—quiet and calm on the outside but liable to erupt into steaming screams of hysterics at any minute. I was dying to find out which one of my drawings had made the final cut. Trying hard not to disturb the orc, I finally shimmied my way to a place where I could see over the scowling creature's shoulder, and there, staring back at me with big sad eyes, practically covering half of Ding-Dong's upper arm, was...

Eeyore.

Mother. Fucking. Eeyore.

The depressed donkey from *Winnie-the-Pooh*, little pink bow on his tail and all, was gazing up at me from the very spot where my own face should have been—no, *shouldn't* have been. No part of me ever belonged on this man, especially not *for*ever.

Eeyore took a bullet for me that day, Journal. And he looked absolutely miserable about it.

I glared at Ding-Dong, who was totally oblivious to my fury.

He just smiled stupidly and slurred at me, "It's Eeyore. You know, 'cause people call me Eeyore 'cause I talk all slow like, *Muh tail…fell awf…agaaaain.*"

That was it. I was done.

I don't know how Ding-Dong got home that night, but I do know that, in my haste to get out of there, I put at least one more hole in that already crumbling ceiling.

Eeyore? *Eeyore??*

Goddamn, that man was a dumbass!

15

Hocus Poke-us

Email Conversation with Sara

FROM: BB EASTON
TO: SARA SNOW
DATE: WEDNESDAY, OCTOBER 2, 9:27 A.M.
SUBJECT: HUMMERS

OMG Sara.

It's working! It's actually working!

So, a couple of weeks ago I wrote my first bullshit
Subliminal Spousal Bibliotherapy journal entry and left
it in a file on my computer that I literally named Super
Private Journal That Ken Is Never, Never Allowed to
Read Ever. It addressed all 4 objectives, and I made
extra sure to emphasize Harley's impressive oral skills
seeing as how it had been at least 18 months since
Ken had gone down on me.

(For real, Snow. I grew and expelled an entire human
being from my body in half that time.)

I was nervous as shit that Ken was going to light my computer on fire after reading it, but when a few days went by and nothing happened I started to worry that he was actually going to respect my privacy and not read it at all. Then he surprised the shit out of me after I put the kids to bed last night.

Ken came up behind me while I was doing the dishes, wrapped his arms around me, and pressed a full-blown goddamn erection against my back. I was super confused about why Ken had a hard-on at 8:30 on a Tuesday night when all he'd been doing was watching the news in the other room, but I don't question these things.

I assumed that he would guide me into the dark safety of our bedroom before anything got started, per his absolute abhorrence of fun and spontaneity, but instead that bastard slid my running shorts and panties down and started finger-fucking me right there at the sink. And he was really into it, too—grinding his cock against my ass and practically making out with my neck and earlobe.

So then, when I turned around to kiss him, Ken hoisted me up onto the counter, spread my legs, and for the first time in a year and a half, that motherfucker went Downtown Julie Brown.

But that's not even the best part: He fucking HUMMED while he did it.

I almost cackled out loud like a goddamn voodoo priestess! That is exactly what I wrote about in the "top secret" journal I planted for him to find, Sara! He must have just read it! And it fucking worked! Mwa ha ha ha ha!

Of course, I still need to work on getting him to compliment me, give me a nickname, and get a BB-themed tattoo, but so far this Subliminal Spousal Bibliotherapy shit is turning out to be marital black magic! I want to kiss your evil brain!

FROM: SARA SNOW
TO: BB EASTON
DATE: WEDNESDAY, OCTOBER 2, 11:14 A.M.
SUBJECT: HUMMERS

Thanks a lot. I was supposed to have some girl's dissertation read by noon, but after reading your email I ended up wasting the entire morning looking for the perfect outfit to wear on Good Morning America. I think I've settled on a Stella McCartney sheath dress, nude Kate Spade pumps, and I want to wear some nerdy professor glasses for credibility but I'll need to find some without the lenses, like actors on TV wear so that the lights don't cause a reflection.

Sara Snow, PhD
Associate Professor, Department of Psychology, (name of university deleted)

16

Oh No, I Incest

BB's Secret Journal

October 19

Dear Journal,

I had an epiphany this afternoon.

It's the weekend, and my goal for the weekend is always the same: get my kids to take their naps at the same time so that I can bang Ken during daylight hours. It's when we're usually both at our best. He's not too tired. I'm not too drunk. It's delightful.

So after waiting all goddamn day, two o'clock was finally upon me. Nap time. I flew up the stairs, my arms full of children, read a shamefully truncated version of *The Cat in the Hat* to my son, speed-nursed my daughter to sleep, and bounced back down the stairs and onto Ken's unsuspecting lap in twenty minutes flat. Unfortunately, he was clearly absorbed in a riveting episode of *Politically Incorrect* with Bill Maher that he'd found on our DVR while I was gone, so I knew I had my work cut out for me.

When Ken's breath finally became ragged and our clothes

finally started coming off, I unsnapped the cups of my nursing bra and folded the soft cotton over, exposing my swollen breasts, while leaving them sexily trussed up by the underwire. As Ken pulled one straining pink nipple into his mouth and massaged the other, I held my breath and crossed my fingers, praying silently that he wouldn't get a shot of milk to the eye.

And that's when it occurred to me. Not ten minutes ago, that exact same nipple had been in the baby's mouth. And a few years ago, it had been in my son's mouth. *So, this is what a family is,* I thought. *Just a houseful of people who've all sucked on your tits.*

And have also been inside your vagina.

17

Hoodie and the Blowjob

Super Private Journal That Ken Is Never,
Never Allowed to Read Ever

Dear Journal,

I fucking love it when Ken has a cold. I know it sounds sadistic to take pleasure in someone else's misery, but Ken is so incredibly cute when he's sick. He never complains. He just cocoons himself into the softest, warmest, comfiest hoodie he can find, flips up the hood, and quietly watches TV with his arms crossed over his chest. So, basically, sick Ken is just regular Ken with a comfy hoodie on. And it drives me wild.

Fucking hoodies and beanies get me every time. Some girls like men in uniforms. I like men who look like they were just dismissed from a police lineup, preferably the young, hard-bodied B-and-E suspects who clear the six-foot mark painted on the cinder-block wall and are only let go because their tattoos don't match the victim's description. You'll notice I didn't say, "armed robbery suspects," because those are ski masks, not beanies, Journal. Turn-*off.*

So, last night, when I got done putting the kids to bed, I came downstairs to find my husband curled up on the couch, totally working the sexy sick Ken combo. The image of that masculine square jaw covered in stubble and those usually sparkling blue eyes shrouded by an inky-black hood screamed danger and mystery while the aged softness of his cotton sweatshirt and vulnerability of his posture whispered, *Hold me. Love me.*

Unable to help myself, I climbed onto the couch next to him and slid my hands around his torso under the warmth of his sweatshirt. What I really wanted to do was straddle him and shove my tits in his face, but knowing that he didn't feel well, I simply rested my cheek on his shoulder instead, settling for some serious unreciprocated cuddling. I purred into his ear and murmured something about him being adorable when he's sick, content to just be near this paradox of hotness for a little while.

It was a sweet moment, but like every other instance of intimacy I've had with this man, I eventually realized, lamented, and then bitterly accepted the fact that the feeling was not mutual. Ken was probably on Ken Island somewhere, a place with a population of one where the white noise of baseball stats and stock-market tickers filled the air. He probably didn't even realize I was there. Or worse, he was gritting his teeth and tolerating my touch while trying to bore me out of the room with *Fantasy Football Live.*

So, I was nuzzling and kneading and trying to siphon every ounce of tenderness I could get when Ken turned his adorable hooded face to mine, leaned over, and began planting soft kisses on my neck just below my ear.

He then whispered, "I don't want to give you what I've got… but I want to give you what I've got." He gyrated his hips a little for emphasis.

I looked down and—

Holy shit!

Ken hadn't been off on Ken Island at all. He was here, with me, soaking up my affection and responding with a huge vulneraboner.

Aw!

Needless to say, I wasn't about to let a little cold come between me and this breakthrough. I dragged Ken by his hoodie strings into our bathroom, deftly maneuvered the childproof latch on the nose-hair trimmer/fiber supplement/facial wax/suppository/ glue stick/spare change/sex-toy drawer and feverishly began rummaging through the assorted bullshit before locating the finger-sized vibrating bullet we kept stashed in there. If we couldn't make out to get things going, what with his cold and all, I was going to need backup.

Not wasting any time, Ken began disrobing on the spot, so I immediately followed suit. As I shimmied out of my jeans, his delicious hoodie hit the floor beside me. The pang of loss I felt over seeing that sexy garment in a heap at my feet was quickly replaced by a throbbing need between my legs as my gaze trailed back up his body. They slid over Ken's muscular calves and thighs, danced up and around the head of his impressive erection, crawled up the ridges of his firm abdomen, slid over his toned chest, licked across the rough stubble of his square jaw, and landed softly on chiseled lips that were parted ever so slightly (probably because he was too stuffed up to breathe through his nose, but whatever). Ken looked like he'd just stepped off the set of an Old Spice commercial, probably after being fired for not being able to contain that nine-inch battering ram under his towel.

Before I could tackle him, Ken reached for my hips and turned my naked body so that I was facing the giant mirror hanging above the sink. Shifting to stand behind me, he let his hands move to my swollen breasts, heavy with milk, and buried his face into my neck. I stared with abandon.

I'd never watched myself making love before. Sure, I'd stolen a few glances whenever I'd found myself having sex in a bathroom or a cheap beach hotel with mirrored closet doors, but standing there, watching Ken knead and lick and suckle my body, made me feel empowered and adored.

At only six months postpartum, I don't make a habit of looking at myself in full-length mirrors. I'm not back to my pre-pregnancy weight yet, and as someone who spent more of her adult life living with an eating disorder (or three) than without, I've learned that mirrors and scales lie. They whisper things to your soul that are untrue—about your beauty, about your worth. Typically, the fewer mirrors and scales I encounter, the better.

But last night, in that mirror, the body I saw before me was… surprisingly hot.

Still nursing, my usually small breasts are a full cup size, maybe two, larger now, and with my arms resting on the top of my head, my stomach at least had the illusion of being taut. My hips, slightly wider than before, balanced out the added fullness in my chest and gave me a gentle hourglass silhouette that I'd never in a million years thought my boyish figure was capable of. There was nothing boyish about the wanton sex goddess gazing back at me. She was curvy. She was feminine. And she had a tall sandy-brown–haired drink of water wrapped around her like a mink shawl.

Ken rotated me slightly to the side, granting his mouth access to my right nipple, the one that had been pierced three times in as many years when I was a teenager.

(My body had rejected the piercing on that side, twice, and

I'd kept saying, "Fuck you, body! You will have TWO pierced nipples, not just ONE. You don't tell me what to do!" So, I'd kept getting it re-pierced because when you felt like the only girl on the planet without boobs, you really, really needed pierced nipples to make taking your shirt off in front of a boy feel okay. It's a miracle I can breastfeed at all out of that nipple, given all the scar tissue left behind in the wake of my self-mutilating youth.)

Ken caressed it with his tongue only momentarily before capturing it at the base and slowly dragging his teeth down its length. The sensation made my toes curl, as did the sting of chilly air when it eventually slipped free from the buttery warmth of his mouth.

The master bathroom in our house is a dark, high-ceilinged cavern of a place, encrusted in wall-to-wall stone tiles. The entire expanse is hard and cold, and I half-expect to see stalactites hanging overhead whenever I go in there.

The room had every inch of my body craving the warmth of Ken's mouth. And I could think of at least one place on his body that was craving the warmth of mine.

I reached out and snatched the bullet-shaped vibrator off the counter. Twisting around, I grabbed Ken by his strong shoulders and rotated our bodies so that he had his back to the counter. Beginning with his clenched jaw, I trailed open-mouthed kisses down his neck and chest while suggestively slipping the vibrator into his left hand. Bending at the waist, I took Ken's straining cock in my hand, licking from base to tip in slow wavy patterns while shifting my hips to the side so that my ass was within his reach.

I heard the hum of the vibrator and moaned into Ken's manhood as his hand traveled down my back, the vibrator between his index and middle finger, leaving trails of gooseflesh over my eager skin. Taking his length deep into my throat, I sucked hard, swirling my tongue around the ridge of his slick head, before plunging him back in. I heard Ken groan in appreciation as he sent the vibrator sliding down the base of my spine, through the parting of my ample ass, and into my slick folds, coming to rest firmly at the base of my clit.

Yes!

I bobbed my head faster, alternating between sucking and swirling, while stroking and cupping the rest of him. Ken responded by buzzing my swollen clit with the vibrator faster and faster, occasionally dipping his ring finger into the achingly empty spot just below. Just as I began to feel my core tighten, Ken's cock jerked in my mouth. He pulled me off him before either of us could come, and then pressed me against one of the few bathroom walls not plastered over by icy-cold tile.

Lifting my thigh to his waist, Ken settled between my legs, bending at the knees to make up for our height difference, and kissed my throbbing slit with the head of his perfect penis. He entered by only an inch or two before withdrawing, and then he did it again. Ken was teasing me, giving me just a taste of what I craved, while exhaling steamy breaths into my collarbone. Unable to delay my gratification any longer, I grabbed his hips and pulled him to me in one hard, satisfying thrust. We both stilled, relishing the moment, before I pushed his hips away from me and drove him back in, harder than before. The next time I pushed him away Ken pushed back, careening into me with a force that let me know he was taking control.

Again and again we pushed and pulled, and with every collision I felt closer to *him*. But not close enough. Not yet.

Flipping around, I stood, spread eagle, on my tiptoes with

one hand against the wall, my free hand reaching between my thighs to guide Ken back into my needy body. Ken bent his legs as he entered me from behind, then stood slowly, almost lifting me off my feet once he reached maximum penetration.

That! Yes! Please!

My clit throbbed, and almost instinctively, Ken pressed the forgotten vibrator into that swollen little swath of flesh.

Ah!

Reacting to the intensity, I cried out and constricted my muscles around Ken's cock, squeezing it hard as he stood to fill me again, pushing him over the edge. Ken gripped my hips with both hands and jerked inside me, finding his release on a strangled moan.

I dropped my forehead to my hands, still planted firmly on the wall in front of me, in defeat. As Ken gently withdrew his already softening cock, I braced myself for some half-assed finger-banging.

If there's one thing I can count on, it's that Ken is—*How do I say this?*—remarkably unenthusiastic after he comes. He can usually barely muster the strength to stay awake, let alone continue to pleasure his kinky wife.

And because of his cold we couldn't even kiss.

Goddamn it.

Just as I began to seriously consider snatching the vibrator out of his hand and locking myself in the closet with it, I felt Ken's breath on the back of my neck as the vibrating bullet probed my swollen apex again.

Hmm...nice.

I tilted my ass up and rolled my hips in slow circular motions, savoring the hum between my thighs. I was going to need more than that though. I felt so empty.

Grabbing his free hand, I brought Ken's fingers to my mouth and began to lick and suck the thickest two, hoping he would take the hint and fill me with them. As soon as I released his palm, Ken brought his hand down to my ass, spanking the smooth skin once, before sliding his wet middle finger inside a different entrance. My breath caught as I let out a surprised gasp. Between the screaming intensity of the vibrator between my legs, the semen languidly seeping from my body, and the pumping of Ken's thick finger, I was suspended in a state of pre-orgasmic bliss.

As good as it felt, my self-consciousness wouldn't let me surrender to the pleasure. With no covers and no cover of darkness to hide behind, I felt so exposed.

Pushing past my embarrassment, driven by an all-consuming need to come, I took one hand off the wall and pinched my left nipple *hard*. A jolt of electricity, almost matching the one from the vibrator below, raced straight down to my clit. As I rolled the tender flesh between my fingers, I was reminded that I actually have tits now. I ran my free hand across both swollen breasts, kneading them appreciatively, before capturing my right nipple and giving it a twist.

The sensation was like a lightning storm of ecstasy, and without realizing it I had begun rocking back onto Ken's probing finger, moaning, "Mmm...fuck my ass," into the cold night air.

My surroundings were gone. It was just me and my nerve endings and the building rumble of thunder that would crash over me at any second. Sensing how close I was and emboldened by my moans, Ken pressed the vibrating bullet directly against my clit and thrust a second wet finger into my thrumming, needy body.

Boom.

My core constricted in a violent, pulsating torrent. Where my senses had been alight with fire just moments before, I found myself plummeting into orgasmic darkness, only remotely aware that I was also convulsing and moaning and cursing as my knees buckled and I dug my fingertips into the wall for support.

When I came to, Ken was leisurely washing his hands in the sink, watching me out of the corner of his eye and looking all too pleased with himself. I half-walked, half-hobbled over to him and rested my cheek on his bicep, gazing drunkenly at his reflection in the mirror.

My wild, wavy auburn hair stuck out in all directions, my face and lips were flushed pink, and my forehead had a bright red patch on one side from being pressed against the wall. Ken's hair had that freshly fucked look, too, but it was from being tucked up under his hoodie just a few moments ago. I glanced down at the cozy black sweatshirt, still in a pile on the floor, and failed to hide the shy smile spreading across my face.

When I glanced back up, Ken's expression matched my own.

Yeah, I definitely have a thing for sick Ken.

Postscript: I just Googled the going rate for a petri dish of rhinovirus—and did a Craigslist search—to no avail. Evidently, I'm the only asshole in America interested in stashing the common cold in my freezer to infect my husband with year-round. I can't decide if that makes me a monster or a genius. I'm leaning toward...meanius?

18

Hard Work (Pun Intended)

BB's Secret Journal

FROM: BB EASTON

TO: SARA SNOW

DATE: WEDNESDAY, NOVEMBER 1, 10:27 A.M.

SUBJECT: CUNNILINGUS

Remember how I was all excited because Ken gave me a hummer after reading the Harley entry and I was like, "This shit is magical!" and "Mwahahaha"? Yeah, well, I might have been a little overenthusiastic.

After that entry shit pretty much went back to normal almost immediately. So this time I decided to try a different approach and write an SSB entry about Ken. I thought maybe if I combined positive reinforcement with the Subliminal Spousal Bibliotherapy technique I might get longer-lasting results.

A few days ago I wrote (in pornographic detail) about this really good bathroom sex we had recently when

Ken was sick. That shit made ME blush, Sara. Well, Ken must have read it while I was getting ready for bed the next night because just as I was finishing my shower he climbed in with me, already fully hard, and blew...my... fucking...mind.

He was so confident and aggressive, Snow. Within like thirty seconds Ken had me bent over with my forearms against the shower wall, smacked the shit out of my ass, and then pushed into me with his cock AND his thumb at the same time. UGH it was soooo good...for all of 2 minutes before he came.

I didn't even care. I was so astonished by his behavior that I wanted to start a slow clap right there in the shower. I also, stupidly, assumed that I'd just seen a glimmer of things to come. (Pun intended.) That THIS time the effect would last longer than one fucking hour.

Welp, yesterday, we were right back to mediocre, me-on-top, muted-TV-in-the-background, cadaver sex, so there you fucking go. Evidently I have to write a 2000+ word pornographic journal entry just to get 2 minutes of kinky fuckery out of Ken. This shit is exhausting. And don't even get me started on lack of compliments, nicknames, and personalized tattoos around here.

I hope you haven't taken the tags off that Stella McCartney sheath dress, because at this rate you're never going to meet Robin Roberts.

FROM: SARA SNOW

TO: BB EASTON

DATE: WEDNESDAY, NOVEMBER 1, 10:29 A.M.

SUBJECT: RE: CUNNILINGUS

A journey of a thousand miles begins with a single step.

Sara Snow, PhD
Associate Professor, Department of Psychology, (name of university deleted)

FROM: BB EASTON

TO: SARA SNOW

DATE: WEDNESDAY, NOVEMBER 1, 10:37 A.M.

SUBJECT: RE: CUNNILINGUS

WTF?

Text message from Sara approximately one minute later:

Sara: I can't believe you sent that to my university account

Me: Ha! So THAT'S what your Chinese proverb was all about!

Sara: What was I supposed to say?

Me: "I don't know you."
Me: "Never contact me again."

Sara: You're going to get me fired

Me: Seriously? You should see the shit you email me from that account. Why are you suddenly…oooooooh. Wait. I get it now.

Me: You're stoned.

Sara: Shut up

Me: Ha! I knew it! You're stoned. I can always tell. You get sooo paranoid.

Sara: Goddamn it

Me: Why are you baked at work?

Sara: That hippie guy Sophie set me up with last week took me to lunch
Sara: I couldn't just let him smoke by himself
Sara: I'm not an animal

Me: Well, that makes perfect sense.

Sara: Good job with Ken, btw

Me: Hardly. This shit is so much work, Snow. Is it even worth it?

Sara: My Audi R8 says it is. Now get your ass back in there and get me some tenure

Me: Meh
Me: Do I have to write about this shower fiasco? I'm so tired. Manipulating people is hard.

Sara: Just copy and paste that email you sent me into your notes

Me: You're a meanius, Dr. Snow!

Sara: Mean genius?

Me: See??

19

BB Suffers

BB's Secret Journal

November 9

Dear Journal,

I wrote a haiku today. I call it "BB Suffers."

Today, you told me
You rub Baby's feet at night.
Not my feet, Ken? Why??

So, this afternoon, while I was holding the baby, I noticed that she kept doing this weird thing where she'd contort her leg into an awful-looking position just so that she could stick her foot into the palm of my hand.

When I brought it to Ken's attention, he nonchalantly explained, "She just wants you to rub her foot. I rub her fee—"

Ken's mouth snapped shut as a wave of regret and fear washed over his beautiful face. He'd just fucked up. He knew it, and I knew it.

My eyebrows shot up, and I pulled my mouth into a homicidal pucker. *You do what now?*

Hesitating for a fraction of a second, Ken decided that he'd better try to smooth over his little admission, lest he be castrated.

"I-I just rub her feet sometimes, at night, when it's my turn to put her to bed, so now"—clearing his throat—"she always sticks her foot in my hand when I'm holding her."

Now, I realize that the idea of a tall, handsome man with a good job and zero felonies rubbing his infant daughter's feet sounds all swoony and charming. And yeah, sure, Ken being a doting father is sexy and all, but let me tell you something, Journal. This motherfucker[4] has NEVER touched my feet. In fact, he *prides* himself on having never touched my feet, and they're really cute feet! It's not like they're all hairy and man-sized and riddled with bunions and hammertoes. They're tiny and pedicured, and all ten digits point in the right direction. One of them even has a cute little freckle and everything.

Regardless of the amount of buffing and bedazzling that my feet have undergone, if I so much as graze Ken with one of them while we're on the couch, he will all but get up and move to the other couch.

Why, you ask?

Because, in his words, "Feet are gross."

---

[4] Just for the record, sometimes when I feel bad about calling the father of my children a motherfucker, I remember that he *is* a motherfucker—as in, he is literally fucked by a mother, approximately once a week, while he lies there and fantasizes about his Google stock splitting. Then I don't feel so bad.

Are they? Are they, Ken? Evidently, you don't think the baby's feet are gross, and she gets shit on them at least once a week when I'm changing her diaper and I don't move the poopy one out of the way fast enough. And she's always putting them in her mouth. She's not a cat, Ken. Licking herself does not make her cleaner than me. Quite the opposite. In fact, if anyone in this house has gross feet, it's the fucking baby!

So, it would appear that Ken doesn't have a "problem with feet" after all. I'd be willing to wager that he doesn't even have a problem with *my* feet. (I mean, how could he? They're fucking adorable.)

I think what Ken actually has a problem with is doing something, *anything*, that I want him to do. In the world of psychology, we call that oppositional defiant disorder. In this marriage, however, I just chalk it up to reason #983 why Ken is an asshole.

20

The Worst

BB's Secret Journal

November 16

Dear Journal,

How is it that you can have the worst sex of your life with someone you've been fucking for the last ten years? I'm kind of stunned. And angry, actually. I really thought that, after all the first times and one-night stands and sloppy drunk sex and cramped car sex and pokey-itchy outdoor sex and got-walked-in-on-by-somebody's-mom sex and over-in-two-and-a-half-thrusts sex and questionable make-you-wish-you-had-a-time-machine-and-five-fewer-pomegranate-martinis sex and I-pulled-my-meniscus-trying-to-do-the-cunnilingus-cartwheel-experimental sex and the depressing you're-finally-about-to-fuck-the-super-hot-guy-you've-been-lusting-after-for-months-and-you-just-discovered-he-has-a-minuscule-penis-and-now-you-have-to-go-through-with-it-so-you-don't-hurt-his-feelings-but-you-know-this-relationship-is-going-to-end-in-about-ten-minutes-when-you-fake-an-orgasm-followed-by-a-stroke sex and the awkwardly violent you-just-realized-you-and-the-guy-you're-with-are-both-doms-and-things-just-kind-of-devolve-into-a-fistfight sex, that I had had about all the bad sex I was ever going to have by the age of twenty.

Then, last night happened.

Just thinking about it makes me want to go punch my husband in the face—or at least grab him by the shoulders and never stop shaking him.

Last night, I wanted so badly to just squeeze his gorgeous chiseled face and scream, *For fuck's sake! Get your head in the game! At least pretend like you don't have a central processor!*

But I didn't because that would have been an insult to the entire cyborg community, who I'm pretty sure could have done better.

So, instead, I let out a dramatic sigh and hissed through my teeth to prevent myself from screaming, "Jesus, Ken. Will you just go get the vibrator?"

He complied, of course, and I used his absence to take some deep breaths.

Don't be mean. Don't be mean. If you attack him, it will just make it worse—if that's possible. Actually, who are we kidding? It can't get any worse.

So, upon his return, I might have given him an eat-shit-and-die look, and I *might* have said something to the effect of, "Wake up, Ken. At least pretend like you aren't thinking in ones and zeroes. You've got to be rougher with me than *that.*"

It sounds harsh, but it was that bad, Journal. That sex was an insult to intercourse.

Let me set the stage for you. Per our usual, Ken and I began kissing in the bathroom after getting ready for bed because we'd just brushed our teeth, which makes it seem like a great time to make out, but in actuality, it's quite the opposite because Ken is tired by then, making him even more lethargic and apathetic than usual, and my old-lady-smelling face cream always smears its way into our mouths, making it taste as though I'm kissing my grandmother.

So, there we were, kissing through the geriatric taste of night cream in our freezing cold bathroom. I was periodically wiping my mouth off on Ken's shoulder, trying to void my lips of the slimy source of the mothball stench, while Ken was robotically touching random parts of my body.

Bored and cold, we awkwardly made our way into the bedroom where I basically masturbated on his lifeless body in the glow of the muted *Channel Two Action News* for all of three minutes before he unexpectedly and unceremoniously blew his load.

Goddamn it.

Ever the optimist, I pressed on, grinding my clit harder into his lean pelvis and squeezing my pussy tighter in a desperate attempt to hold on to his rapidly shrinking cock, passionately licking and sucking his neck, his lips, his tongue, only to be met with...nothing. I felt like a reluctant necrophiliac.

Hoping a change in locale would inspire a little more gusto, I yanked Ken's ass off the bed and slowly walked backward, making sultry eye contact and pulling him toward me by his hard biceps, until I was sandwiched between him and the wall. Wrapping one leg around his waist, I tilted my head back and placed his hand between my thighs, hoping he would accept the invitation to kiss and nuzzle my neck. Instead, I was caressed by a frigid blast from the air conditioner, which found plenty of space for swirling in the chasm between us.

So, there I was, throbbing and freezing and posed like a Grecian goddess on the front of a Harlequin Romance novel, while Ken was absentmindedly fiddling with my clit, staring at the reflection of the TV in a framed wedding photo just above my head. Knowing the Braves highlights were on, I even gave him the benefit of the doubt and waited a full two minutes until the sports segment was over to see if his enthusiasm would improve—it didn't—before sending him on the vibrator mission of shame.

I should have just gotten it myself and left him alone with Bryant Gumbel. Somehow, the battery-operated appendage, coupled with Ken's unyielding apathy, made him seem even more mechanical. Eventually, I just gave up and retreated to the shower to brood.

Ken's inability to show me so much as a whisper of intimacy felt like a roundhouse kick to the gut. And it made me want to roundhouse kick *him* in the nuts.

21

Somebody Call Oprah

BB's Secret Journal

November 15

Dear Journal,

I just had an *a-ha* moment. For a solid decade, I've been under the impression that Ken was just tolerating my affection because he liked having a dual income.

Then, last night, during one of his particularly corpselike performances in the bedroom, I finally just came out and said it. The phrase that had been on the tip of my tongue and the forefront of my mind since 2003.

"I feel like you're just not into this."

Such simple words. Why hadn't I said them sooner?

I realize that to you I probably seem like the kind of bitch who would shame her husband's lackluster lovemaking right to his face, but I actually try to tiptoe around the issue as much as possible. For starters, I'm a psychologist. I know that the male ego is a fragile thing. Make a man feel inadequate about sex or pressured to perform and you might as well buy his boner a bus ticket and a prepaid calling card because that fucker won't be back for *a while*. But I also haven't said anything to Ken about it because I really do love him—oppositional defiant disorder and all. I don't want to hurt his feelings—if he has any.

Besides, Ken is amazing in so many other ways. His easy-going introversion complements my mania perfectly. He's smart as shit and quietly sarcastic in a way that nobody seems to get but me. He's the most honest, trustworthy human I've ever met, and he takes care of all the shit I don't want to do. Plus, he's pretty damn nice to look at. I simply accepted his lack of passion as proof that nobody's perfect. But that was ten years ago.

Now I'm starving.

Now I'm screaming at him from inside my head to make me feel something.

Now I'm talking to my journal like some kind of imaginary friend.

Now I'm fantasizing about my loser ex-boyfriends and devouring bad-boy romance novels like they're my last meal.

Now my hunger for passion, for love, has finally overshadowed my desire to protect Ken's delicate male ego.

And now I'm kicking myself for not bringing it up sooner.

You want to know what he said, Journal?

"I'm trying not to come."

It was like a bomb exploded in the room.

Kapow!

Those five words echoed and ricocheted in my head until their meaning slowly began to emerge.

So... wait. This means that, for ten years, Ken has been lying underneath me, doing his best impersonation of someone getting a CT scan, not because he's not into it, but because he's too into it? Okay... so, this means that he does *want to pull my hair and claw my ass and claim my mouth and grab me by my hips while he thrusts into me faster, faster, faster, but he fights the urge because he'll come too quickly?*

It was all coming together—no pun intended.

I thought about the mind-blowing sex we'd had in the shower a few weeks ago that lasted all of two minutes and the recent vulneraboner he'd gotten when he was sick on the couch. During both of those encounters, Ken had actually allowed himself to get into it a little bit. Have a feeling. Cop a feel. And on both occasions, he'd come pretty quickly and gotten all flustered about it.

That's it! Holy shit, Journal! This motherfucker has been acting like a beached porpoise in the sack since the Bush administration because he was trying to avoid that exact scenario!

The blank look on his face, the muted TV, the lifeless prone body—it's all just been an exercise in self-control! (Only, I was the one doing all the exercising, thank you very much.) It's like he thinks the only way he can outlast me is to pretend he's watching a baseball game on the ceiling of a dentist's office while being waterboarded!

Ugh. I've been feeling undesirable and upset for a fucking decade over his lack of enthusiasm when the whole time he's just been gritting his teeth and trying not to . . .

Oh, *hell* no.

Now I'm just pissed. Doesn't he know that *all* men come quicker than women! It's a scientific fact! That's why foreplay was fucking invented! There's nothing wrong with Ken—he's just fucking lazy!

You know what? The gloves are coming off, Journal. It's about time for a certain rock star named Hans to show that motherfucker how it's done . . .

22

Hansel and Metal

Super Private Journal That Ken Is Never, Never Allowed to Read Ever

Hans.

The first time I ever laid eyes on Hans Oppenheimer, he and his band, Phantom Limb, were playing to a crowd of thirty or so at a party being thrown by my friend, Goth Girl.

Goth Girl had recently dropped out of high school in order to devote more time to her burgeoning drug habit, which was being bankrolled by her much older yet equally gothy boyfriend whose house she'd just moved into.

To show off her new digs, Goth Girl threw a total rager, and just to make extra sure that the cops got called, she'd hired her friend's heavy metal band to play in her manfriend's living room.

I wasn't a fan of metal—I've always been more of an alternative-rock kind of girl, even when I was pretending to be punk—but the band covered just enough Nine Inch Nails songs to keep me from leaving the room. And the fact that their bass player was a tall, dark drink of Heineken didn't hurt either.

Once the band finished their set, I disappeared to the kitchen to get another beer. After freshening my Solo cup at the keg, I spun around and careened, face-first, into an unyielding wall of hot muscle and sweat. Stumbling backward, I watched in horror as half of my beer landed with a dramatic splash on the floor, just missing one of the human barricade's massive black Adidas. Luckily, the giant reached out and grabbed my upper arms to steady me before I completely busted my ass on the keg behind me.

As my eyes made the long journey from his boat-like shoes up to his face, I took a quick mental appraisal. *Baggy black pin-striped slacks, chain wallet, slightly damp wifebeater plastered to a seriously bulbous set of six-pack abs, obviously tall as shit, seeing as how I haven't even made it up to his face yet—*

Oh my God! The fucking bass player!

Hoping he was a friendly giant, I donned my best please-don't-hurt-me-mister smile as I continued to crane my neck the rest of the way back, finally taking in his looming face. This dude could have gotten a walk-on role as one of the German bad guys in a *Die Hard* movie, no problem. His features were severe—jet-black hair violently headbanged into a mop of stabby, sweaty little spears, heavy brow impaled with a silver barbell on one side, prominent nose. But his playful gray-blue eyes and pouty lips, which were upturned into an adorably dimpled smile, fought hard to betray his otherwise villainous appearance.

Just looking at him made me feel as though I were standing under a streetlight on a hot summer night. While he was imposingly tall and slender and dark and hard, the glow he cast down on me was nothing short of sunshine.

"Hey, kitten. Going somewhere?"

I managed to squeak out an apology, but when I went to scoot around him to get out of his way, the giant simply snickered and tucked me under his arm. Holding me firmly to his side, he wrapped his long, strong callused fingers around my shoulder and steered me back into the living room. It was a bizarre move, but for some reason, I was helpless to stop the forward progression of my steel-covered toes. It was as if I had been sucked into his cool, self-confident aura, suspended in a magical fairyland where strange men don't rape drunk teenage girls at parties. Plus, with our height difference, my head fit perfectly under his big tattooed arm.

Mmm...

The raven-haired rocker steered me toward Goth Guy's black leather sofa, but rather than release me to sit, he effortlessly flopped onto the couch, twisting me on the way down so that we both landed side by side, his arm never leaving my shoulders. During our descent, he also managed to maneuver me so that my legs landed across his lap—his free hand coming to rest on my thigh.

Holy shit. This fucker is good.

"So, what's your name, Tinker Bell?"

As the dimple-cheeked devil beamed at me, I became aware that he was also nonchalantly rubbing a slow circle on my thigh with his thumb. I felt my cheeks heat with a blush that I was sure could be seen from outer space. I was sitting on the lap of quite possibly the sexiest man I'd ever encountered, and my brain chose that exact moment to take a smoke break. All it could process was heat and rhythm—heat in my face, heat where his massive hand was absentmindedly kneading my body, a virtual fire being stoked in my belly, and the tempo of his fingers strumming my thigh, which seemed to be in perfect concert with the blood thrumming between my legs just inches away.

When my brain finally registered that the expectant look on his face meant I was supposed to be answering a question, I frantically searched my recent memory for whatever the fuck it was that he'd asked me.

Something, something, Tinker Bell. Something...

Shit.

Taking a lucky guess, I blurted out, "BB?"

Why did that sound like a question? Oh God. He's going to think I'm wasted.

I swallowed and tried again, forcing myself to meet his gunmetal-blue gaze. "I'm BB. Hi."

Jesus, that was smooth.

"So, Bumblebee, why were you in there, getting your own beer? Don't you know it's against the rules for pretty girls to get their own drinks? You're lucky I found you."

He could say that again.

It was a cheesy pickup line, but the tattooed mystery man delivered it with such a flirty playfulness that I felt myself relax a little and blush even more.

I looked down and continued our conversation through my eyelashes, trying in vain to hide my hot pink cheeks. "Well, who else was gonna get it for—"

"Me," he interrupted with an arrogant grin.

Mr. Tall, Dark, and Tattooed tilted my chin up with the hand that had been resting on my shoulder, encouraging me to look at him.

"I have a feeling I'll be getting *all* your drinks from now on, Bumblebee."

Squeal!

To anyone else in the room, I'm sure it probably looked like I was being glamoured by a sexy vampire who was about to dine on my jugular. This cocky stranger had absolutely no boundaries, and my inner rape whistle should have been blaring, but for some inexplicable reason, I felt completely safe. There was no desperation, no salacious neediness, no predatory pheromone being emitted from him at all—just a warm, fuzzy cloud of flirt and familiarity.

Although I'd literally *just* met the man, he made me feel more secure, beautiful, and interesting than any man I'd ever met. And I didn't even know his name. Not that it mattered. He was seventy-five inches of snuggle bunny disguised as a pierced, tattooed rock star.

I was home.

―――

Standing in the pit waiting for Phantom Limb to take the stage always made my stomach do back flips. Not because of all the PBR I'd funneled in the parking lot. Not because I was nervous for Hans. But because of my stupid fucking territoriality.

Everyone with a uterus in that audience was about to find out how incredibly sexy and talented and gorgeous and *tall* my boyfriend was, and I might or might not have to pull one of those bitches off of him before the end of the night. Hans was just too goddamn nice. If some coked-up cock-nest monster started dry-humping his leg backstage, he'd simply let her and possibly pat her head sympathetically while she came. God forbid he hurt her feelings or embarrass her by pushing her away.

Seriously, Journal.

So guess who got to run groupie recon after every show? I'll give you a hint. She's the jealous type, and her last name rhymes with deceaston. (As in, "You're gonna be deceaston about thirty seconds if you don't get the fuck up off my boyfriend.")

On one such night, Phantom Limb was finally headlining at a legitimate venue and had been given the star treatment backstage. They had a private greenroom filled with every kind of charcuterie imaginable, and plenty of champagne. Not bad for a bunch of twenty-year-old high school dropouts.

Headlining also meant a higher caliber of groupie—as in, they had enough self-respect to hide their track marks and cutting scars on the insides of their thighs, *like ladies.* They were working on their retirement plans, goddamn it, and they weren't going to let a little thing like me (or a condom) get between them and eighteen years of rock star–sized child-support checks.

So, there I was, shoulder to shoulder with the competition—or should I say flat chest to bouncing breasts?—right there in the front row. I was a boy among women. And boy, did I feel threatened. It didn't help that Hans looked like sex on a stick that night.

What is it about a man in eyeliner? With spiky black hair? Who happens to have a full sleeve of horror movie–themed tattoos on his right arm, which he uses to violently slap and strum the strings of his bass guitar while on stage in front of thousands of people?

Honestly, guyliner aside, what made Hans even sexier on stage was his complete lack of ego. When he was up there, it was as if the audience didn't exist. He just played his heart out, stomping around his side of the stage, banging his head and swinging his bass, occasionally giving a knowing smirk to one of his bandmates or a head nod to signal this or that, but he never acknowledged a single one of the star-fuckers in the audience, which—unfortunately for me—only made them want him more.

After finishing their second encore with my favorite cover song, a killer version of "Terrible Lie" by Nine Inch Nails, the guys exited stage right to the deafening sound of screaming and declarations of love from the front row, which no longer included me. I was already clawing my way out of the pit, making every effort to get my scrawny ass backstage and into Hans's pinstriped pants before my competition.

Once I finally extracted myself from that undulating sea of pumping fists and steamy bodies chanting, "We won't go! We won't go!" I ran toward security with my backstage pass thrust out before me as if I were an FBI agent waving a badge.

Not that it mattered. I was already too late.

After sprinting through the dark corridors backstage and repeatedly getting lost, I finally caught sight of Phantom Limb's lead singer through the greenroom's cracked door.

Trip (which was short for his stage name, *XXX*) was one gangly, goofy motherfucker. He wore his dyed black hair parted in a blunt bowl cut that fell just above his ears, and he was astonishingly perverted, like in a thinks-it's-completely-appropriate-to-watch-sick-Japanese-Bukkake-porn-in-mixed-company-and-then-pause-it-at-the-"best part"-so-he-can-run-in-front-of-the-TV-and-do-his-own-pantomimed-Kabuki-theater-version-of-a-money-shot-for-everyone-while-screaming-*WOOOOOOO* kind of way.

Once I got a little closer, I could see that Trip was hovering over a tray of cold cuts, eating a rolled-up slice of turkey, while some Grade A piece of Southern white trash was on bended knee, massaging his balls with both hands through his leather pants.

Fuck!

Instantly, I knew that if there was already a woman desperate enough to worship over Trip's weaselly, measly little pecker, that could only mean one thing.

With a balled fist at the ready and my pounding heart in my

throat, I slowly pushed the greenroom door the rest of the way open. There, on the couch, was my tall, dark, wickedly sexy rock-star boyfriend flirting with a juicy piece of jailbait. She was wearing a tank top so low-cut that he could've used her cleavage as a beer koozie. Hans looked totally at home with his arm draped over the back of the sofa, his posture open and inviting, his mouth pulled to one side in his signature self-confident smirk.

I watched in suspended strike mode as Valtrex handed Hans a Sharpie, then hooked an index finger into the top of her tank top, as if she were about to expose her left tit for him to sign. Just as I reared back to launch myself at her, Hans caught a glimpse of me out of the corner of his eye.

"Hey, Bumblebee!"

The smile that illuminated his face was temporarily disarming, and I almost forgot how mad I was when he leaped from his seat with so much speed and enthusiasm that Valtrex had to grab handfuls of the (probably cum-encrusted) upholstery to keep from falling on her stupid fucking face.

Hans snatched me up in a lung-crushing bear hug, which was definitely *not* reciprocated. Feeling my resistance, he slowly set me back on my feet. Not releasing my arms, which were pinned to my sides by his gargantuan, callused, bass playing hands, Hans held me in front of him at arm's length, looking me over with a furrowed brow.

"What's a matter, Bee?" His jovial mood turned sour in the blink of a black-rimmed eye. "Seriously, what's wrong? Did something happen to you out there?"

Really? Really, Hans? You have no idea why I'm upset?

I huffed and shook him off, stomping out of the green-room and back into the labyrinth. The halls were lit at random intervals by red party bulbs, ominous shadowy darkness filling the stretches in between. It looked underworldly.

Fitting, I thought, seeing as how I was already in hell.

I'd finally found the perfect man, and I was doomed to watch other women try to fuck him for the rest of eternity.

Following the exit signs, I eventually found an external door to thrust myself out of. Only instead of being revived by a crisp, invigorating blast of cool night air, like I'd hoped for, I barreled headlong into a hot, sticky viscous concoction that would have only passed for oxygen on a molecular level.

I don't know why I had expected any different. I live in Georgia. The air here is exactly the same temperature and consistency as simmering gravy—boiling hot clear air gravy—for at least five months out of the year.

Choking down that first breath of molten-hot ectoplasm completely took the wind out of my sails. I leaned over and placed my hands on my knees, trying to catch my breath and psych myself up for the five-block swim I would have to make through this putrid liquid oxygen to the nearby neighborhood where my car was parked. I might not have been throwing up, but I probably looked like I was, and so did my purse, because when I leaned over, it effectively barfed its entire contents onto the finely ground bed of broken bottles and cigarette butts under my feet.

Nice.

Before I could rescue my assorted lip glosses, fake IDs, and cigarettes from the ground, five long, sinewy fingers reached out and grasped everything in one pass. Without standing, I lifted my gaze just enough to capture Hans's spiky-haired silhouette crouched down next to me. Although we were technically eye-to-eye, I couldn't see his face at all, thanks to the backlighting from the club behind him, which only helped to keep the disconnection I felt from him intact.

Hans quietly asked me if I was okay in a tone that made me realize he must have thought I was sick.

Oh my God, with the way I ran away and how I was now doubled over in the parking lot—Ugh! He still didn't get it!

I snatched my shit out of his talented fingers, stood up as straight and tall as I could, and told him to "Fuck off, Hansel."

Nobody but his German-American *mutter* called him that, and even she'd only do it when he was in trouble.

"I'm not sick, you dumbass. I'm *pissed*! Were you really going to sign that gash's tit? Were you going to let her ride your cock a little, too, just until I got there? I can't do this anymore! I guess I'm just too fucking jealous to be your girlfriend. I'm sorry."

With those departing words, I was going to turn on my heel, whip my imaginary long hair over my shoulder, and march off in the direction of my loyal Mustang. I was going to write Hans off as just a good time—just a beautiful nurturing soul inside a towering darkly sexy figure—with lickable tattoos and flickable piercings whose perfect smile radiated from his wicked face like a crescent moon in a midnight sky. I was going to hold in my tears until I made it safely to my car. Then, I'd crank up the AC and sob myself unconscious.

I only made it half a step away before I was completely immobilized by a pair of massive hands clamping down around my midsection. Hans rotated my body back around so that I was facing him once again. Only, now, he was kneeling in front of me instead of crouching beside me. With his hands on my hips and his head tipped back to gaze up at me, it reminded me of the way I'd been craning my neck up to see him all these months. Hans might have been physically restraining me, but with our reversed height differences, he was making it clear that I was the one with the power.

His usually smooth, strong eyebrows were pulled tightly together, forming a deep V of pain above the bridge of his nose. His mouth, which was so often pulled to the side in a playful smirk, now formed a tight frown. And his eyes, which usually sparkled like blue diamonds in a coal mine, now sparkled with unshed tears.

Not only was this beautiful man—inside and out—groveling at my feet, but he still had his rock-star eyeliner and sweat-soaked stage clothes on, reminding me that I'd just watched this Adonis perform in front of thousands of screaming fans. Only, instead of getting his cock smoked backstage like the heavy metal deity he was, Hans was on his knees in a parking lot full of what appeared to be broken light bulbs and human teeth. I felt like shit.

"I'm sorry, Bumblebee. God, I'm so fucking sorry. I'm such an idiot. That girl had a media pass and said she was with Y105 and wanted to do a quick interview. I was just going to sit down and answer a few questions until you made your way backstage, but once we started talking, it was pretty obvious that she wasn't from any fucking radio station. She was just some dumb girl who got her hands on a press pass and wanted an autograph."

"Oh, I think she wanted more than just an autograph." I couldn't help myself.

Even though Hans was obviously beating himself up, it was the same story every time.

This girl just needs a ride home because her boyfriend left and took her car.

This girl is getting kicked out of her apartment and doesn't have anyone to help her move.

This girl only needs a couple more bucks to be able to quit stripping and put herself through astronaut school.

Either he had some serious self-esteem issues that made him think women wanted his help but not his dick, or the altitude from his height was making his brain all foggy.

"I didn't know. I swear, Bee. I just thought she was going to interview us."

"Hans, this is exactly what I'm talking about. You're so fucking naïve you don't realize girls are hitting on you until they're practically sitting on your face! I won't always be around to swat away the competition, and obviously, you're just not up to the job."

I practically spat my words down at him with a seething, unfairly accusatory tone. I knew he couldn't help what'd happened. He was just too optimistic and sweet to see the bad in anyone, and that was part of why I'd fallen in love with him.

According to my interpersonal relationships professor, there was a name for what Hans and I had—*fatal attraction*. It's a phenomenon where the very qualities that attract you to someone, in turn, cause the death of the relationship. I adored how kind and gentle and romantic Hans was, especially considering that my parents had taken a life insurance policy out on me when I broke up with Knight.

"Just in case," they'd said.

No, Hans was a real honest-to-goodness dyed-in-the-wool sensitive artist type. Whenever he wrapped those bulging tattooed arms around me, I felt as though I'd just shrugged on a fur coat made from live puppies that could sing "Lovesong" by

The Cure a cappella. The only problem was, Hans made every-body feel that way. And this Cruella de Vil was not down with sharing her puppy trench.

"Let me go, Hans. Your fans await."

As angry as I was, the look of consternation and despair on his face after that statement made me want to rent a time machine so that I could take back everything I'd just said. This man was a unicorn. A myth. A fairytale. I'd somehow managed to score a tatted-up bad boy with a heart of gold and a cock of lead, and what was I doing? Guilt-tripping him while he knelt in a bed of rusty screws and asbestos shards at my feet?

He should be the one leaving me. I opened my mouth to retract my words, but the only sound that came out was a sur-prised gasp as Hans wrapped his arms all the way around my waist and buried his face in my belly.

He turned his head sideways, just enough to speak, but kept a death grip around my midsection. "You can't leave, Bumblebee. Please. Please stay. You want to know why I don't realize when women are hitting on me? It's because all I can think about is you. I don't see girls or groupies or fans out there—I just see people who aren't you, and you. That's it. As far as I'm con-cerned, everyone else is just a walking, talking hunk of flesh that I need to get around to get to you."

He shook me a little out of frustration, then looked up at me with glistening kohl-rimmed eyes—the V of pain between them only deepening. "You're like this pretty little Tinker Bell with your pixie hair and big green eyes, but then you're smart as shit and full of fire and sass and all I want to do is put you in my pocket and never fucking share you with anyone."

His grip tightened fractionally, but his voice grew significantly louder and more frantic as he continued, "Haven't you noticed that I don't look at you anymore when I'm on stage? It's because I can't, Bee. I can't fucking look anywhere near the audience anymore because whenever I do there always seems to be some meathead trying to buy you a drink at the bar or knock you down in the pit or press his dick into your ass when you're in the front row. Every five seconds, I see some shit that makes me want to leap into the crowd and smash some motherfucker's teeth down his throat. It throws me off my game so bad that I can't even watch. I just grit my teeth and try to focus on the music and pray that you'll come find me backstage, still in one piece, when it's over. All I want to do is protect you and I'm fucking helpless up there."

Tears and mascara and relief poured out of me as the implications of Hans's words sank in. I grabbed his face with both hands and pulled him up to meet my salty wet mouth. I kissed him with everything I had and realized in that moment that the real problem was never Hans. Clearly, he was even more perfect than I'd feared. It was that I'd never truly felt worthy of him.

I saw the women who hung around these bands, and I didn't exactly fit in with my flat chest, narrow hips, and freckled skin. My wardrobe didn't help either. I looked like something that crawled out of the movie *Tank Girl*. I'd even tried to tone down the punk that night by wearing a little black dress, but it still had white Jolly Rogers embroidered all over it and was paired with my signature mid-calf steel-toed Grinders. It was as if someone had handed Pippi Longstocking a big pair of boots, a big pair of scissors, and a bottle of forty-watt hair bleach.

What the fuck could this icon of rebellion and sex possibly want with me?

Hans kissed me back like I was the last canteen in the Sahara, and I decided that my self-doubt and jealousy had to stop. Hansel obviously loved me if he was willing to breathe this fluorocarbon emulsion bullshit *and* kneel in broken glass just to keep me from leaving him.

Until that moment, I hadn't even known that kind of love existed. Skeletor would have chased me down, tackled me in the parking lot, and then dragged me kicking and bleeding over his shoulder back inside. Harley wouldn't have even noticed I'd split until after he'd safely deposited at least a gallon of his semen into the groupie with the media pass. But Hans—my sweet, sweet, beautiful, sensitive artist—was the real deal.

Hans broke away from our kiss and pressed his forehead to mine. Clutching my face in his colossal callused hands, he said, "Say you'll stay."

"I can't," I whispered. Hans's face crumpled before I could get out the rest of my sentence. I grabbed his chin and forced him to look at me. "No! Hans! I meant I can't stay *tonight*, because I have school in the morning, but I'm not going anywhere, okay? I promise. I don't know why you want to keep me around, but I'm yours for as long as you'll have me."

With those words, Hans's expression flipped from devastated to perky in the blink of a kohl-smudged eye. It was adorable. He took my arm in the crook of his elbow and said, "Well then, allow me to walk you to your car, milady."

The walk was magical. I'd parked a few blocks away from the club in a gorgeous recently gentrified antebellum neighborhood where I knew I would not only find a free parking spot, but could also possibly walk to and from said parking spot without getting chloroformed. Even though it was a good half-mile to my car, and trying to stroll through that thick, hot summer air felt more like trudging through quicksand, Hans and I might as well have been floating overhead in a love bubble built for two.

Although my relationship with Hans had been love at first sight—the way he swept me off my feet (literally) at Goth Girl's party set the tone for our entire whirlwind romance—I had always secretly had one foot out the door.

No matter how perfect things were, a small, nagging part of my psyche was constantly whispering, *He's too good to be true. Rock stars aren't faithful. He's going to break your heart. Don't get too attached.*

But after seeing Hans on his knees before me in full stage attire, that whisper was forever silenced, replaced by a pulsing, deafening need. For the first time in the eight months since I'd met Hans, I was all in, and all was right with the world.

Holding hands and cooing in hushed tones at each other, Hans and I turned the last corner on our way to my car. Just as the taillights of my trusty black Mustang were coming into view, Hans began leading me off the sidewalk and into someone's perfectly manicured backyard.

Goddamn it.

Hans, like most bass players, had the attention span of a goldfish, so this wasn't the first time that he'd been distracted by a few twinkling lights. I was quietly protesting and trying to tug him back toward the street when I looked up and caught a glimpse of the ethereal wonderland he was dragging me toward. The backyard of this particular McMansion had been wrapped, swathed, and wallpapered in thousands upon thousands of white Christmas lights—in the middle of July.

Obviously, there must have been a party or wedding, some

grand celebration, here earlier, but there was no evidence of life anywhere. The rustic Italian grotto-style pool in the center of the yard was as still as a pane of glass, which allowed it to better reflect the twinkling lights coiled tightly around every tree branch and deck post within a hundred-yard radius. And speaking of the deck, the entire main floor of the three-story modernized plantation-style house was equipped with a wooden deck that boasted an outdoor kitchen, a stone fireplace, and a hot tub the size of my bedroom, all illuminated by gauzy paper lanterns suspended overhead.

Below the main floor was a patio tucked away under the deck, which was furnished with a perfect row of at least six expensive-looking teak lounge chairs with overstuffed red cushions and at least three ceiling fans, still rotating on high speed. The rustic stone tile that surrounded the pool fed right into the patio area and ended at a set of double doors that probably gave entrance into some grand basement bathhouse that was fully equipped with a spare pool, just in case.

I couldn't even process all the beauty at once. The way my attention was flitting from one shiny object to the next must have been what Hans's brain felt like all the time. As my head swiveled and my eyes darted around that sparkly, glowing jewelry box of a backyard, I failed to notice that Hans was pulling me farther and farther onto this obviously very private property.

It wasn't until my body plopped down onto Hans's lap (his signature move) that I realized he had escorted me all the way down to the patio, and we were now sitting on one of the cushy lounge chairs under the deck.

Oh no. What the fuck is he doing?

These people obviously had a stupid amount of money and

probably owned a state-of-the-art *Hunger Games*–style security system with invisible lasers and paralysis-inducing mist. I knew Hans was impulsive and needed me to be the voice of reason, but it was too late. Between Hans's strong arms around my waist, the secluded coziness of the covered patio, and the majesty of a hundred thousand tiny lights dancing in the trees and water before me, I was already paralyzed.

Hans and I just sat in silence, enjoying the view. The fiery tree branches flickered in concert with the sounds of crickets and cicadas and air conditioners in the distance, weaving a tapestry of white noise and white light that made the dark stillness of our patio hideaway feel even more secluded. As we watched the show, tucked into and around each other, Hans and I had an entire conversation telepathically, one that was full of promises and shiny rings and *I do*s and baby names.

Beyond the scenery and intimate seclusion, I was also enjoying the feel of Hans's tattooed arms around my body and his desire, hard and ready, against my hip. He always did have a sensitive cock—and by sensitive, I mean, *emotionally.*

Hans began trailing featherlight kisses from my shoulder up to my neck and then just behind my ear.

Mmm . . .

He repeated his delicate assault on the other side. Only, this time, when his mouth reached my neck, he bit down on one of the tails of the bow holding my halter dress up and yanked. Within seconds, the black fabric covering my chest was replaced by warm, damp air.

My first instinct was to snatch my dress back up and scurry off before the owners had a chance to let loose the hounds, but when Hans took both of my pierced nipples between his talented fingertips and tugged gently, I was a goner. My head rolled back onto his shoulder, and my back arched involuntarily. The psychological rush of having my breasts exposed in such a dangerous yet romantic setting took the already intense physiological experience and pushed it over the edge. That sensation alone was worth the risk of being attacked by trained killer bees.

Just as I was about to cry out from the exquisite pleasure, Hans abruptly stood up, came around to the foot of the lounge chair where I was sitting, and knelt before me. It was reminiscent of our postures from just minutes ago in the parking lot. Only now, everything had changed. Hans's signature smirk had been returned to its rightful place, and I was ready to book a flight to Las Vegas instead of booking it to my car to cry.

Oh, and my tits were out.

After gazing at me for a moment, his eyes soft and loving, his mouth failing to hide a mischievous grin, Hans bent down and captured my left nipple ring between his lips. He swirled his tongue around and around the sensitive pink flesh until I could feel my panties dampen and my knuckles turn white as they tightened around the wooden frame of the chaise.

Reading my body language, Hans grabbed the hem of my dress with both hands and slipped it off over my head.

Oh my God.

I was naked, except for a red cotton thong and some combat boots, on a stranger's patio.

And I fucking loved it.

Hans then turned his attention to my other breast, fondling and sucking, while I desperately tore at his wifebeater. Ignoring me, he made his way down my torso, planting torturously unhurried kisses in a trail that could only be leading to one place. Meanwhile, he used his hands to simultaneously pluck at the silver hoops in my nipples and guide me down onto my back in the lounge chair. Just as my head hit the cushion, his mouth hit the apex of my already drenched panties. The feel of his tongue and nose and lips probing me through that thin piece of fabric was a glorious electric agony. I wanted it to never end, yet somehow culminate into a screaming days-long orgasm all at the same time.

No! I can't come like this. Not in my fucking underwear! Hans, please!

My hips began to thrust involuntarily, begging him to dive into me, to end the torture.

Please!

And that's when I felt a thick finger hook the sopping wet fabric between my legs and slowly drag it to the side.

No sooner had that finger slid aside the barrier between us than it was sliding inside my slippery folds, thrusting in and out at an excruciatingly unhurried pace. My womb felt like it had been pumped full of boiling hot napalm. I was going to die. It was too much. I was spread-eagled, practically naked on a stranger's chaise longue, with my breasts exposed to the steamy night air, my wet pierced nipples cooling into sharp points by the humming ceiling fans. Fingers that had just skillfully shredded a bass guitar in front of thousands of people were stroking my G-spot, and the playfully wicked black-rimmed eyes of a rock star were gazing up at me from between my thighs where his expert tongue was flicking and teasing the barbell piercing my clit.

Just as I felt my sweet release beginning to build, I could hear the sound of Hans undoing his belt and fly.

Oh, thank God! Fuck me, Hansel! Now!

His tongue and magical fingers never left my pussy while he easily shimmied out of his skater shoes and baggy pants. The instant his mouth left my flesh, Hans peeled off his tank top and scooped me up into his arms in one fluid motion. I wrapped my legs around his waist and my arms around his neck, hoping he would lay me down on the chaise longue and plunge into me—or better yet, plaster my sweat-soaked body against the wall of the house so that we wouldn't have to worry about any unexpected squeaks from the patio furniture.

Hans began walking. The feel of his callused hands gripping my ass cheeks and his thick, firm cock grazing the inside of my thigh had me writhing with need. I thrust my hands into his sweaty hair and sucked at his swollen lips, which were slick and tangy from my own juices. My senses were so overwhelmed with desire that I didn't even notice that Hans was carrying me away from the safety of the covered patio...until I felt lukewarm water slosh into my boots. My eyes shot open immediately to the realization that Hans was carrying me

into

the motherfucking

pool!

Before I could yelp or thrash in protest, he thrust his tongue and the head of his massive, diamond-hard cock into me at the same time, effectively shutting me up.

My awareness dived below the surface of the water to where our bodies were now joined. Hans was all I could feel. There was simply no room in my consciousness to process anxiety, fear, wet, dry, hot, cold, past, future. Every sensation was flooded with Hans, and I wanted him even deeper—in every sense of the word.

Once we were completely submerged, Hans pressed my back against the cool tiled wall of the pool and filled me with not only his throbbing length, but also himself. Every achingly slow withdrawal felt as though it was peeling away another layer of separation between us until we were no longer two people in a pool. We were the pool. We were the unending, undulating sea.

Hans broke our kiss just long enough to whisper into my neck, "I love you."

Tears pricked my eyes. Sure, Hans had said those three words to me a thousand times before, but I'd never really allowed myself to *hear* them until then. Until that night I had assumed that *I love you* was just something cute Hans said to all his girl-friends, and that sooner or later he'd be saying it to someone better. But I saw it in his face in the parking lot. I heard it in his voice. And I could feel it with every thrust of his hips. Hans actually *loved* me. And I was all in.

I grasped his beautiful face with both hands and urged him to look at me. When he finally complied, tiny white lights from the trees behind me danced across the shiny surface of his eyes, giving me the sense that, through those black holes of eyeliner and dark lashes, I could see directly into the heavens.

I smoothed the worried V between his brows with one thumb and whispered back, never breaking eye contact, "I. Love. You."

Hans tightened his grip on my ass and buried himself into me as far as he could go, pressing his forehead into mine. "I love *you*."

Hans's words were more forceful, insistent, and resolute than before. They echoed through me, bouncing into and out of all the hollow places they'd never managed to reach before, leaving a satisfying vibration in their wake.

After a moment of reverie, Hans slowly withdrew and then plunged into me harder than before. I moaned unintentionally into his mouth.

Shit!

If he kept that up, I was going to wake up the homeowners and their ravenous pet cobras for sure. Hans's next thrust was harder still.

Ugh!

I bit my lip to keep from groaning with pleasure as I grabbed a handful of his messy black hair and hissed into his mouth, "I love you."

My sentiment was immediately rewarded with a pounding so forceful that water sloshed over the edge of the pool.

Kissing me just below my ear, Hans growled as he ground his hips into mine, "I love *you*."

Abruptly, Hans tightened the grip he had on my ass and stood upright, exposing both of our naked torsos to the warm night air. I reached behind me and propped myself up with my arms on the ledge of the pool, baring my breasts to the bad boy before me and my soul to the sensitive artist within. Hans responded to my submission by taking my left nipple ring between his teeth and thrusting fully into me just as he bit down.

Fire.

I might have been submerged in water, but my loins and heart and lungs were ablaze with pleasure. I could only writhe and hump and moan, "I love you. I love you. I love you," with every thrust.

I arched my back and squeezed the head of Hans's cock with everything I had. He grunted in response and slammed himself into my tightened pussy again.

Hans withdrew and attacked, harder and faster, until the once mirrorlike body of water around us had become an uncontainable riptide of waves and lust spilling over the edges of the pool and crisscrossing through the cracks between the surrounding terra-cotta tiles.

With my right nipple between his teeth, Hans wickedly flicked his tongue across the sensitive pierced flesh until my eyes rolled back and my core contracted and my body erupted into a volcano of seminal fluids and whimpers and curse words and tears.

Hans quickly slid two wet fingertips into my mouth to silence me and growled, "God, I fucking love you," into my neck as he poured the rest of himself into me.

We stood there in the water, eye makeup running down both of our faces, slumped over one another, panting in a tangle of postcoital bliss until our brains were able to acknowledge and process outside information again.

How long? Who knows? Time doesn't exist in heaven.

But I do know that when I finally looked up at the house, something was different.

"Um, Hans? Was that light on before?"

"What light?" Hans's head snapped around, and the look that flashed across his face as soon as he caught sight of that illuminated third-floor window was all the answer I needed.

Fuck! I started sloshing my way through the pool toward the stairs, but quickly realized it was going to take me until next Tuesday with those water-and-steel-filled wrecking balls on my feet. Walking through quicksand on the lunar surface would have been easier than getting out of that pool with those goddamn cement shoes on.

That's when I heard the sirens.

Luckily, Hans had the reaction time of a fucking ninja. Within five seconds he had scooped me up and set me on my ass on the edge of the pool, hoisted himself out, made a mad dash for the covered porch, and returned wearing his shoes and clutching our clothes under his tattooed arm like a football. Although his face was playful, Hans wasted no time in pulling me up with his free hand and whisking me and my eighty-pound boots away from that twinkling fairyland.

Hand in hand, we tore through the neighbors' backyards in the direction of my car. The sound of our shoes sloshing and slapping the earth ricocheted through the darkness and silence and affluence surrounding us. I just prayed that the owners of the million-dollar yards we were destroying were adrift on a creamy turquoise Ambien-induced sea somewhere and couldn't hear us cursing and giggling and tromping all over their perfectly manicured flower beds and shushing each other every time we accidentally knocked over a water feature or bumped our heads on their Corinthian wind chimes.

With every hot, humid, panicked yet elated breath I sucked in, the approaching sirens grew louder. Finally, the 'stang was in sight. Hans and I tiptoed around the far side of the castle it was parked in front of and peered around to see if the coast was clear.

I looked at Hans and exaggeratedly grabbed my fisted arm in what I hoped was the universal TV cop show signal for *hold*. He waited next to the house as I scampered across the front yard, remembering on the way that I'd locked my purse in my trunk and tied my car key to one of my bootlaces since I'd worn a dress with no pockets to the concert that night.

Thank fucking God I still had my boots on! If Hansel had untied and taken them off before our little tryst in the pool, that key could have been anywhere!

I slung my forty-pound foot up and rested it on the ledge of the driver-side window. Although I was topless, I at least still had on my red thong, which had somehow shifted back into place during my five-hundred-yard dash. Inexplicably, the realization that my cooter wasn't hanging out as I stood in the middle of the street with one leg up, water pouring out of my boot, while fumbling with my car door at three in the morning made me feel about a thousand percent better about the situation. I mean, I was practically wearing a whole bikini. I'd just lost the top part.

No big deal, officer. I'm sure this sort of thing happens all the time.

Finally!

I got the door open and hit the unlock button as I dived inside. I watched in awe as Hans's naked, muscular six-foot-three-inch silhouette sprinted across the yard toward me. I knew he'd played soccer when he was in high school, but with that physique and speed, he could have been a professional.

Could this man be any more perfect?

Just as he slammed his door shut, my rearview mirror was illuminated by flashing blue lights.

I spun around to look behind us and let out a relieved sigh when I saw that the cop car had stopped in front of the McMansion and wasn't right on my tail. Although I was parked at least a block away in the shadow of a huge magnolia tree, I still didn't want to draw any attention to the suspicious 1996 Ford lurched on the curb in an obviously garage-kept-import-car-driving kind of neighborhood, so Hans and I just slid down in our seats and decided to wait them out.

Even though we were naked and hiding from the police, Hans flashed me a confident rock-star smile and reached over to brush my cheek with his thumb. "That was amazing."

"Best night of my life," I muttered, quickly looking away as a familiar heat crept into my cheeks.

Thank God it was too dark for him to see me blush.

Hans was just so, so fucking sexy. I'd been trying to play it cool and keep my emotional distance from him all these months because I knew there was simply no way this man could ever see me the way I saw him, love me the way I feared I loved him, or be faithful to me for the rest of our lives.

And now that I was vulnerable and exposed (literally), I could barely look him in the eye out of fear of what I might find there. Would I be just another lovesick fangirl to him now that he knew he had me? Would the chase be over?

I had already begun to mourn the impending death of my relationship when Hans tilted my chin back toward him, forcing me to return his gaze.

"There you are," he said with that signature sideways smile. "Thought I'd lost you for a minute."

Mmm...

Looking into that dreamy face was like mainlining Xanax. The familiar fog of calm and contentment I usually felt whenever I was around Hans clouded the car until I couldn't even remember what I'd been so worried about. Just then, I heard the sound of a car door slam shut, and I remembered pretty quickly what I should be worried about.

The fucking cops!

I fished my dress out of the pile of clothes in Hans's lap—whose smoky eyes were now glued to my side view mirror—and shimmied it on over my head. Unfortunately, I couldn't quite tie the halter top from my fetal position under the steering wheel, but at least my bottom half was covered. Of course, the oh-so coordinated Hans managed to slip his pants back on without ever taking his eyes off the show unfolding behind us.

Curious to see what had Hans looking so serious, I climbed out of my hidey-hole and leaned across the center console to get a look at his mirror. On my way, I was momentarily distracted by the bare tattooed chest of a long, lean bass player slumped down in my passenger seat. His skin was damp and hot and smelled like chlorine, bringing to my attention the fact that I was also still topless.

Damn. If I could just tilt that seat all the way back real quick . . . Where was I? Oh, yes.

I shook off my hormones and rested my cheek on Hans's chest so that I could see what was going on in his mirror without sitting up and blowing our cover. The cruiser still had its headlights on, and one police officer was at the ready behind the wheel.

Shit.

The cop who'd been riding shotgun was now standing in the doorway of the McMansion, talking to a middle-aged man wearing a bathrobe. I couldn't make out much from that distance, but I distinctly saw the homeowner raise an angry-looking finger and point directly at my car.

"GO!" Hans yelled, prompting me to mechanically stomp on the clutch, crank the engine, and peel out of there, all without ever turning on my lights.

Shit, shit, shit!

Luckily, I'd driven through that neighborhood looking for free parking enough times to know an alternate way out. The sirens screamed to life the instant I pulled away.

Oh my fucking God.

My body operated that machine on muscle memory alone as my consciousness completely abandoned ship and spiraled in a million different terrible directions.

Let's see. Where to begin? Evading the police, indecent exposure, trespassing, being in possession of false identification, underage drinking, engaging in a public sex act, disturbing the peace, speeding…

What I thought was going to go down in history as the most glorious sexual experience of my life would now be forever remembered as The Night I Got Raped in Jail. Although I've never heard of lady-on-lady rape, I was an underweight teenager who'd been raised by hippie pacifists. I had no self-defense skills (other than clumsily swinging my ten-ton steel-toed boots in the general direction of other people), and my only undergarment that night was a sopping wet red thong. If there had ever been a prime candidate for lady rape, it was me.

I turned right onto the first street I came to, stomping on the accelerator halfway through the turn to build up speed as quickly as possible.

I'd learned how to drive fast back when I was dating Harley. There had been an abandoned housing development down the street from his mom's house where people used to race. Everybody called it The Track because the streets had all been paved, but not a single house had been completed before the builder went belly up. And because it wasn't technically private or public property, we could blow off steam without the cops fucking with us.

Whenever I pushed it too hard and threw a belt or something, Harley would just call his redneck buddies from the shop where he worked, and they'd come out with their big-ass trucks and their headlamps and their Natty Ice and fix that shit while singing David Allan Coe songs like we were all in *Snow White Trash and the Seven Hicks*. Thanks to them, I now have the lyrics to "Don't Bite the Dick," "Little Susie Shallow Throat," and "Cum Stains on the Pillow" tattooed on my brain.

But I also know how to tail-brake a corner without spinning out.

In fact, that particular memory actually seemed to calm my nerves. My consciousness was back, and it decided to press the Play button on "You Never Even Called Me by My Name" for a little nostalgia.

I was drunk... the day my mom... got out of prison...

Just pretend like you're back at The Track, B. You used to do this all the time. It was fun. You're having fun.

Redlining in second gear, I braked hard just before the next turn to transfer some weight to my front end before cutting the wheel. As soon as I was halfway through the turn and my RPMs were at a perfect 3500, I punched the gas and hit the straights, shifting into third within seconds.

"Damn, Bumblebee! Where the fuck did that come from?"

It was the first thing Hans had uttered since we peeled out, and I could hear the surprise in his voice. I glanced over and found my rock-star boyfriend gripping the Oh, Shit bar (I don't actually know what that handle hanging from the ceiling in cars is called. In the South people just call it the Oh, Shit bar.) with one hand and the center console with the other, a look of shock and awe on his face. It was all the encouragement I needed.

After spending almost a year feeling inadequate around this man, I'd finally found a way to make my mark, to set myself apart from the hordes of ho-bags beating down Hans's door. I could drive this fucking Mustang, and I could do it topless. My consciousness turned up the volume:

And I went... to pick her up... in the raaaain...

I redlined her again and muscled through the last turn in the neighborhood. I could still hear the sirens right behind me and see the occasional reflection of a blue light off a house or a street sign, but I'd managed to keep enough distance and turns between us that the police hadn't been able to get a visual on me.

The next turn would make or break us though.

But before I could get to the station in the pick-uuuuuup truck...

If I could pull out of the neighborhood and onto the highway without having to stop, we'd be home free. I could have us tucked away into the club parking lot within ten seconds. I downshifted to second and held my breath as we approached the intersection.

Please be clear, please be clear, please be clear...

She got runned over by a damned old traaaain!

"It's clear! It's clear! GO, GO, GO!" Hans was on the edge

of his seat, looking left and right and left again, making sure I wasn't about to kill us both.

Ha!

I crushed the accelerator with all forty pounds of wet steel and leather strapped to my right foot and was rewarded with a satisfying yelp from my well-worn BFGs (that's what the rednecks call BF Goodrich tires) and an even more satisfying glimpse of Hans's head being slammed backward into the headrest by the torque.

I flicked on my headlights as I raced toward the entrance of the club's parking lot, just a little over a block away. A few hundred yards, and we'd be in the clear.

Two hundred, one hundred...

Hans was now turned around completely backward in his seat with both fists gripping the headrest and wide, excited eyes scanning the expanse behind us for any sign of the police cruiser. I bit my lip just in time to squelch the very smug, very self-satisfied grin threatening to destroy my cool, took a deep breath, and made the final turn into the parking lot, barking the tires a little just for show. The instant all four tires were off the highway, I killed the headlights and careened into the first available parking spot I could see.

Hans erupted into a fit of hysterics, pounding the headrest with his fists and yelling "WOOOOOO!!!" as if he were greeting a sold-out stadium.

I'd never seen anybody so amped in my life.

The moment I killed the engine and turned to face him, Hans had his giant hands around my shoulders and was practically shaking me like a rag doll.

"Holy shit, Bumblebee! You lost 'em! You motherfucking

lost 'em!" A manic grin split his face. "You turned into fucking Angelina Jolie from *Gone in Sixty Seconds* back there! Where the fuck did you learn to drive like that?"

Ever distractible, I watched Hans's eyes flick down to my still-exposed breasts mid thought, and his hand impulsively reached out to stroke one of my nipple rings. Hearing my gasp, Hans glanced back up at me, as if he'd just remembered where he was.

He shook his head and continued in a more serious tone, "That was the sexiest fucking thing I've ever seen in my life."

Before I could formulate a response to all that flattery, I found myself plastered against the driver-side door as seventy-five inches of tall, dark, and tattooed ravaged my mouth, neck, still bared breasts, and still swollen pussy with every appendage in his arsenal. I'd never seen Hans so ravenous.

And knowing I had done that to him made me feel like maybe I was special after all. Maybe, just maybe, I did have things to offer him that other women didn't.

From that day on, anytime my old familiar insecurities reared their ugly flat chests, I would simply pull that shiny memory out of my pocket and rub it like a talisman until all the self-deprecating feelings melted away in a blaze of twinkling lights and churning black water and hushed *I love yous* and high-speed pursuits with happy endings.

23

I Was in a Basement, Surrounded by Phantom Limbs

BB's Secret Journal

December 7

Dear Journal,

So...I might have gotten a little carried away with my last SPJTKINNATRE entry. In reality, the best sex I ever had was significantly colder, dirtier, and just all-around more dungeony. Rather than a luxurious, magical, liquid fairyland in the sultry heat of summer, the actual act took place in a dingy linoleum-floored, wood-paneled basement...in a bed blanketed with dust and mouse droppings...in the dead of winter. And instead of being enveloped by the majesty of a million twinkling lights, we were surrounded by Hans's hopefully sleeping bandmates, who were scattered all over the floor.

After most of their shows, Hans and the rest of his Phantom Limbs bandmates would head over to the lead singer's redneck dad's house to crash for the night. (Trip got every bit of his perverted personality from his dad. The first time I went to his father's house the man stumbled over, reeking of brown liquor and creepiness, winked at me, and then handed Trip a tiny flashlight, "To shine a little light on the situation.")

Exhausted from a particularly badass show and wasted beyond belief, the guys shuffled into the basement one by one and pretty much passed out the moment their faces met the linoleum floor. Except for Hans.

Watching him perform always turned me on, but on that particular night I was ravenous. I couldn't keep my hands off him in the car on the way to Trip's dad's house, and once we arrived the only thing on either of our minds was finishing what we'd started on the ride over.

By the time we made it down to the basement the place looked like a crime scene. Unconscious bodies were strewn around the room as if a bomb had been detonated nearby. There was no rhyme or reason as to why the guys landed where they did, especially considering that they left the bed in the corner of the room untouched. It did have a bunch of boxes and shit piled on top of it, so maybe through their beer goggles it just looked like too much work.

Hans and I tiptoed over his snoring bandmates on our way to the bed, removing the debris—and our clothing—as quickly as possible. Within seconds we were joined under the cover of some scratchy woolen nightmare, trying our damnedest to be quiet. The bed was squeaky, so we had to move slowly and deliberately. We paid attention to our breathing, our pace, every sound, every movement. While it seemed at first like a pain in the ass, all that care and intention caused us to be more present. Every exquisite drag and pull felt *significant*. Time moved fractionally, if at all, and each time we returned to one another, three tiny words always seemed to escape on a sigh, despite our best efforts to be silent. Fallout bed be damned, Hans and I were cloaked in a silken womb of soul-baring love, and it transcended our meager, mothball-littered surroundings.

I like to think of that experience the way people describe the first time they smoked crack. They say the first time is always the best, right? So maybe love is just like any other drug. Maybe the reason I haven't experienced that magical interconnected love-bubble sensation since that night in the basement is because I'm doomed to chase that high for the rest of my life. It wouldn't matter who I ended up with—a cold, limp fish or a sensitive artist.

But deep down, I know that's not true.

I *could* have that feeling again. In fact, every time I close my eyes and go back to that night, I feel it. It's not some elusive high I'm chasing. It's accessible. Simply remembering how the ambient light in the room turned Hans's kohl-rimmed gray-blue eyes into liquid pools of mercury, the way my hands slid over his tattooed torso and found a home in his unruly black hair, the way his lips caressed my ear like butterfly wings as he whispered the words "I love you," has that exact combination of pheromones and endorphins queued up and ready to go...for nothing.

Whenever I try to initiate a love volley like that with Ken, he simply throws his hands up and takes a step backward, as if I just tossed him a live rattlesnake. It's like he's an extra on *CSI: Miami*. There might as well be a chalk outline around his body while we—no, while *I* have sex.

If Ken would just have a fucking feeling once in a while,

make a little eye contact, cup my face in his hands, press his forehead to mine, say something sweet—I'm not even looking for complete sentences. He can fucking tap *You are beautiful* into my ass in Morse code if it's really that excruciating for him to express himself out loud—that entire entry would have been about him. Actually, that entry wouldn't even exist. There would be no need. We'd be John and fucking Yoko.

Speaking of musicians, I'll tell you a little bit about the *real* Hans Oppenheimer after I explain myself . . .

Complete and utter lack of passion aside, I still love the shit out of Kenneth Easton. In fact, he's my all-time favorite person. I think I even like him more than our kids. (Honestly, what have those little shits done for me lately?)

He just accepts me and supports me and quietly goes about making all my dreams come true without the need for affirmation or thanks of any kind. He's the kind of man who waits to eat until everyone else is seated; who stands on the train, no matter how many seats are empty; who folds the laundry simply because it needed to be folded; and who always lets me choose the restaurant. Despite his inherent sense of responsibility and courtesy, Ken also curses like a sailor (even in front of children, and not just our children, either) and never fails to shoot me a smart-ass one-liner whenever I acknowledge any of his gracious gestures. And somehow, he manages to be both the most handsome and most humble man in any room.

I want to take him with me everywhere. I want us to live a hundred years and die at the same time. I want them to mix our cremated remains together, dump us into a river, and watch our mingled ashes swirl like coffee creamer all the way to the ocean. I want our souls (okay, my soul and his, whatever he has, operating system?) to find each other on the other side as soon as possible just so that we can fall in love and make more babies and do it all over again.

I just *also* want him to fuck my brains out.

It's a beautiful life Ken has given me, one filled with security and laughter and intelligent conversation and honeymoons in Paris and well-behaved children with long attention spans and cute noses and his-and-hers sinks and 401(k)s and well-manicured lawns. I just wish the orgasms matched the drapes, if you know what I mean. And I wish the drapes had my name tattooed on them somewhere highly visible and brazenly unprofessional.

Is that so much to ask?

24

Bass Players Do It with Rhythm

BB's Secret Journal

December 14

Between his height, bone structure, unruly black hair, and giant, left-leaning cock, Hans could totally have been a body double for Tommy Lee in that Pamela Anderson sex tape—if it weren't for all the tattoo discrepancies, that is. He was a sensitive, romantic soul camouflaged by the body and attire of a six-foot-three-inch heavy-metal bassist with a raging case of ADHD. Bless His Heart, as I've taken to calling him, might have ruined me for everyone.

That motherfucker would tell me I was beautiful *every day*—with sincerity, and eye contact, and a gentle caress of my cheek with his giant callused man hands. He would buy me big, ostentatious bouquets of flowers—for no reason. He would hold my hand—in public. He'd paint my toenails while we watched *Sex and the City*. And whenever his parents were out of town, Hans would drag a TV into their opulent master bathroom so that we could soak in the clam-shaped splendor of their garden tub as Leeloo and Korben Dallas fell in love all over again.

Hans was also every bit as distractible and impulsive as I described him in that bullshit journal entry I left for Ken to find. In fact, the part about him veering off course due to a bunch of twinkling lights was based on actual events. It was a steamy summer night, much like the one in the story, and we were driving across a dam near Bless His Heart's parents' house. Before we could make it to the other side, BHH slammed on the brakes, lurched his ancient BMW over to the shoulder of the bridge, yanked me out of the car, and plopped us both down on the guardrail, doing his patented twirl-me-in-the-air-and-set-me-down-sideways-on-his-lap move along the way. I held on to his big shoulders for dear life and shut my eyes tight, thinking this crazy tattooed motherfucker was about to jump into the lake.

At that point, nothing would have surprised me. I'd learned pretty quickly that, with Hans, all I could do was hang on and enjoy the ride.

When I finally realized I was not about to plummet twenty-five feet into the inky black water below, I opened my eyes and saw what had him so enraptured. The surface of the lake looked as if someone had taken the night sky and spread it out like a picnic blanket before us. A million crystalline points of light billowed and swayed below while a million more floated just out of reach in the thick summer air above. I wanted to stay there forever, but BHH's emorection wouldn't allow it.

Eventually, we retreated to the car where we spent the next hour and a half cuddling, gazing into each other's souls, and making love while Jimmy Eat World competed with the sound of rushing water plummeting below us. It felt as though we were in our own personal snow globe of ecstasy, only the white flecks swirling around us weren't snowflakes but stars. Stars everywhere—in the sky, on the water, splashed in ink across his skin and in my eyes as they rolled heavenward on a crest of pleasure.

The only thing that prevented *that* particular lovefest from going down in history as the best sex of my life was the fact that it took place in a *car*. I damn near required skin grafts on my knees after all the grinding they did against the door and center console that night.

I guess that's how you know you're a grown-up, Journal. If you're old enough to complain about the upholstery burn, you're too damn old to be getting plowed in a sedan on the side of the road.

Dating a rocker (even one who lived in the bonus room above his parents' garage) was kind of like having your cake and eating it, too. Actually, it was more like having a gay best friend and being able to sit on his face. While both are into fashion and makeup and gossip and feelings and experimental anal play, the rock star wouldn't insist that you wear a strap-on and douse yourself in Drakkar Noir first. He'd merely *appreciate* it.

Sounds fantastic, right?

It is.

Until it's *not*.

Do yourself a favor, Journal. If you happen to fall in love with a rock star, good for you. Congratulations. Don't marry him. Trust me on this. You'll want to have his freakishly tall, dark, inattentive babies. Don't do it. You'll want to sign a six-month lease on an apartment and get a betta fish with him. Don't fucking do it.

Because when that shit goes south—and it will, in spectacular fashion—who do you think is going to lose all her deposits and have to fashion a tiny Viking-style funeral pyre for sweet little Betta Bob Thornton all by herself? Who do you think is going to find her bestie in bed with him the next day? Who do you think is going to get a phone call at five a.m. a week later to come get him from the hospital because he was sad and wanted to be put on suicide watch, but the attending psychologist sized him up in ten minutes and knew he wasn't going to hurt himself or anyone else (other than you, emotionally, some more) and told his uninsured ass to take a hike?

I'll give you one hint. Her name rhymes with pee-pee, and she's been royally shit on.

So, here's what you do in the event that you find yourself in love with a rock star. You have passionate, consummate, paradigm shifting sex with him while keeping separate residences, bank accounts, credit cards, cell phone plans, and even fucking Netflix accounts. If you can get away with giving him a fake name, all the better. Especially if he happens to be a bass player. Bass players and drummers all have ADHD. Every last one. It's a scientific fact. And for that reason, they cannot be expected to keep a stable job, show up anywhere on time, remember to pay fucking bills or put gas in the tank, not overdraw their accounts, or resist free drugs or pussy. But *damn* can they keep a beat. The bumper stickers are true, Journal. Bass players *do* do it with rhythm.

Now, don't get me wrong. I'd had some incendiary, life-affirming (and at times, life-threatening) sex well before Bless His Heart ever came along. Knight had bent me into shapes that only the cartilage of a barely post-pubescent would allow, and Harley had a vibrating tongue ring. (Yes, they make those, and they are *glorious*.)

But Hans is the only man I've ever been with who I can say, beyond a whisper of doubt, truly *made love* to me. He took sex and wove into it something transcendent, arresting, and . . . well, *deep*. I mean, he was the only guy I'd ever met who not only got a hard-on watching *The Notebook*, but also insisted that we reenact the peel-our-wet-clothes-off-on-our-way-to-the-bedroom-after-the-rainy-canoe-ride scene. *No shit.*

This guy exists, Journal, and he will ruin your credit and gene pool if you let him.

25

Bonerversary

BB's Secret Journal

December 20

Dear Journal,

I think my husband might have just made actual love to me. Hang on, let me mark my calendar. I don't want to forget this shit. Every year from now on, December 20 is officially going to be BB and Ken's Bonerversary. I'll drop the kids at my parents' house, prepare (pick up) a lovely meal, and then Ken and I will sit with our heads bowed in quiet remembrance of the one time he didn't behave like a cold limp fish during sex. Our annual Bonerversary will keep me going. It will sustain me.

Ken and I got ready for bed at the same time tonight, which doesn't happen that often because I'm practically nocturnal and he's practically narcoleptic, so I was optimistic that I might actually get some action. Only instead of climbing into bed with me—or on top of me, like I'd hoped—Ken went back into the living room so that he could finish watching the Falcons game that he had recorded on the DVR.

So there I lay, alone, in the dark, resigned to the fact that the Atlanta Falcons had won again—not the game, but the war.

An old, familiar blanket of defeat settled over my naked body. I tried to fight it off by thinking happier thoughts. I thought about Ken singing a Bob Marley song to the baby after dinner. No one would ever guess by looking at his suave, clean-cut appearance that the man absolutely loves funk and reggae music.

I thought about how he surprised me with movie tickets last weekend, and kept it a secret from me until the babysitter arrived. I was excited at first, but then quickly realized that I didn't have on a lick of makeup and my hair was pulled back in a frizzy poof of a ponytail. When I said something to Ken about it he simply shrugged and said, "It'll be dark in there." Fucker! Not, *I like your hair pulled back—it shows off your pretty face!* or *You're so beautiful, you don't need makeup!* but *Don't worry about your ugly mug. Nobody's gonna see it anyway.*

Just as I was beginning to remember why I'm always want-ing to knee my husband in the balls, the bedroom door opened. Ken padded lightly across the room, only instead of slipping into bed on his side of Chastity Mountain—the person-sized hump that has formed in the middle of our mattress due to a total lack of spooning, cuddling, and other fun middle-of-the-bed activities—Ken climbed into bed right behind me and wrapped his arms around my waist.

"I love you," he whispered into my shoulder, grazing it with his lips.

Wha?

"I love you, too," I said back, my words laced with confusion. I hadn't meant for it to sound so much like a question, but his behavior was completely out of character. Ken only tells me he loves me whenever one of us is about to leave the house, and even then I think he's just doing it to cover his bases in case one of us dies in a horrible car accident or something.

I felt Ken's hand gently brush the hair away from the side of my face. Warm breath bathed my ear as he whispered again, "I love you."

I brought my hand up behind me and touched the side of his head. This time my voice shook with concern when I said, "I love you, too, baby. Is everything okay?"

Ken ignored my question, pulling my earlobe into his mouth and pressing his cotton-covered erection into the crease of my ass. My inner psychologist immediately switched the sign on her door from OPEN to CLOSED, as I no longer gave two fucks about the cause of Ken's atypical behavior. The only thing I cared about at that moment was getting those goddamn boxer briefs off.

"I love you," Ken whispered again as his hand disappeared between my legs.

"I love you, too," I replied, this time without a shred of inquiry in my voice, then sucked the words back in on a gasp as he slipped a finger into me. I opened my legs to him wider and rocked back against his still-clothed manhood.

I turned my head to the right, searching for the lips that had just been on my ear. When I found them they gave me one soft, lingering kiss that held more emotion in it than I thought I would ever experience again.

"I love you." His words floated into my open mouth, down my throat, and into my belly where they blossomed and took root.

Ken hadn't been watching sports in the living room, he'd been reading my SPJTKINNATRE entry about Hans!

I'd almost completely forgotten about that journal entry, and Ken was doing an amazing job of making me forget all over again. After our kiss Ken rolled me onto my back, pulled his boxer briefs off in one fluid motion, and positioned himself between my legs.

Planting my feet firmly on the bed, I lifted my hips toward him and accepted the love he was offering. Once Ken and I were completely joined I embraced him with my legs, clutched his beautiful face in my hands, and whispered, "I love you, too, baby. I love you so fucking much."

Once we began to move the air became charged with an intensity that made me feel like I was being worshipped in the front seat of a faded black BMW all over again. Unfortunately, it had the same effect on Ken. Even though he came first, it just provided further proof that Ken really had been overcome…by an emotion.

I'd finally broken through.

I felt like I was in one of those movies where the main character sits faithfully beside her comatose partner, night after sleepless night, in defiance of everyone who says it's hopeless. Except the only one telling me it was hopeless around here was Ken—every time he'd roll away from me when I tried to cuddle with him in bed, every time he'd fold up one of my frilly little calligraphied love poems and shove it in his pocket with a "Thanks, man," every time he'd tap me on the ass five seconds after coming.

Ken has been in an emotional coma for ten years, but something I wrote woke him up. He might slip away from me again, but now, I have hope.

And every year on December 20, I will make sure that, though his emorection might be gone, it will never be forgotten.

26

Guard Your Thighs

BB's Secret Journal

January 18

Hans used to get emorections all the time. All I had to do was tell him I loved him and he'd be hard as a diamond. He was my first roommate, and at first, I loved playing house. I decorated the walls with my paintings and stocked the kitchen drawers with miscellaneous gadgets and cutlery that I'd stolen from either my parents' house or the housewares department at Macy's where I worked part-time.

But I didn't love how Hans couldn't get his shit together enough to help me pay for the place, clean it, or after a few months, even come home to it at all.

Turns out Hans had been spending his weekends doing blow and blowing all his money at the strip club down the street. I know, Journal. I know. My rock-star boyfriend partied like a rock star. I should have seen that one coming. You don't have to rub it in.

After discovering that he had also failed all of the college classes I'd signed him up for *and* lost his job without telling me,

I finally flipped the fuck out about his partying. And get this—*he* had the audacity to break up with *me*!

The next day at work, I was so distraught that I tearfully clocked out mid shift, snatched an armful of boxes from the Macy's warehouse on my way out, and decided to race home and dramatically move all my shit out while Hans was...wherever the fuck he went during the day. Only, when I went to pull into my usual spot in front of our building, Hans's ancient black BMW was already there with one tire lurched up onto the sidewalk, windows halfway down, and keys still in the ignition.

Goddamn it! Of course he's home! It's noon on a Tuesday! Where else would he be? Obviously not at work or school!

Up to that point in my life, I'd only experienced two kinds of breakups—the kind where your boyfriend turns into a violent, terroristic stalker and the kind where you just quit answering the phone and they go away. I was wading into uncharted waters. And while I was a thousand percent sure that Hans wouldn't ever physically hurt another human being, I was about to discover that I couldn't say the same thing about myself.

As soon as I opened the door, two things immediately grabbed my attention by the balls. They were both black. They were both stilettos. And they were both tossed in a heap on the stairs. The stairs that led to *our* motherfucking bedroom. I short-circuited. Physically. Mentally. Digestively. My first instinct was to barf up my fucking spleen into those cheap pleather knee-high boots, but I never got the chance because my body beat my stomach and my brain up the stairs.

By the time my out-of-shape rational mind caught up with what was unfolding up there, huffing and puffing and pausing to light another cigarette, I'd already kicked open the door to

our bedroom, ripped the sheets off the bed, and started screaming, "Get the fuck out of my bed!" while slapping Goth Girl
repeatedly on her bare thigh. It watched the assault taking place
like an innocent bystander, absentmindedly thinking, *Really, B?*
The thigh? That's kind of a weird choice, don't you think?

I guess it was the first part of her body I could get my hands
on. I dunno. At least I didn't bite her.

Unfortunately, before I could select a cooler place to strike
Goth Girl, Hans leaped out of bed, dragged me into the hallway, locking Goth Girl inside *our* bedroom on his way out, and
escorted me into the living room. After chucking three remote
controls, a four-pound crystal ashtray—also stolen from my
parents—and all of our ceramic coasters at his head like Chinese stars, I finally ran out of ammo and simply melted into a
screaming, rocking, hyperventilating puddle on the couch.

Eventually, through the rushing sounds of blood and bile, as
well as my own shrieking, I slowly began to make out Hans's
calm, repetitive mantra.

"Nothing happened. Nothing happened, Bumblebee. I
swear. Nothing happened."

When I finally calmed down enough to process visual stimuli
again, I noticed that Hans was wearing boxers and a T-shirt. (He
usually slept naked.) And when I mentally replayed my assault
on Goth Girl, she had been wearing one of Hans's T-shirts and
a pair of boxers, too.

Goddamn it.

Hans explained while I trembled and sniffled and chain-
smoked on the couch that he had gone to a bar after our big
fight the night before, gotten plowed, and called Goth Girl for a
shoulder to cry on.

Evidently Goth Girl had just broken up with Goth Boy, so she decided to head on up to the bar and drown her sorrows as well. She wound up crashing at our place because she was too drunk to drive home. (Based on Hans's parking job, he was, too.)

I actually wanted them to have had sex so that I could be justified in my rage, but I knew that Hans was telling the truth. It didn't make it hurt any less that he'd run to another girl's arms just hours after our breakup, but the fact that it was just for comfort made me feel like an even bigger psycho for all the thigh slapping.

Eventually, Goth Girl tiptoed out from the safety of her little cage, and we cried and smoked together on the couch while Hans paced around, looking lost. Once I was all cried out I asked both of them to leave so that I could get on with packing up my shit in peace...

Then I gutted that fucking hole-in-the-wall so bad that you would have thought I was the Grinch trying to stop Christmas from coming.

I took the shower curtain, the rod, and the little rubber drain stopper. I took the toilet paper. I took the blinds, and I didn't even have a screwdriver. I just ripped that shit right out of the wall. I took the pillows, comforter, and twenty-five-thread-count Walmart-brand sheets. (The mattress stayed only because it wouldn't fit in the 'stang. The TVs wouldn't fit in the 'stang either, but that didn't stop me from taking the remote controls.) I took every pot, pan, dish, scrap of food, and drawer knob from the kitchen. Hell, I even took the last can of Who Hash.

And you know what, Journal? It made me feel a little bit better.

You know what made me feel *a lot* better? Finding out that Hans got evicted the next month and lost his deposit due to all the missing appliances and chunks of drywall.

You know what made me forget Hans had ever existed? Meeting my soul mate.

27

Skynet Has Become Self-Aware! Skynet Has Become Self-Aware!

BB's Secret Journal

February 2

Mayday, Journal! Mayday!

You've been compromised! There's no other possible explanation! Ken went from giving me head about as often as he changes the AC filter to going down on me *every time* we have sex. Every. Time. Um, yeah. You don't go from never doing a thing to *always* doing a thing unless there's a serious fucking intervention, especially Ken. His behavior is so calcified that I don't think he could sit on the other side of the couch if you held a gun to his head. There's only one thing that could make this motherfucker suddenly feel the need to eat pussy all the time, and it's my journal entry about his oral dry spell. Fuck.

What else did he read in here? How much does he know??

This is so bad. It's so good, but it's so, so bad. I totally underestimated him, Journal. Of all the husbots in all the world, why did I have to wind up with the evil genius TL 9000 version?

I've been writing a lot lately, so I'll bet he went to sneak a peek at Super Private Journal That Ken Is Never, Never Allowed to Read Ever to see what I've been up to, then got suspicious when there was nothing new in there and went on a little fishing expedition.

Did he figure out how to search for recent files? Is that how he found you? I thought that asshole was computer illiterate! Has he just been malingering as a technological simpleton this whole time when in reality he's some kind of diabolical data miner?? Is he Kevin Spacey from *The Usual Suspects*?? (Spoiler alert if you haven't seen *The Usual Suspects*.)

Wait a minute! Oh my God, I know what happened! Ken hasn't read you at all, Little Guy! He read my email! My EMAIL! That entry about him never going down on me was actually just cut and pasted from an email conversation with Sara, right? And Ken totally has access to my email because we're too cheap to get our own iPads, so anytime he wants to check his email while he's on there, he literally has to get all up in my inbox to log me out. Usually, I don't worry about it because everything in my inbox looks like it will immediately inject you with a lethal dose of estrogen upon opening—daily affirmations from Oprah, OB/GYN and hair appointment reminders, half a dozen receipts for romance novels I purchased on Amazon—but I'm sure the subject line *Cunnilingus* piqued his interest.

It's so simple! This explains why Ken has been giving me head every other day instead of stabbing needles into an auburn-haired voodoo doll like he would if he'd actually been reading this shit. We're safe, Journal! We're safe!

It's a Groundhog Day miracle! Free oral sex, on the regular, and I'm not going to be smothered in my sleep? Thank you, universe! Thank you, Oprah! Thank you, Deepak Chopra! Namaste! Namaste!

28

When the SUV's A-Rockin'

BB's Secret Journal

February 8

Dear Journal,

I had sex in a car last night. In a random neighborhood. At eleven p.m. It was not a first for me, but it was a new low for my Mother of the Year contention, especially considering that I sprayed breast milk all over Ken's Oxford shirt mid coitus and used an emergency stash of baby wipes to clean myself up afterward. Goddamn it. I really wanted that trophy, too.

The evening started classily enough. Ken and I had concert tickets, so we got a babysitter and went to dinner at a cozy little Italian restaurant on the way.

(Side note: I'm never going to stop writing Super Private Journal That Ken Is Never, Never Allowed to Read, EVER. The steady flow of date nights and oral sex is definitely still in full swing. Unsolicited compliments and a tattoo of my name can't be far behind!)

It was a general admission show, so when we got to the concert venue, I dropped Ken off at the end of the line, so he could grab us good seats while I scrounged up a secluded place to park so that I could pump my breast milk, *like a lady*.

(See, Journal? This is why I was a contender for Mother of the Year in the first place! Who else is conscientious enough to still be breast-feeding nine months postpartum, keeps a hospital-grade breast pump fully equipped with a car charger on hand at all times, AND has the foresight to empty her breasts *before* ordering a double Jameson on the rocks? At this point in the story, I'm basically June Cleaver.)

When my boobs were sufficiently deflated, I deftly snapped the flaps back up on my nursing bra, adjusted my designated I'm-going-to-a-rock-concert black tank top, ripped off the nursing cover I'd worn to keep from flashing innocent bystanders, and stashed the bottles of milk away in the little cooler I kept inside my breast-pump bag.

Hoping I had enough time to pee and grab a drink before the show started, I cheerily repeated, "No, thanks. I'm good," as I ran-walked through a sea of scary-looking scalpers and vaga-bonds into the venue.

When I emerged from the least feculent restroom stall I could find, I noticed a group of teenyboppers huddled around one of the sinks, primping and preening. All three of them looked nearly identical with their matching skeletal, fifteen-year-old bodies and perfectly straight waist-length hair. I delighted in eavesdropping as I washed my hands.

Teenybopper #1: "Did you notice that guy sitting next to us? He's so hot!"

Teenybopper #2: "No! What does he look like?"

Teenybopper #1: "He's wearing, like, a button-down thing and looks kind of stuffy, but whatever. I just like looking at him."

My ears perked up. *Hot? Button-down? Stuffy?*

There was only one guy in that audience who could possibly match that description. Ken had come straight from work and was looking positively GQ when he met me for dinner in his pale-blue dress shirt and navy basket weave tie.

Tween #3 rolled her eyes: "Don't be creepy."

I smirked as I dried my hands.

You should listen to your friend, bitch.

I made my way up to the balcony, following the directions Ken texted me while I was pumping, and spotted him sitting in the back row. He locked eyes with me immediately like he'd been watching the door and smiled, casually saluting me with two fingers. I happily drank in his Christian Grey–esque business attire.

Damn. He does look hot.

Ken's smile got wider as I approached, obviously noticing my appreciative stare. I stopped in the walkway behind his seat and bent over to kiss him hello before I made my way to the bar. When I stood back up, he flirted with me by taking a little nip at my thigh with his teeth.

Wha—who is this guy??

Flirting back, I said, "I stopped by the restroom on my way up here and overheard some little teenyboppers talking about some hot *button-down* guy sitting next to them. I assumed they must have been talking about you."

Ken nudged his head to the right and replied, "Was it those girls?"

I looked past him to a cluster of giggling waifs about ten feet away who were just taking their seats. And holy fucking shit, it *was* them! Those little bitches really did want my husband!

I can't explain what happened to me after that, Journal. To call it jealousy would be egregiously dismissive. This was visceral, physiological. Knowing that a gaggle of younger, skinnier, straighter-haired females wanted my husband caused my body to start pumping out pheromones on a nuclear level.

By the time I got back to my seat with my half-gallon of Jameson, I was a virtual mushroom cloud of sexual energy. I don't know if the pulse I was emitting was a defense mechanism meant to warn off the bitches sitting next to me or if it was an offensive tactic intended to scramble Ken's thoughts and keep his attention solely on me, but whatever it was, Ken picked up the scent loud and clear.

While we watched the opening bands, I sat up on the back of my seat so that I could see better, which also gave me a height advantage over Ken and those little skanks. I used the power differential to assert myself by resting a protective arm on his shoulder while lightly scratching his head with my fingernails. I felt ridiculous, like I was some high school quarterback trying to prove to everybody in the lunchroom that the big-tittied blonde cheerleader was mine, but I couldn't help it. I stared straight ahead like a gangsta, never acknowledging the cast of *Hannah Montana* sitting next to me, and fantasized that they were staring at me out of the corners of their eyes thinking, *Who is that woman with The Suit? Is she playing with his hair? Oh my God, she's such a badass. He looks like some rich business executive, but Rocker Chick has her arm around him like he's her fucking bitch. I'll bet she has tattoos. And rides a motorcycle. And keeps a pair of brass knuckles in her vagina.*

Just as I was beginning to worry that I was making Ken feel emasculated with my possessive posturing, he leaned over and rested his head on my tit! It was fucking adorable. At that point, any energy I was expending on warning off the jailbait next to me got redirected to my now throbbing pussy. This gorgeous, well-dressed, five o'clock–shadowed tall drink of water was cuddled up next to me like a teddy bear. He was mine. And all I could think about was how badly I wanted to throw my leg over the wooden armrest between us and dry-hump him for the rest of the show.

And it was a really good show—until it wasn't.

There were two opening bands, and both of them were actually pretty fantastic. Ken and I bobbed in our seats, never breaking physical contact with each other, and surrendered to the noise. By the time the headliner finally came on, the crowd had been worked into a frothy, foaming, hormone-fueled frenzy— Ken and myself included. We leaped to our feet like everyone else and jumped and danced with abandon.

People without children will never truly appreciate the majesty of a night out. The exquisite freedom from responsibility is intoxicating, especially after polishing off a feedbag full of Jameson.

Then, two songs in, the music stopped. A cloud of murmurs and reverb wafted through the air as the lead singer was led to the side of the stage by a roadie who whispered in his ear entirely too long for it to be good news. The hush was deafening. When the roadie finally returned our beloved front man to the mic, he was beaming with pride.

"You guys are so fucking crazy you broke the floor!" he exclaimed, just before being ushered off-stage.

Broke the what?!?!

The house lights came up, but no one so much as flinched,

seeing as how we had just been told that the floor might or might not be crumbling beneath us.

The same roadie (who was obviously developing a semi from standing on stage in front of a sold-out crowd) told everyone, in his best authoritative voice, "Remain calm. Don't make any sudden movements. When security tells you, move slowly to the exits."

Move to the exits?? Show's over?? NO! No no no no no no no!!! They just got started! We have a babysitter until one a.m.! You can't make us go home! PLEASE don't make us go home!

As it turned out, when the headlining band came out and everyone rushed toward the stage, all the little bitches in the emo club down in the basement freaked out because they heard a "loud cracking sound" and "felt the floor shudder." *Pussies.*

Not that I was surprised though. The venue is in an ancient building, and anyone who's ever seen a show there has feared for his or her life at least once during the experience—except for me because I am a cock-eyed optimist. Even though the floor always seemed to bounce and sway in a way that made me question the most basic laws of physics, I felt secure in the assumption that *surely* the fire marshal/building owner/safety-code-person-man wouldn't let thousands of people pile into the place night after night unless it was absolutely, positively one hundred percent safe. Right?

I know, Journal. I know. It's a miracle I've survived this long.

While we waited for our section to be dismissed, everyone remained standing, craning their necks to try and see what was going on down below, but Ken and I were too enveloped in our own little foreplay bubble to notice. He had pulled me into his arms and was seductively rubbing his hands up and down my back. Between the jealousy-fueled pheromone beacon I was emitting, my belly full of Irish whiskey, and the frenzy we'd been worked into from the music, it was taking every ounce of my already limited self-control to keep from tearing my tank top off like Hulk Hogan right then and there.

When I couldn't take it anymore, I stood on my tiptoes and growled into his ear, "I'm not going to be able to wait until we get home."

Ken just smiled and said, "What do you have in mind?"

As soon as we got the go-ahead from security, I grabbed Ken's hand and took off down the fire escape, bobbing and weaving through the unfortunately dressed, sexually ambiguous heart-broken teenagers slowly shuffling out of the crumbling building. We sprinted three blocks, pushing past panhandlers and hurdling over hobos, until we finally made it to the car.

Once we were safely inside, Ken raised an eyebrow at me and asked knowingly, "Where am I going?"

I gave him directions to Sara's old neighborhood, the sketchy one she'd lived in back when she was just a lowly school psychologist, like me. It wasn't ideal, but it was the closest poorly lit secluded place I could think of. It was so poorly lit, in fact, that when I'd left my car there for a couple of nights while Sara and I were at a school psychology conference, we'd returned to find that all four of my tires had been slashed without any of the neighbors so much as batting an eye. It would be perfect.

As soon as we found a good spot, Ken killed the engine and looked at me with concern in his eyes. "So...how are we going to do this?"

I was already in the process of tearing off my boots, jeggings, and underwear. Foregoing the foreplay, my only instruction was to "Switch places with me" as I climbed out of the passenger seat and onto the center console, perching up on my tiptoes like an owl, to allow him enough room to slide over.

There, facing the backseat, crouched half-naked on the armrest while I waited for Ken to get situated, I could feel those two empty child safety seats staring back at me, judging me.

Fuck you, car seats! I'm still a good mom! You're lucky I'm even letting you watch!

Ken eased over to the passenger seat, unzipped his fly, and shimmied his pants down just enough to allow his eager cock to spring free. Still high on pheromones and territoriality, I almost came just from looking at it. Although I tried to straddle Ken as gracefully as the quart of Jameson in my bloodstream would allow, I failed in spectacular fashion when my left knee completely missed the seat and slipped down between the door and passenger seat.

Shit!

Trying to be smooth, I immediately attempted to pull my leg out of the crack as if I had just placed it there for leverage or something, but ... but ... it was fucking stuck!

I panicked and yanked on my leg like it was being crushed under a boulder in the middle of werewolf country during a full moon until it finally popped loose. Trying to salvage whatever was left of my sexiness, I pinned Ken with a sleepy-eyed sultry stare and placed my left foot (instead of my knee) in the seat next to his hip, causing me to end up in a weird half-squat/half-straddle position.

Real sexy, BB.

Bruised ego aside, I soldiered on. The instant the warm, naked parts of Ken came in contact with the warm, slippery parts of me, I let out a breath I hadn't realized I'd been holding. This...this was what made waiting until we got home an impossibility.

Mmm...

As I began to rise and fall, Ken pulled up my shirt and snapped open both cups of my nursing bra simultaneously. At that point, it had been almost four hours since the last time I pumped, and my breasts were full to bursting. The moment Ken took them in his hands, I felt a familiar tingle and watched with detached horror as my left breast shot a stream of milk directly onto his blue button-up shirt. The right one, which has always been a little gimpy from having been pierced three times in the past (I call her 50 Cent[5] now), just dribbled onto his lap.

Oh my fucking God! My milk let down!

When I finally released my cringe long enough to peek at Ken for his reaction, I noticed that his head was tilted back against the headrest, and his eyes were closed in ecstasy. He hadn't seen it! He didn't know!

However, the relief I felt was quickly overshadowed by the realization that Ken was really, really enjoying himself.

Shit.

It suddenly occurred to me that this was going to end the way almost all of my kinky sex experiments had ended—with Ken

---

[5] For those of you who aren't up on your hip-hop trivia, 50 Cent is a rapper who survived being shot nine times and went on to become a gazillionaire superstar. He got to fuck Chelsea Handler, got interviewed by Oprah, acted in a movie with Al Pacino and Robert De Niro, launched his own line of condoms, and was given a personal meditation mantra by none other than Deepak Chopra himself. He's pretty much my right nipple's hero.

coming too soon and apologizing profusely before half-falling asleep/half-trying to get me off with a vibrator that somehow always had an almost dead battery.

The thought made me sad. I really, really wanted to come. My pent-up sexual energy was whistling so loud that I'm surprised the neighborhood dogs weren't howling in pain.

I knew what I had to do. It was time to take matters into my own hands—er, *hand*.

Reaching deliberately between us, my fingers found their target. Swollen and sensitive, it didn't take long before my entire lower half was on the verge of eruption. Ken met my enthusiasm with his own, grabbing my ass with both hands and thrusting into me fully, taking care not to pull out so far that I would hit my head on the ceiling above.

Ever the gentleman, that Ken.

I thrust my other hand into his hair and claimed his mouth with mine. As soon as he hissed into my mouth that he was about to come, I felt myself detonate around him, whimpering as I squeezed and clutched and clawed and bit whatever I could get my hands on.

We held each other for a few moments as our heart rates returned to normal before Ken broke the contented silence. "So, what are we going to clean this up with?"

Um . . . crap.

I hadn't thought that far in advance.

Taking a mental inventory of the items in Ken's SUV, I suddenly flashed on a package of baby wipes I'd stashed in the glove box months ago in case of an emergency. This definitely counted as an emergency.

I reached behind me, careful not to make any sudden movements, and retrieved the package.

Ken raised an eyebrow at me as if to say, *You have got to be fucking kidding me.*

I simply shrugged and handed him one nearly dried out square of cloth.

In my defense, just in case any of you actually serve on the Mother of the Year judging committee, I want to make it known that I did, in fact, hold on to both our soiled baby wipes until we got home so that I could be sure that they made it safely into our trash can. I could have easily tossed them out the window like a common hoodlum, but no, not me. I care about the environment—and world peace.

As it turned out, that was Ken's first time having sex in a car. *Ever.*

How does a person live thirty-four years in suburbia and never resort to fucking in a car out of convenience or necessity?

Looking back, I'm beginning to realize that our entire relationship might have been based on one big, fat false assumption.

29

Mark McKen

Super Private Journal That Ken Is Never,
Never Allowed to Read Ever

When I first began dating Ken, I had just moved back in with my parents after my brief stint of cohabitation with Hans had devolved into a violent (on my part, not his) contentious nightmare. I'd been super pissed off about the whole thing because I was soooo ready to be a grown-up, and my parents were super pissed off about the whole thing because it meant they could no longer walk around naked and smoke pot out in the common areas of the house at all hours of the day. Apparently, in the few short months I'd been gone, my childhood home had turned into a virtual opium den of hippie hedonism.

When I showed up there after my impressively dramatic breakup with Hans, at ten o'clock at night, screaming and crying and trying to shove my eight-foot-long dresser back up the stairs to my old room, my parents didn't...even...get off...the couch. I had imagined them mourning my absence and holding nightly candlelit vigils in my old bedroom while I was gone, not blasting CCR and flopping around naked in a psychedelic stupor on a plastic tarp covered with finger paint on the living room floor.

I, on the other hand, hadn't done drugs in, like, a whole year. I had a 4.0 college GPA and good credit, and I was applying to graduate schools. I might have looked like a fuck-up with my half-shaved head and python-print pleather pants, but somehow, the responsibility torch had been passed while I was away, and I was now more of an adult than my parents. I'd just gotten back, but clearly, it was already time to go.

Right before my knock-down-drag-out fight with Hans, I'd met and begun chatting with Ken almost bimonthly at my friend Jason's weekend house parties. For some reason, Hans never came with me. Oh, yeah, because he was too busy doing blow off of strippers with his bandmates every weekend. Whatever. I didn't mind going alone. There was always booze, which is kind of a big deal when you're still ten long months away from being twenty-one, and pool—both billiards and swimming— and plenty of opportunities for some harmless ego-boosting flirtation. That place was a total sausagefest. There were the regulars, which included me and a few guys I'd already boned, and then there was a revolving door of extras, all of whom looked vaguely familiar. Ken was one of the extras. We'd gone to the same giant suburban high school, but because he was a senior when I was a freshman our paths had never crossed before.

When I'd first made Ken's acquaintance, he was in his pajamas and I was living with Hans, so it was hardly a love connection. That motherfucker was always in his pajamas.

(Whenever I tell this story in Ken's presence, he never fails to rudely interrupt me and insist, "Those were not pajamas. They were running pants."

To which, I say, "Tomato, tomato."

That saying doesn't really work in print, does it?)

Whenever I saw him at Jason's house, Ken would just be sitting there on the couch, all cozy in his fucking PJs, watching sports or whatever with the guys, which just so happened to be exactly where my attention-whore, cock-teasing ass always wound up—wherever the guys were.

Without fail, Ken and I would somehow strike up a conversation. He never hit on me. He was never drunk. He would simply make eye contact, smile at appropriate times, and speak to me like one intelligent being to another. We would go back and forth about museums we'd been to, music we loved, and movies we'd seen. In fact, Ken was the manager of a movie theater at the time and had seen every film released since 1995 (except for *Meet the Feebles*[6]).

Ken wanted to go to Egypt one day. I was taking an Egyptian art history class. I wanted desperately to go to Europe. Motherfucker had been twice. He had not, however, been to a Cirque du Soleil show, which blew my mind considering that they came to Atlanta every year.

I wish I could say it was love at first sight. But, honestly, at the time, I didn't give Ken a second thought.

Journal, you know my track record. The friendly-guy-in-the-PJs-without-a-criminal-record-or-a-single-visible-tattoo isn't exactly my type—or at least it wasn't until Jason's Super Bowl party.

---

[6] (Let me spare you an IMDB search and tell you right now that *Meet the Feebles* is sick, sick shit, Journal. Way before *The Lord of the Rings* trilogy, Peter Jackson was evidently in a dark, mixed-up place. It's basically *The Muppets*, if the Muppets were drug-addicted, sexually deviant depraved pornographers. I knew that one would stump him.)

Hans had just dumped me, and I was soul-crushingly depressed about it. All I wanted to do that night was sit on a couch near other people and get really, really drunk. Jason's Super Bowl party was the perfect distraction.

After being there just long enough to grab a beer and a seat on the sectional, I noticed someone entering the room. Time stopped, an imaginary wind machine inexplicably roared to life, and the first few bars of Sugar Ray's "Fly" began to play in my head. This mysterious figure was tall and lean, had short light-brown hair that flipped up in the front, and was wearing black from head to toe—black dress shirt with the sleeves rolled up, black slacks, and a skinny black tie. My heart stopped. It was as if Mark McGrath himself had just walked in.

(He was still a big deal in 2003, I swear!)

Mystery Man greeted Jason with a sexy, perfect smile/head-nod thing and disappeared from my sight.

Who the fuck was that??

Not that it mattered. I was going to fuck him. I was going to break him. I was going to have him safe-wording on me by the end of the night. I was going to—

Just as I began to march off in search of Mr. McGrath's doppelganger (and something nice and firm to flog him with), he came back into my line of sight...and had changed into a pair of running pants and a white T-shirt.

No. Fucking. Way.

I suddenly understood how so many people had been successfully duped by Clark Kent.

I used to think, *Really, Superman? A pair of glasses and a tie? Frankly, you are insulting the whole human race with that disguise. How stupid do you think we are?*

But there he was. Ken, the quiet, articulate, pajama-wearing introvert whom I'd been having long, intellectually stimulating, undeniably platonic conversations with on a bimonthly basis had been able to ignite my libido with as little as a change of clothes and a dollop of hair gel.

I was so confused. Ken was as far from my type as a person could get without having a vagina: nary a tattoo, piercing, warrant, GED, or vice to be found. He didn't even drink! He'd just sit on the couch, sipping Gatorade in his running pants and Nikes every weekend. But damn, he cleaned up good. And with that tall, fit, lean body, he must actually put those athletic clothes to use.

Maybe he's a runner? Would that be so bad? A hot, responsible grown-up who takes care of himself and has a decent job and can engage me in discussions about art and travel?

Considering that I was still in the process of unpacking my shit after being dumped by a wannabe rock star who couldn't scrounge up three hundred and fifty dollars a month to pay his half of the rent because he'd blown it all on nose candy and girls who were probably named Candy down at The Frisky Pony, a guy like Ken actually sounded fanfuckingtastic.

I didn't talk to Ken at all that night. He sat and watched the game while I sat and watched him, absentmindedly warding off unwelcome advances from the Alexander brothers.

Ethan and Devon Alexander were a couple of good-looking, cocky, charismatic man-whores who competed with each other over everything. Ethan had just turned eighteen and was giving his big brother a run for his money in the categories of Funniest Story Told at the Party, Guy Who Fucked the Hottest Girl at the Party, and Tallest Brother, but never in the category of Who

Sleep-Pissed in the Weirdest Location After Passing Out. That title will always be held by Devon, the shorter, angrier older Alexander who had once urinated on his own parents while they lay snoozing in their bed.

Rumor had it, when they'd woken up and begun screaming at him to stop, Devon had reportedly held up his hand midstream and screamed back, "Shut the fuck up! I know what I'm doing!"

I love that story.

In defense of the Alexanders, I kiiind of had a reputation for getting drunk and taking boys into the bathroom to show them my piercings at parties, so I'm sure, in my depressed state, I probably looked like low-hanging fruit.

My only other clear memory from that night, besides Ken's slow-motion entrance and mindfuck of a wardrobe change, is of Jason randomly asking Ken what his last name was. I thought it was an odd question to ask someone out of the blue, and I remember listening intently for the answer, idly wondering why I was so interested in hearing Ken's response.

Maybe it was because whatever came out of Ken's mouth next, no matter how unfortunate or unpronounceable or lacking in vowels it might be, would one day be my last name, too.

—⚬⚬⚬—

The days came and went, and for some reason, I just couldn't shake my two-second glimpse of Mark McKen. I wanted to see him again. I wanted to see if I could synthesize that panty-soaking black-clad hunk with his platonic conversationalist alter ego. They were still two different people in my head.

Then, about two weeks later, the universe delivered my in.

On my way to school, I happened to hear a commercial on the radio announcing that Cirque du Soleil was coming to Atlanta and tickets would be going on sale that week. Instantly flashing on a conversation Ken and I'd had months prior, I seized the opportunity and called Jason.

Before he could get the words "What's up?" out, I squealed into the phone, "Please, please call your friend Ken and tell him that he's taking me to Cirque du Soleil! Plea-plea-please!"

The very next day, on my way into my Egyptian art history class, my cell phone rang. It was an unknown number.

Oh my God. It could be Ken!

It had to be. It was far too light outside to be Skeletor calling. I could usually count on Knight to keep his drunk dials predictably stationed somewhere between midnight and four a.m. This person, however, was calling me at two in the afternoon, which gave me just enough hope to answer the phone. I took a deep breath, subconsciously bracing myself for an explosion of expletives out of habit, and pressed the little green button on my Nokia. I exhaled giddily as soon as I heard Ken's smart-ass opening line.

"So, I hear I'm taking you to the circus."

Ken offered to buy the tickets, but by buy, what he really meant was, *I will physically purchase the tickets and allow you to pay me back for your half.*

He's lucky I came from a home in which I had absolutely no model for male monetary provision. My mom was the cook, maid, greenskeeper, primary breadwinner, primary caregiver, and CFO. My father was the chain-smoking, pill-popping, perpetually unemployed, former garage-band guitarist, very entitled white male. A typical evening in our household would involve my mother coming home from her full-time job, cooking us a lovely meal—which my father always managed to roll out of bed in time to enjoy—and then recruiting me to help her do the dishes. Meanwhile, my father would sit on his ass in the living room, drinking, smoking, and otherwise fueling his depression and generalized anxiety disorder with a steady stream of doom and despair (CNN) until the wee hours of the morning.

Ken should really send them a thank-you card.

After I hung up the phone and floated into my art history class, it slowly began to dawn on me that I had a date scheduled with a guy I really liked in a *month*. That's like a decade in single college girl years. I could be pregnant with a senator's baby by then. I could be getting matching salt-and-pepper shaker tattoos with a waiter I had fallen in love with at Waffle House. I could be in prison for "accidentally" rolling all my parents' incense sticks in arsenic.

Luckily, Jason was having another get-together that weekend.

———

Ken looked fucking adorable. He wasn't wearing the black that I so loved, but his light-blue button-down shirt made his eyes sparkle, and his dark gray pants were made out of something soft that hung from his hips. It wasn't edgy. It wasn't punk or emo or rockabilly or biker. It was what a grown-ass man with good taste (and a very nice body) wore to a party after work. And I was surprisingly into it.

We talked all night. It was so weird hanging out with someone I was "dating" but had never even touched. So, I touched him—a lot.

If I went outside to smoke, I'd drag Ken by the hand into the cold March night with me. If I needed another beer, I'd tug him by the pinkie over to the mini fridge in the corner of Jason's basement. I'd clutch his arm and whisper in his ear whenever I was talking shit about somebody at the party. And he let me, all the while smiling and making eye contact and leaning in to tell me his own funny stories about people there that I didn't know.

It was a fascinating dynamic. I was obviously the alpha, but Ken held his own and carried himself with a strong, quiet confidence. I could totally picture him in his crisp shirt and tie, sitting behind the desk in his office, stoically firing people like it ain't no thang.

Boom. You're fired.

Boom. Collect your belongings.

This man was a boss. And he was *letting* me dominate him.

When it was time for me to leave, I didn't drag Ken out to my car (even though it looked that way). He chose to let me pull him. And when I lunged at him and threw my arms around his neck in an overzealous good-bye hug, the intensity with which he held me took my breath away. I had expected to peck him on the cheek and scamper off in a cute little tee-hee-hug-kiss-see-you-around kind of way, but instead, I found myself caught against the length of his body, like an unsuspecting stick that had just been tossed into an electric fence.

I don't even remember if my feet were touching the ground. I just know that Ken's strong arms clutched me to his body for what felt like an entire courtship.

The sizzle was almost audible. Just as I was about to thrust my hands into his hair, wrap my legs around his waist, and invade his beautiful, sculpted mouth with my tongue, Ken released me and turned to go.

NO!

Before he could make it out of arm's reach, I caught his hand and tugged as hard as I could. I tugged as if I were Patrick Swayze, and he were Jennifer Grey. When I successfully spun him all the way back around to face me, I grabbed two fistfuls of his sable-brown leather jacket—and, instead of lifting him over my head to the musical stylings of Bill Medley—I attacked him with a bizarrely aggressive closed-mouth kiss. It was like the worst TV kiss you've ever seen, or when a ten- (make that twenty-)year-old girl kisses the back of her hand pretending like it's Ryan Gosling.

WHY was my mouth closed? WHY did I have to do the arm-pull-spin move from Dirty Dancing*??*

I still want to die when I think about the awkwardness of that first kiss.

Thankfully, Ken must not have been completely deterred by my enthusiasm because he stopped by Macy's the next day to have lunch with me (which in those days consisted of a smoothie and three Camel Lights). It was the best. Surprise. Ever.

Unfortunately, I was so excited to see him that my now patented overzealous hug made a second appearance, prompting Jamal—the body-building, customized-Honda-Civic-driving, cologne-wearing slut of a sales associate I shared the cash stand with—to pull me aside and whisper-lecture me about "needing to slow my roll."

Lunch was fucking delightful, and it was over all too soon.

As Ken walked me back to my register, I dragged my feet and valiantly fought the urge to cling to him like a spider monkey. Probably sensing that he was about to be bound and gagged, Ken threw me a bone and asked what I was doing the next day.

Um, making your babies. Duh.

After making some quick dinner plans, our lunch date ended exactly the way it had begun—with me plastered to Ken's chest and Jamal shaking his head in disappointment.

The next day, at six o'clock sharp, I whipped the old 'stang into a prime parking spot in front of the aging local movie theater that Ken presided over. As soon as I swung open the heavy theater door, time stood still, and Sugar Ray launched into a serenade about halos and four-post beds that only I could hear.

He does exist.

Mark McKen was standing in the lobby, like a fucking Pegasus in a skinny tie, directing a handful of zit-faced employees. And he looked every bit as delicious as I remembered from Jason's Super Bowl party—sexily mussed sandy-brown hair, hands casually tucked inside the pockets of those memorable black slacks, biceps straining against the rolled-up sleeves of his black button-up shirt, and that goddamn matte black tie. For weeks, I'd been fantasizing about tying Ken's wrists to my headboard with that silken strip of fabric.

After spending the last few days with Ken McKhaki, I was beginning to doubt that his black-clad alter ego had ever really existed. Maybe he was just a figment of my imagination, the product of a hazardous combination of breakup and beer goggles.

But there he stood, in the flesh, and he was breathtaking.

When Ken finally made his way over to the doorway with my

immobilized body in it (which took him about an hour, what with the imaginary wind machine and all), he leaned down and wrapped his arms around my waist, pulling me to him in another one of his now familiar electrifying embraces. Barely letting me go, he held the door open with one hand while ushering me into the brisk March evening with the other.

Once we were in the parking lot, Mark McKen released me—*no!*—and asked where I'd like to go to dinner.

I really, really wanted to come across as cool and relaxed, but after the short-circuiting my brain had just experienced, I simply defaulted to being my hyper, bossy self and blurted out, "Oh my God, I looove Italian and there's this place not too far from here that I've been wanting to go to and if we take highway twenty we'll be going against traffic and I think they have a buy one entrée get one free special on Mondays!"

I immediately cringed, embarrassed that I was showing my spoiled, only-child ass so soon.

Ken simply replied with a twinkly-eyed smile, "Really? Italian is my favorite."

We went to the restaurant I squealed about, of course, and I don't know if it was the food or the company, but to this day it remains our favorite restaurant.

During the course of that evening, I came to realize that, in addition to our taste in food, Ken and I had *everything* in common. We liked the same music. We had even been to some of the same concerts. We had the same favorite movie (*Braveheart*). Ken was completely apolitical and atheistic, so my counter-culture political and religious beliefs, which had stemmed from being raised by hippies and Oprah Winfrey, weren't even an issue.

The only thing we didn't have in common was our need for control. Ken made absolutely zero decisions. He let me steer both the conversation and his body wherever I wanted them to go—childhood memories, *Seinfeld* episodes, outside to smoke, inside for dessert.

Just when I had begun to mourn the end of the best dinner of all time, Ken asked if I wanted to come hang out at his house.

Now, in my experience, when a man asks you to come back to "his house," what he means is, his mom's basement, bonus room, or garage. That's it—basement, bonus room, or garage, where he lives rent-free and still can't afford to pay for his own cigarettes.

So, you can understand my confusion when I followed Ken's little red sports car into the driveway of a sprawling white two-story traditional, dripping with charm and encircled by dozens of blooming azalea bushes. We're talking window boxes, plantation shutters, and a covered front porch that spanned the entire width of the first floor and culminated in a fucking gazebo with a bench swing on the far corner of the house. This place was what dreams were made of—at least for a girl who had moved around a lot and grown up overhearing her parents whisper-shout words like *bankruptcy* and *apocalyptic tick infestation* in the middle of the night.

With a surprising amount of animosity, I followed Ken inside the estate, racking my brain for a polite way to ask him who owned it. This was not a single man's house. This was my house, goddamn it, and I needed to know who lived there!

The interior was equally charming and immaculate. The front door opened into a living room with stairs immediately to the right. Straight ahead, through the main room, was an entryway into the kitchen. And to the left, the living room was painted a cozy shade of sage green. A stacked stone fireplace took up almost the entire far left wall, and the centralized camel-colored suede-like couch was an inviting overstuffed marshmallow surrounded by contemporary espresso furniture, satin-nickel light fixtures, and an eclectic collection of original paintings and pen-and-ink sketches of the Eiffel Tower.

No, seriously. Who the fuck lives here??

It was too sparsely decorated to be his parents' house. This place looked like an Ashley Furniture showroom, and there were exactly zero family photos or personal mementos anywhere. No, this was definitely somebody's first home, and I wanted it to be *mine*!

When I finally choked back my envious rage and complimented Ken on the decor, he simply said, "Thanks. My dad helped me with the crown molding."

Aha! "Oh, does he live here, too?"

"No, but my sister rents a room from me. She agreed to pay me extra if I gave her the master bedroom and a spot in the garage."

So, a woman does live here. That explains all the Eiffel Towers. "Did she help you decorate?"

"No. I did all the painting and decorating. She just moved in a few months ago."

"Really? You did all this yourself? It's beautiful! Where did these paintings come from?"

"Oh, I got those in Paris. There are these street artists on every corner there who just draw and paint the Eiffel Tower all day long. Their work is amazing, and it's really cheap."

So, not only was he hot and smart and employed and fit,

but he also owned his own home and had decorated it himself with paintings he bought in Paris. It was as if he had known I was coming. My reverie was quickly shattered when I realized that, if I *were* to move in one day, Ken and I would probably be sharing a twin-sized bed in one of the tiny secondary bedrooms since his asshole sister had gone and snatched up the master.

Trying to feel out the sleeping arrangements, I probed, "I can't believe you own your own home, and you don't even sleep in the master bedroom."

"Oh, I don't mind. I just had the bonus room finished, so I sleep in there."

And there it was. *Boom. Basement, bonus room, or garage. I fucking knew it!*

Just as I was beginning to get a handle on Ken's living situation, a tiny Asian girl emerged from the kitchen. She looked like she was around my age, maybe younger, and was no more than five feet tall. When she noticed that Ken had company, she sheepishly averted her eyes and scurried up the stairs.

Okay, seriously, who the fuck lives here??

Noticing my horror, Ken explained, "That's Robin. She works at the theater and needed a place to stay, so I'm renting out one of the other bedrooms to her."

This motherfucker was savvy. He probably had these bitches paying his whole mortgage for him AND doing his housework. Ken *was* a boss!

And here he was, letting me drag him around like a rag doll and call the shots. It didn't make sense. Why would someone who exercised so much control over every aspect of his life surrender all that power so willingly? It wasn't even necessary. I was just a twenty-year-old college girl who worked at Macy's and lived with her parents. Ken, on the other hand, was a twenty-three-year-old *man* who owned multiple neckties and a house big enough to board a small army of female indentured servants.

Clearly, Ken didn't answer to anyone, yet when we were together, it was as if the man had been born without an opinion. Radio stations, restaurants, wherever we went, whatever we did, he deferred to me. Why?

Oh my God.

Ken wants me to hurt him.

It was the only explanation. Ken was some kind of masochist. He'd sized up my fiery, headstrong bad-girl vibe, heard about all the piercings, and thought maybe I'd be down to pour searing hot wax all over his balls.

Now, don't get me wrong, Journal. I was no stranger to S and M, and *maaaaybe* I did have a closet full of pleather and bondage accessories, but wasn't it I who was always being handcuffed to things? I mean, I was no *dominatrix.*

Or was I?

From the moment I'd laid eyes on Mark McKen that night at Jason's Super Bowl party, I'd had the overwhelming urge to tie him up and whip him a little.

And I was really enjoying getting my way all the time. And whenever I'd started to manhandle him or physically push him around, he always responded with an amused little smirk and zero resistance.

Oh, Jesus. Ken did want me to hurt him.

And I kind of wanted to hurt him.

30

Mission(ary) Accomplished!

BB's Secret Journal

February 21

Dear Journal,

I just wrote the story of when I first met Ken and left it in my Super Private Journal That Ken Is Never, Never Allowed to Read Ever file. It was all true, for once, and I hope it gave him a little ego massage. That being said, Ken's ego does *not* need to hear what I really thought about our first sexual experience, so I'm moving over here to the safety of your arms, dear sweet, secret Journal, to continue the story.

Ken and I didn't have sex right away.

Okay, okay, I know what you're thinking.

BB? Not behave like a whore? Did she have mono that month?

But it's true, Journal. I swear!

I would just go over to his house on non-school nights and make out with him on his supple microsuede cloud of a couch, and then we'd fall asleep watching *Highlander* or some shit. He never pressed me to have sex, and for some reason, I never initiated.

I think I was still too confused about how I felt about him. Ken wasn't dangerous or rebellious, other than his potential masochism. He didn't play games. He was…a gentleman. And I think all that chivalry dried my vag right up. Even though my eyes liked what they saw and my head knew that Ken was a good, solid choice, my wild heart kept searching for some spark, some flaming, naughty ember, and coming back wanting.

It also didn't help that Ken was as emotionally available as a tomato. The man wouldn't know a feeling if it dry-humped his leg. Skeletor, Ding-Dong, Bless His Heart—those boys could *feel*…about a thousand different emotions an hour. They'd go from gazing into my eyes and asking me to marry them before the condom even came off to screaming and throwing a trash can through their basement, bonus room, or garage window because *somebody* made Velveeta Shells and Cheese for dinner when they'd specifically asked for the OG Kraft kind!

So, it was a double-edged sword. I appreciated that I wasn't constantly patching sheetrock and walking on eggshells around Ken, but after a few weeks, it became very clear that I wasn't going to be getting hearts and flowers anytime soon.

Whether it was in spite of his flat affect or in light of it, the more I got to know Kenneth Easton, the more I liked him— like, as a person. His introversion and stoicism were in perfect harmony with my extroversion and emotional sensitivity. He was fucking beautiful, and we loved all the same things.

"No way. You have Marvin the Album by obscure one-hit wonder '90s band Frenté? Me too!"

"Your favorite pizza is ham and black olive from Papa John's? Mine too!"

"Oh my God, you like to put Peeps in the microwave with little toothpicks under their wings and see which one stabs the other first once they start to puff up? ME TOO!"

It took about three weeks for me to get past Ken's lack of tattoos and emotional range, but once I finally realized how stupid I was over this guy, I knew it was time to do what I did best—spread my legs.

Our first time wasn't *bad*, per se, but it was missionary, and I don't usually get down like that. But I was on a mission (no pun intended), and getting off was low on my list of priorities. My first objective was to investigate whether or not Ken really was a masochist, and if so, to what degree. My second objective didn't become evident until we started in with the foreplay. I needed to boost the man's confidence, stat.

After we'd started making out, Ken touched me so cautiously that it was as if I were the meanest goat at the petting zoo, and he was one wrong move away from losing a finger.

It made no sense, Journal. We'd been dating for over a month. I was ninety-five percent sure he wasn't gay or married. Neither of us was drunk. And an erection of more-than-respectable size was pressed against my naked hip. Why was he so hesitant to make a move?

At first, I assumed it was just because I'd never been with a gentleman before.

Perhaps he just doesn't want to overstep my boundaries, I thought. *Perhaps there's some secret bat signal of consent that I haven't given him because I don't know what it is because I've never been with a nice guy before.*

But then I remembered that I'd brought an overnight bag with me. I'm pretty sure if there were ever a universal sign for *down to fuck*, that would be it.

Whatever the reason, my cool, calm, collected Ken was behaving like a mime trying to get out of an invisible phone booth, so I decided to help the poor guy out. Rolling him on top of me, I shifted my hips until the head of his impressive cock was poised at the entrance of my impatient, thrumming body. Then, I kissed the shit out of him.

There, motherfucker. I consent. Bring it.

But still he didn't relax. Ken's body remained stiff above me, and his breathing was quiet and shallow, like he was concentrating on something. I, on the other hand, couldn't concentrate on anything with him hesitantly sliding the entire length of his manhood back and forth over my slippery flesh.

Gradually, his pace quickened. Over and over, with each successive pass, Ken would graze my entrance, just enough to cause me to lift my hips in invitation, before denying me again. Confused and frustrated, I glanced up at his face in search of an explanation.

Is he afraid to fuck me without a condom?

(He should have been.)

Is he reliving a childhood trauma? Is he having a seizure?

While the man looming over me did look tense, for reasons I didn't understand at the time, it was the familiar smirk and the twinkle of mischief behind his aqua eyes that made me realize this motherfucker was playing a game. He was going to *make me* call every shot, just like he always did.

Kenneth Easton had all the power, and he was using it to make me take control. As much as I didn't appreciate being manipulated, I couldn't deny how empowering it was to be the puppet master of this hunky, mysterious, real-life Ken doll.

Submitting to his impossibly strong will, I reached between us and stroked Ken's slick girth, which felt rigid and ready and so right in my hands. Guiding him into my body, I gasped at the way he stretched and filled me. It wasn't painful. It was perfect, like a puzzle piece locking into place. I held him to me, appreciating the exquisite fullness, and he waited.

I don't know if he was feeling what I was feeling or if he was still just stubbornly refusing to take the lead, but once we began to move, it became pretty obvious that Ken was feeling a whole lot of *something*. Finally letting go of all his self-imposed restraint, Ken pulled my thigh up around his waist and rocked into me with everything he had. His mouth crushed into mine. His hands claimed my hair, my hips, my ass. He was feral and free and sexy as fuck, and I wanted desperately to reward him for that.

The only problem was that no man had ever or would ever make me come missionary-style. It's just not how I'm built.

Rather than risk Ken's newfound confidence by flipping him back over so soon, I decided to noisily fake an orgasm around the three-minute mark just to give him a little positive reinforcement.

Because I'm selfless like that, Journal.

With my second objective taken care of (Confidence boost? Check!), I moved on to priority number one—figuring out whether or not this hottie really wanted me to hurt him. While pretending like I was still in the throes of the mind-blowing orgasm he'd just given me, I sank my nails into Ken's shoulder blades as hard as I could. Instead of hearing him suck in a pained breath or feeling him flinch in response, which would have been the appropriate reaction, I felt Ken's taut muscles soften like putty in my hands.

The fuck?

I'd just stabbed the man with ten little razor blades! He should have reared back and cold-cocked me in the mouth, not slumped into a puddle of ecstasy, as if I'd just shot him full of heroin!

Okay, so clearly my suspicions were accurate. Ken liked pain.

Now, it was time to find out how much.

Without lessening the pressure even a smidge, I proceeded to drag my claws at a torturously unhurried pace down the entire length of Ken's back.

It was practically medieval, Journal, and Ken...fucking... loved it.

Before my charcoal-gray talons had even made it past his waist, Ken was clutching my body to his and quietly shuddering his release.

Holy shit.

Okay, so I had a bona fide masochist on my hands. (Literally. His DNA was under my fingernails.)

There were worse things to discover about your boyfriend, right?

It was just a little kink. And if my track record proved anything, it was that I could handle kinky, especially if it meant that I would get to see Ken in all his relaxed postcoital glory.

With his ego sufficiently fluffed and the welts on his back sufficiently raised, Ken was a new man. We spent the next few hours cuddling and talking and laughing, and when we went for round two (during which I made sure to be on top) it was a thousand percent better (for me, at least).

Before I knew it, the morning sun was peeking into the charming little eyebrow window above Ken's bed. As I admired the pink and orange streaks of light splashing across his white sheets and settling into the topography of our entwined bodies, I realized that, not only was it possible to be attracted to someone stable and responsible, it was actually easy.

⚬

Within a couple of weeks, the subject of our *numbers* inevitably came up. I sort of lied and told Ken eight. It was only *sort of* a lie because I *had* slept with eight people—*before* him.

I don't know why I didn't just say nine. I think because, once you hit nine, you're just a hop, skip, and a hump away from those dreaded double digits. Plus, I wanted to seem fractionally chaster than I really was.

Says the girl with her nipples and clit pierced.

Ken's number, you ask? Three—as in, me and two other people.

By the age of twenty, the number of dicks that had been inside me could man a baseball team. Meanwhile, Ken was three years older and could fit all his conquests comfortably in the backseat of a Toyota Tercel.

And here, Little Guy, is where my big, fat false assumption occurred. You see, I *should* have taken Ken's performance anxiety and low number of sexual partners for exactly what it was— proof that he was an inexperienced lover who could use some gentle guidance. But you know what I told myself instead, just to keep from feeling like such a used-up, dirty old cock-socket? I told myself that Ken had probably had sex *thousands* of times.

After all, by the time *I* had slept with three people, I had already been with both Skeletor and Ding-Dong—those kinky bastards. I had loooooong matriculated from car sex and was mastering some serious, post-graduate level shit.

So, Ken's dainty little number didn't really mean anything. It certainly didn't mean that I was a whore. No, definitely not. Ken could very well have been *just* as experienced as me, maybe even more so!

Numbers schmumbers!

In reality, gorgeous, introverted (and definitely masochistic) Ken could have counted his pre-BB sexual experiences without taking off both socks, and I was already throwing Reverse Wheelbarrows and Two-Headed Crabs at him. I'm sure those first few months with me felt like finding out he'd been hired to pilot the first manned expedition to Uranus (pun intended) with nothing but a GED and a snazzy jumpsuit.

Poor guy. No wonder he'd insisted I take the lead.

Besides car sex, I wonder what other prerequisite teenage sexual experiences Ken missed out on. Slow sex under a blanket in the same room as at least three of your friends while pretending like you're just watching a movie? Sex in a neighborhood pool in broad daylight? Sex in the restroom at your minimum-wage job while a sign on the front door implores potential customers to ~~Cum~~ *Come back in 10 minutes*? Sex in a tree house? (Not *my* tree house, obviously. Hippies don't build their kids tree houses. They squat barefooted in the driveway drawing mandalas with sidewalk chalk while eating undercooked pot brownies out of the pan. Which, in their defense, totally feels like quality time to a five-year-old.)

Jesus, I think I might have overestimated the value of teenage rites of passage. I mean, there are worse things in life than never having to pick someone's pubes out of your braces.

In fact, I think Ken owes *me* a thank-you card for saving him from all that bullshit—full of coupons redeemable for childfree brunch and cunnilingus—but not at the same time. Or maybe at the same time? Mmm...most *definitely* at the same time.

31

Stupid Safe Word

BB's Secret Journal

February 28

It's been eleven years since I first sank my claws into Ken's taut muscular flesh, and after all this time, that move still never fails to please—either of us. I've got to say, I do not mind hurting that man. Before I met Ken, I had no idea how gratifying it could be to chomp down on a grown man's clavicle and feel his back arch in ecstasy under me. To twist his nipple and feel his appreciative moan reverberate through my mouth. To yank his hair and feel his grip tighten around my waist in excitement.

The fact that he's into pain also makes him seem like a little bit more of a badass. Ken might be a quiet cubicle dweller with hands as soft as the supple pink underbelly of a newborn cockapoo, but under that buttoned-down intellectual exterior is a man who can take a beating. And if a little pain is what it takes to get his rocks off, well then, I am more than happy to oblige.

Only, I'm realizing that a little pain might just be the tip of the iceberg.

Last night, I had one of my classic over-poured pinot Gs before hitting the sack with Ken, and thus, might have under-estimate the amount of pressure I employed when executing my signature nails-down-the-back move. It did the trick though. The second I brandished those little daggers, Ken thrust himself as deeply into me as he could get and came for the entire ten-second journey it took me to make it from his shoulder blades down to his ass. Although I suspected I'd been a little rougher than usual, Ken collapsed on top of me and almost purred in appreciation when it was over, so I figured it couldn't have been too bad.

Then, while Ken and I were washing up in the bathroom under the harsh compact fluorescent glow of reality, I caught a glimpse of what I had actually done.

Holy fuck.

I felt like I was in some kind of horror movie where you wake up and realize that you mutilated your own lover while under alien mind control or some shit. Ken's back looked like a Jackson Pollock painting. Pink and red welts ran the length of his torso, so angry and raised that they looked like eight spare spinal cords.

As soon as I saw the damage I'd done, I began kissing and coddling and examining every inch of him from shoulder to sitz bone while he simply continued to wash his hands, watching me in the mirror with a quizzically raised eyebrow, as if he had no idea what I was being so dramatic about.

If only he could see what I saw! He'd be disgusted! He'd be horrified! He'd be...

I grabbed Ken's biceps and turned his body to face mine, urging him to look over his shoulder in the mirror, so he could at least acknowledge the carnage that was once his back.

"Look at what I did! I'm so sorry, Ken! I had no idea I was scratching you that hard!"

Upon glancing at himself in the mirror, rather than taking the kids to his mother's house and obtaining a restraining order, Ken dismissively muttered, "Pssh. You *can't* do it too hard," and turned back around to brush his teeth.

Excuse me?

Now, I know deep down in my soul that Ken meant that statement to be a commentary about himself, about the depths of his masochism and his freakishly high pain tolerance, but the only sound my self-absorbed only-child ears could register was the smack of his words slapping me right across the face.

Oh, really? I can't do it hard enough, huh? Well, challenge accepted, motherfucker! You'd better find yourself a safe word because I'm . . . gonna . . . carve . . . you . . . up.

Postscript: Ken found himself a safe word. It's scrumpets.

Me: "Why is your safe word *scrumpets*, Ken?"

Ken: "I dunno. I just like that word."

Me: "It's not a word."

Ken: "Yes, it is. It's what British people eat with their tea."

Me: "Those are crumpets."

Ken: "Bullshit. A crumpet is like a Bugle."

Me: "No, that's a trumpet."

Ken: "The other kind of Bugle."

Me: "You mean, those crunchy, salty cornucopia-shaped things people pretended to like in the '90s?"

Ken: "Who was pretending?"

I don't even know why I felt the need to have that conversation. Anytime you're doing something to a man and he responds by uttering the nonsensical word *scrumpets*, your next move should be to immediately stop what you're doing and check the other three signs of a stroke because he just met one.[7]

---

[7] Because I'm in the business of saving lives here, the acronym you need to remember when identifying a potential stroke is FAST. The F stands for *Face drooping*. The A stands for *Arm weakness or numbness*. The S stands for *Speech difficulty*. (Ahem, *scrumpets*.) And the T stands for *Time to call 911 if you see any of these signs*.

Of course, if Ken is safe-wording on me, I should probably call 911 anyway because I might have just accidentally clawed out his pancreas.

32

Leprechauns Love Anal

BB's Secret Journal

March 7

Dear Journal,

I must be drunk. I just flipped off my husband. I don't feel that dru—

Shit.

I do totally, actually feel that drunk. But I only had one glass of cheap pinot G!

(FYI: When I say one glass, I mean, one teeny, tiny little glass filled all the fuck up. I have to compensate, Journal. These wine glasses are miniature. They're basically aperitif flutes, I swear!)

Whatever. It doesn't matter how I got here. What matters is that I am presently at that magical, elusive, just-right amount of drunkenness where I could either instigate a fistfight OR anal sex (two things that would never, ever happen, EVER, unless I've had the perfect amount of white wine on a slightly empty stomach and Mercury is in retrograde) and still be conscious enough to actually show the fuck up and perform.

So, we've established that Ken refuses to compliment me.

But it's almost like a phobia, Journal. In fact, I just Googled *fear of giving compliments*, thinking surely there's a term for this sick pathology. And guess what? I got nothing. There is a fear of receiving compliments, which, of course, Ken does graciously, but not of giving them. You know why? Because no one has ever been pathologically averse to complimenting his or her spouse *ever*. Because it's not a thing.

There's no term you can hide behind, Ken. No support group. You're not mentally ill. You're just an asshole.

Here, Journal. Let me give you some background so that you can weigh in on this bullshit…

I'm into photography. I've taken classes. I have a fancy camera with fancy lenses. It's my hobby. I used to paint, but with a baby and a toddler demanding my attention now there is no scenario in the foreseeable future where I will be gifted with ten blissful hours of solitude to smear paint around on a canvas and sing along to Death Cab for Cutie, so if I'm going to make any art at all, it has to occur at the push of a button and with a baby on my hip.

I really like photography. I also really like to think that I'm good at it, but I can't be sure because the only people who've ever validated that hypothesis are my closest friends and family. And let's be honest, their opinions are pretty fucking worthless. Not that they necessarily have shitty taste, they're just a little too supportive and awesome to sit me down and say, *Honey, maybe don't spend so much money on camera equipment, okay?*

Okay. Now that you're up to speed, let's get back to me flipping off my husband.

So, the kids were in bed and I was sitting on my designated side of the couch, pecking away at my laptop as usual. Only instead of writing, I was ordering a largescale print of one of my favorite photographs because it had just been accepted into an art show. It was a photo I had taken while visiting my ladyfriend Sara in California. We'd been strolling down the Venice Beach boardwalk when I wandered over to the skate park and got this shot:

I love this damn photo. When I mentioned the honor to Ken he leaned over from *his* designated side of the couch and looked at the image on my screen. Rather than take advantage of the opportunity to praise his wife, Ken simply said, "Huh. A skater pic." Then HE GOT UP AND LEFT THE ROOM.

I would have accepted anything, Journal.

Oh, look at that. You didn't fuck it up, or even a condescending, *Looky-wook at the pwetty-wetty picture,* with a matching pat on the head.

Anything.

So, when Ken passed back through the living room on his way to bed and told me good night, I chose to respond by flipping him the fuck off.

Take that, asshole!

I think the desired outcome of that gesture was, in my head, for Ken to be immediately struck down by the same hurt his apathy had caused me, like my middle finger was a magic wand of feelings and effeminacy and boners and unicorn tears. Then, he would rush to my side to apologize and coo over my art and make it up to me with a foot massage, followed by some gentle well-lubricated anal with a vibrator reach-around.

(Yes, yes, I am that drunk.)

Instead he just looked puzzled. Not even surprised yet amused, like, *Oh, Brooke.* (Because that's what Ken fucking calls me—*Brooke*—the name on my driver's license. He is so averse to giving me a nickname that he won't even use the one that I actually go by.) *You're so cheeky. Put that finger away, you silly girl!* But more disappointed and judgy, like, *Really, Brooke? Grow up. Who gives people the finger anymore? Seriously.*

I'll tell you who!

I totally just flashed back to one of my fondest childhood memories. My mother's parents were hard-core Irish Catholics. They'd sent all four of their redheaded, green-eyed, freckle-faced daughters to Catholic school. Every Sunday, my grandmother would play the organ, and my grandfather would volunteer to be an usher at church. Every St. Patrick's Day, my grandfather would organize a parade downtown and surreptitiously dye the city fountain green even though the city would threaten to arrest and fine him for vandalism.

Before every meal, my grandfather would toast, "If I had a ticket to heaven and you didn't have one, too, I'd tear my ticket to pieces and go to hell with you."

They were like real live leprechauns. Full of mischief and whimsy, those two.

Well, I remember once, when I was visiting for the summer, my grandmother had yelled into the living room where my grandfather was watching *Murder, She Wrote* (with the volume at full blast) that she was going to have a beer and scream-asked if he wanted to split it with her.

Seriously, these little elfin lightweights *split* beers. Maybe that's why I'm so drunk off one topped-off thimbleful of Clos du Bois. It's genetic!

After at least fourteen back-and-forths about how he couldn't hear her and the TV was too loud and how she was going deaf—no, he was going deaf—my grandmother, with a flourish of badassery, thrust her brittle, translucent, knobby-twig-like middle finger into the air and stuck out her tongue before sashaying right back into the kitchen where she immediately cracked open a can of Coors Light and proceeded to drink the whole damn thing.

Those two were married for almost sixty years. I can only pray that my inability to metabolize cheap alcohol, love of limericks, and penchant for giving the finger are signs that I—like my fiery, impish grandmother—also have what it takes to keep a marriage intact for the better part of a century. And given that she'd emerged from the baby-booming 1950s a Catholic housewife with only four kids suggests that her secret probably involved lots and lots of anal.

You do the math, Journal.

Guess I'd better stock up on pinot G 'cause it's going to be a long sixty years.

33

We Both Have Gmail Accounts. It's Like We Want to Get Fired.

Email Conversation with Ken

FROM: BB EASTON

TO: KENNETH EASTON

DATE: THURSDAY, MARCH 19, 12:36 P.M.

SUBJECT: FRENCH IMMERSION

Hey Boo Bear,

I just found out that the new elementary school down the street is going to pilot a French immersion program starting next year. I'm so excited! It's going to be the only one in the county! Maybe if I grease some palms, we can get Little Man enrolled for kindergarten. That way he'll be fluent enough by second grade to translate for us while we're summering in Paris.

(BTW- I've decided we're going to start summering in Paris. I'm putting it on my vision board tonight.)

BB Easton, Ed.S.
Oppressed School Psychologist
Conservative Public School System That Probably Still Supports the Confederacy

FROM: KENNETH EASTON

TO: BB EASTON

DATE: THURSDAY, MARCH 19, 12:45 P.M.

SUBJECT: RE: FRENCH IMMERSION

Sounds good. I assume other schools will start picking up these programs, so bribery is probably unnecessary.

You should also put some winning lottery numbers on your vision board, if you want to summer in Paris.

We can revisit this conversation at a later date.

Kenneth Easton
Blah, Blah Financial Money-Stuff Person
AGTBRF—Some Fucking Acronym I Never Bothered to Learn—Telecommunications

FROM: BB EASTON

TO: KENNETH EASTON

DATE: THURSDAY, MARCH 19, 1:15 P.M.

SUBJECT: RE: FRENCH IMMERSION

Why, Mr. Easton, that was so formal. I appreciate your time and input.

Good day, sir.

BB Easton, Ed.S.
Oppressed School Psychologist
Conservative Public School System That Probably Still Supports the Confederacy

FROM: KENNETH EASTON

TO: BB EASTON

DATE: THURSDAY, MARCH 19, 1:18 P.M.

SUBJECT: RE: FRENCH IMMERSION

I think I am going to give you some input tonight.

Kenneth Easton
Blah, Blah Financial Money-Stuff Person
AGTBRF—Some Fucking Acronym I Never Bothered to Learn—Telecommunications

FROM: BB EASTON

TO: KENNETH EASTON

DATE: THURSDAY, MARCH 19, 1:20 P.M.

SUBJECT: RE: FRENCH IMMERSION

Tonight, Mr. Easton?

I never make appointments on such short notice, but for you, I suppose I could clear my schedule. Looking forward to it, sir.

BB Easton, Ed.S.
Oppressed School Psychologist
Conservative Public School System That Probably Still
Supports the Confederacy

FROM: KENNETH EASTON

TO: BB EASTON

DATE: THURSDAY, MARCH 19, 1:25 P.M.

SUBJECT: RE: FRENCH IMMERSION

I hope you can squeeze me in.

Kenneth Easton
Blah, Blah Financial Money-Stuff Person
AGTBRF—Some Fucking Acronym I Never Bothered
to Learn—Telecommunications

FROM: BB EASTON

TO: KENNETH EASTON

DATE: THURSDAY, MARCH 19, 1:36 P.M.

SUBJECT: RE: FRENCH IMMERSION

Mr. Easton! I'm going into a very serious meeting and
have no more time for your tomfoolery.

Until tonight, sir!

BB Easton, Ed.S.
Oppressed School Psychologist
Conservative Public School System That Probably Still
Supports the Confederacy

FROM: KENNETH EASTON

TO: BB EASTON

DATE: THURSDAY, MARCH 19, 1:47 P.M.

SUBJECT: I'LL SHOW YOU IMMERSION

Tom who?

Kenneth Easton
Blah, Blah Financial Money-Stuff Person
AGTBRF—Some Fucking Acronym I Never Bothered
to Learn—Telecommunications

34

867-5309

BB's Secret Journal

April 4

Dear Journal,

Here's a fun fact. I've had the same cell phone number since 1998, yet I haven't actually answered it since 1999.

That's the year that Knight and I had our—now legendary—Halloween party breakup from hell. I had assumed that breaking up with Knight would end our relationship. That's kind of the definition of a breakup, right? Well, evidently in Knight's fucked-up dictionary the definition of a breakup looks more like this:

Breakup (noun): an event that changes the roles in a romantic relationship from boyfriend and girlfriend to stalker and stalkee, respectively.

Because the only thing better than being in a relationship with a skinhead on steroids is being stalked by one—especially one who is *super* pissed that you rebounded over to legendary bad boy Harley James in less than a week. Ronald McKnight's particular brand of stalking included attacks by air (cell towers) as well as by land. You see, when your stalker calls you fifty-seven times a day to no avail, eventually he's going to have to hunt you down so that he can scream at you in person. Only, by then, he's going to be extra pissed off because his monster truck only gets four miles to the gallon, and you just cost him, like, a hundred bucks with your selfish call-screening ways.

Honestly, referring to what Knight put me through as stalking is a bit of an understatement. That shit was terrorism. The word *stalk* implies a certain degree of stealth, which one cannot attain when one's vehicle is louder than a Boeing 737 driving over a fresh bed of M-80s inside an aluminum school gymnasium. I would have welcomed a good old-fashioned stalking…

Oh, you just happened to show up, unannounced, where I am. What a creepy coincidence.

Oh, look at that. There's a random hair doll on my porch… and it's just my color.

Hmm, somebody seems to have left a collage of pictures of me splattered with blood on my car… again.

Child's play.

Instead, Knight used classical conditioning to paralyze me with fear two to five times per week. Like a Pavlovian dog, the instant my highly attuned ears picked up on the inimitable rumble of Knight's piecemeal Frankentruck in the distance, my body would freeze. It didn't matter what I'd been doing—ringing up a customer at Pier 1 Imports, smoking a cigarette in the parking lot, readjusting my thong—the moment my brain registered that ominous engine roar, my simple daily life activities would become suspended in time, as though I were a post-volcanic citizen of Pompeii. I could literally hear Knight's wrath coming a mile away, which gave me plenty of time to dissociate and watch from some safe floaty place above my body as Knight lurched his homemade tank over the curb in front of wherever I happened to be at the time. Then, he'd descend upon the blinking vacant doe-eyed decoy left standing in my place.

The unanswered phone calls and random acts of terror went on until Knight graduated from high school and was deployed to Iraq with the U.S. Marine Corps. During that time I got a little reprieve, but once his tour was over Knight picked up right where he'd left off.

So, now, you are probably asking yourself, *Why didn't she just change her fucking number?*

I know. I ask myself the same thing all . . . the . . . time.

And honestly, up until recently, I didn't have an answer. The damn thing rings day and night. And every time I see *Blocked* on my caller ID, I still have to suppress the urge to scream and stomp on my phone as if it were on fire.

But, for some unknown reason, the idea of changing my number has always been scarier. I was never able to cut the cord, but I had no idea why.

Until May 28, 2009.

The call came from my high school buddy, Tim, whom I hadn't spoken to in years, and luckily, like everyone else under the sun, he still had my cell number. When I called him back after listening to his clipped, foreboding voice mail, he told me what I had been subconsciously waiting to hear since the day I met Ronald "Skeletor" McKnight.

He was dead.

Shot to death.

At the age of twenty-nine.

35

Hasta La Vista, Knight

BB's Secret Journal

April 4, continued

No matter how nasty our breakup had been, Knight never stopped calling me. No matter how many times he lost, pissed on, or crushed his phone into a million pieces with his bare hands; no matter how drunk he was; no matter how long it had been since we last spoke, Knight always remembered my number. It was tattooed on his brain (perhaps literally, knowing him).

Eventually, Knight's calls faded from traumatizing-stalker levels to just typical middle-of-the-night-drunk-ex-boyfriend levels, but good, bad, or ugly, I never answered more than twice a year. Knight was a drug so potent that I knew I could only take a hit once every six months without falling back off the wagon.

Which, I found out once I switched my major to psychology, was just frequently enough to ensure that Knight would continue to call me forever.

I remember the exact moment I learned the term *intermittent positive reinforcement.* I was a sophomore in college. Knight and I had been broken up since my junior year of high school, so I'd already been trying (and failing) to avoid him for three years at that point.

When the hot young grad student teaching my behavioral psychology class explained to us that the hands-down best way to ensure that a behavior continued wasn't to reward it every time it was displayed but to reinforce it randomly, my mind immediately conjured a picture of Knight's icy, spectral face.

Holy shit! He keeps calling because I pick up at random intervals!

The second Cutie Pie asked if anyone had an example, I thrust my cell phone high into the air with a gasp of insight.

I can give you a fucking example!

Knight had joined the Marines the instant he graduated from high school. It didn't change him much. He was already scary, muscle-bound, and militant, so being a Marine just… fit. But after doing a tour of duty in Fallujah, the nature of his phone calls changed. Instead of acting like a crazed, jealous ex or a sloppy, apologetic drunk, Knight would open our bi-annual yeah-sure-we're-just-friends-now conversations by asking for advice. He'd tell me about the bar fights he'd gotten into recently. The blackouts. The panic attacks. He'd talk about the motorcycle club he'd joined and how he was working as a tattoo artist in Atlanta. And he'd talk about all the problems he was having in both settings because of his rages.

The deeper I got into my psychology coursework, the clearer it became that Knight was suffering from post-traumatic stress disorder, and he needed help.

I asked him about it once, and he said, "Yeah. That's what the doc told me. Gave me some pills, but they don't fucking work.

Last night, I tried to kill a guy downtown. He started some shit with me at The Point and before I knew what was happening, my buddies were holding me back and I had a fucking broken beer bottle in my hand. They said I'd smashed the neck off on the edge of the bar and lunged at the guy. I don't even remember doing it. So...I think it's getting worse?"

Jesus. Ya think?

I don't know the half of what he saw, heard, or *did* while he was over there, but Knight was an emotional paradox when he returned. He'd be pensive and candid during our irregular phone calls, yet his behavior had become more violent and reckless than ever.

Whenever I'd finally get off the phone with him, gently complaining about having to get up early or making up some other thinly veiled excuse to let him go, Knight would always close with his patented ex-stalker good-bye, saying that I was still *his* girl, that he'd always love me, and if I ever needed anything, he'd be there.

I'd roll my eyes and sigh into the phone, its battery searing hot against my cheek by the time I finally hung up.

I know, Knight. You poor deranged, psychotic motherfucker, I know.

When Knight was honorably discharged from the Marines and joined the motorcycle club, I remember feeling relieved. Happy, even. I thought he was finally out of the crosshairs. That bullshit skinhead persona he'd had in high school had made him such a target for hate. Then he joined the military and became an actual target. Once Knight came home for good and joined the MC I felt like he might finally be safe. Have a chance at a normal life.

How wrong I'd been.

Not only were the bar fights getting worse, but Knight wrecked his motorcycle. Twice. The second time left him with road rash so bad on his back he looked like one of Hannibal Lecter's victims. His entire back piece, the McKnight coat of arms, was just...gone.

Then, a few years later, so was he.

As the story goes, Knight was trying to break up a fight between his buddy and some asshole from a rival motorcycle club at a bike rally in South Georgia. The media painted him as the heroic veteran, a valiant US Marine caught in the crossfire.

Right.

The Knight I knew had either started that fight or jumped in to finish it. The Knight I knew didn't put out fires, he poured gasoline on them. The Knight I knew was the scariest mother-fucker on the planet, and when he went into a blind rage I could believe that it might take a bullet to put him down.

But maybe that's just the story I want to believe. Maybe I need Knight to be the bad guy so that I can sleep at night. Maybe I want the world to be a just place where people who put their lives on the line to serve our country don't come home just to be gunned down by one of the citizens they'd been trying to protect.

—————

It was bittersweet, knowing that as I was burying my first great love, another great love was growing inside me. I worried the edges of the sonogram photo in my pocket as I gazed into the casket at Knight's face. He looked so different from the fuzzy-headed, freckle-faced boy who had once picked dandelions for me and drawn me stick-figure pornos at school. He looked old. Leathery. Spent. His fair skin, damaged from countless hours in the Iraqi desert with no sunscreen, was already set into deep wrinkles, exacerbated by a lifetime of scowling. His almost transparent blond hair—grown out and slicked back, biker-style—lay thin and limp atop his head. Not much different from when it had been shaved, it was still just a colorless frame around a colorless face.

Without a whisper of pigment in his eyebrows, eyelashes, or sideburns, Knight's leveling arctic-blue eyes with their contrasting black pupils used to provide the only point of reference on his otherwise pallid face. With them closed, his appearance was that of a man wearing an unfinished flaccid, flesh-toned rubber mask. As my brain desperately searched and scanned his pale face for that familiar bite of blue, repeatedly coming up lacking, images from the final scenes of *The Terminator* began to infiltrate my mind.

After being chased and generally terrorized by the T-800 for at least ninety minutes of screen time, Sarah Connor finally manages to lure the evil cyborg into a hydraulic press in an abandoned factory. Exhausted, injured, and suffering from shock, Sarah watches in disbelief as machine crushes machine. It isn't until the piercing red orb of light burning within the killer robot's eye socket fades to black that Sarah finally realizes that the chase is over.

Knight had been my own personal Terminator—obsessed, unrelenting, literally programmed to kill. And as I gazed into that casket, seeing only flesh where the flame-blue light in Knight's eyes should have been, I knew exactly how Sarah Connor felt.

And like Sarah, I was also carrying a very special little boy in my belly at the time.

—⚏—

That little boy is now four years old, and he is all me. All mine. He's a lover, a rebel, an artist, and a very old soul. He's the kind of man I wish the world had more of, and I'm pretty sure the universe sent him here to keep me from killing my husband.

36

Roses Are Red, Violets Are Assholes

Actual Poem I Gave to Ken on Our Anniversary Last Year

HAPPY ANNIVERSARY, ASSHOLE

Eight years of marriage and you still don't compliment me
Or say anything particularly romantic
Or appear to have any emotions at all.
But you gave me the love of a little boy who tells me I'm
    beautiful every day,
That I'm the "best woman in the whole world,"
Who won't go to sleep until he's hugged and kissed me—
Properly.
A little boy who looks an awful lot
Like you,
So much so that when his little Ken face tells me he loves me, I
    know he's speaking for you
Both.

37

What a Difference a Year Makes

Actual Poem I Gave to Ken on Our Anniversary This Year

FOR KEN ON OUR NINTH ANNIVERSARY

You make me want to dance
Like a girl on a pole.
But instead, I watch other people dancing
Gracefully inside the black frame of our TV,
And I shove my lingerie a little deeper in the drawer.

You make me want to paint, create,
But all I've created are some babies,
Which took a lot of time.
And take a lot of time
And leave me with just enough time
To think.

So, I tap out my thoughts,
One-handed in the dark,
Our baby asnooze in my arms,
Because words are all I can produce these days—
Besides people
And milk.

But know that, if given the choice
Between pas de deuxs and oil pastels
Or caring for cherubs
Who look like you and act like me,
Who love to dance and draw on floors,
I'd watch them paint and pirouette instead.

38

Sex on the Beach

BB's Secret Journal

May 27

Dear Journal,

I guess Ken appreciated that I finally wrote him a poem without the word *asshole* in it because he surprised me on our anniversary with an invitation to have sex...with him...on the beach!

How did I not know that nine years was the sex-on-the-beach year? I thought nine years was the wood anniversary! Or maybe it still is...

Hey-oh!

My birthday, Ken's birthday, and our anniversary all fall in the same week, single-handedly disproving the entire zodiac theory. (There is no fucking way that Ken and I are the same astrological sign. We're barely the same species.) So every year we just take that week off and go on vacation. This particular year we (I) decided to rent a little house on an island near Charleston. Only, who the fuck wants to spend a week at the beach with two little kids? So, we invited Ken's parents to come along and *help out* (keep our children alive) so that we might be able to *go on a date* (get drunk and avoid all parental responsibilities) for our anniversary.

Things were going well. We fell into a nice little routine where Ken and I would put the kids down for a nap every afternoon, give his parents the old two-finger salute, and take a long walk up and down the beach together—meaning that I would walk five or ten feet, stop to take pictures, then walk five or ten more feet, and Ken would putter along behind me, entertaining himself by looking up the property value of every beach house we passed.

Traveling with me would probably be annoying as shit to a normal person, but Ken has the patience of a saint. He never complains, never has his own agenda, he is simply content to follow me from shiny object to shiny object as I explore the entire area through the lens of a camera.

On this particular afternoon, however, just as we made it back to our little turd of a beach cottage, Ken took a jackhammer to our comfortable silence.

"So, I was thinking about fucking you on this beach tonight for our anniversary."

Record scratch.

Wha—

Whipping my head around, I immediately began analyzing Ken's facial features for any sign of humor, some tell that he was just fucking with me. There were none. His eyes were masked behind dark sunglasses, and his mouth was set in a determined line with just a whisper of an upturn on one side. When I replayed his sexy words in my head, Ken's voice sounded husky—not playful, not even close.

Not only was Ken serious, I think he was actually daring me.

A heat blossomed in my belly that had nothing to do with the sun beating down on us, and my face erupted into a supernova of enthusiasm. Drunk with glee, all I could do in response was nod and smile and clap vigorously.

It reminded me of how the Little Mermaid, rendered mute by Ursula the Sea Witch in exchange for a pair of human legs, reacted when Prince Eric finally guessed her name. As a child, I always identified with the Little Mermaid because we were both rebellious redheads who liked to sing and collect shiny objects, but now, I find myself identifying with her on a whole new level. I, too, am on a quest to make a certain square-jawed, blue-eyed prince love me back. And like Ariel, I tend to become ridiculously excited whenever he pays me even the slightest amount of romantic attention.

I couldn't believe the acuity of Ken's sexual intuition.

Seriously, who is this man?

I'd *always* wanted to have sex on the beach, but had never dared to bring it up to Ken because I knew he would just shoot it down as being impractical and exhibitionistic and illegal. Which would have left me with no choice but to give him a purple nurple to mask my hurt feelings, which would have, in turn, emboldened him to give me a retaliatory purple nurple. Only, that would have ended disastrously because *my* nipples would have been full of milk, and then I'd be all like, *Who the fuck is going to clean up all this breast milk, asshole?* And there, now I've managed to call Ken an asshole on our anniversary *again*, and now no one is getting beach sex or regular sex, for that matter. And also, the owners of this dilapidated death trap are probably going to keep our deposit because they can't get the putrid sour milk smell out of their carpet.

But happily, none of that had to transpire because Ken is evidently a goddamn mind reader now!

I figured Ken, being the Blah, Blah Financial Money-Stuff

Person that he is, would've had some kind of logistical plan formulated already, but when I regained the use of my larynx and asked him where, exactly, he thought we should do the deed, he just shrugged and waved a hand in the direction of the vast sandy expanse between us and the ocean.

Out there??

No, no, no, no, no.

I couldn't have sex out there. I'd never climax in a million years if I were that exposed and vulnerable.

Now, I have to admit, a little bit of danger is fun, and when I was eighteen, I probably wouldn't have batted an eye, but if you're fucking out in the open on a residential beach at the age of thirty-two, you're basically saying, *You know what? This whole responsible adult thing just isn't for me. I'd really appreciate it if someone would kindly ask the Department of Child and Family Services to come relieve me of my children.*

No, no, no.

We needed a plan. Dragging Ken away from our rented shack on stilts and back onto the beach, I started scouting locations.

"What about over there?" I asked, gesturing to an elevated wooden boardwalk that extended out from a nearby hotel with about five or six stairs down to the sand at the end.

Ken wrinkled up his nose at my suggestion and said, "What, on the stairs?"

"No, not *on* the stairs. *Under* the stairs."

But Ken was all, "That's a ditch."

And I was like, "But no one would see us under there."

And he was all, "Because it's a ditch."

Touché, Ken.

Finally, we compromised and settled on a spot under another

wooden walkway, only this one jutted way out onto the beach and had a nice smooth patch of sand under it. No ditch.

Now that we had our location, it was time to talk logistics. Ken suggested that he could go for another "walk" tonight after the kids went to bed, and he could stash some towels outside before then for us to use as a blanket. I volunteered to wear a dress for easy access. The plan was coming together nicely. (No pun intended!)

After an absurdly romantic dinner at a quaint little Italian restaurant in downtown Charleston that night, Ken and I returned to the Little Shack of Horrors and put the kids to bed. We shot the shit with his parents until it was good and dark outside. Then, with a wink and a nod, we began putting on our shoes and jackets and fumbling for excuses as to why we were going on another walk.

"I want to see if the lighthouse really lights up!" was the best I could do.

Just before we walked out the door, I remembered that we'd need towels, and I hadn't seen Ken stash any outside, like he'd said he would. Dramatically rushing back in to grab one, I could hear myself rambling to Mr. and Mrs. Easton about how I needed the towel because our feet would be sandy, from all the walking, on the beach, so we would need to rinse them off, with the hose, when we got back, from our walk, which would make our feet very wet, and would, in turn, necessitate the use of a towel. My circumlocution was made even more awkward by all the tripping I was doing over said feet as I tried to get the fuck out of there. When I finally made it out onto the deck, my flushed cheeks were met with cool, humid air, and I was greeted by a gorgeous man holding two beach towels, smirking like a smug son of a bitch.

"When did you put those out here?!?!"

"Right before we left for the restaurant. I just pretended like I was laying them out to dry."

God, I felt like a dumbass. Why did he always have to be so smooth?

Letting out a defeated sigh, I dropped my towel on one of the patio chairs and linked elbows with Ken as we made our way to the non-ditch. Surely, we wouldn't need more than two towels, right?

Wrong.

So, so wrong.

Minding the time, Ken and I made a mad dash for our agreed-upon spot under the boardwalk stairs, which was just far enough onto the beach to be considered *on* the beach.

Although we were in a hurry—the last thing on earth I wanted was for one of the senior Eastons to get worried and come looking for us—a *little* foreplay would have been nice. Would have helped me relax, get in the mood. But I guess Ken was more nervous than me because as soon as we made it to our predetermined location, he spread out his towel and lay down just as supine as one of the dead jellyfish I had seen washed up a few yards away.

Great. Ken the Cadaver was back, and his timing was impeccable.

I kicked off my flip-flops and shimmied out of my panties, tucking them inside the front pocket of Ken's hoodie, which I'd thrown on right before we left. I didn't dare take the hoodie off, however, because I was still way too cold to part with any more clothes. Meanwhile, Ken shoved the other towel, still rolled up, under his head as a pillow and pushed his shorts and boxer briefs down over his hips, revealing the very flaccid product of his nerves.

We were not off to a great start, but damn if I don't love a challenge.

Straddling Ken's tense body, I leaned down so that we could make out, but instead, I smacked him right in the face with the dangling drawstrings of his hoodie. At least that broke some of the tension. We both snickered quietly as I tucked the shoelace-like strings into the neck of his gray hooded sweatshirt. Then, I readjusted my game face and dived back in. That time, I got him.

I thrust my hands into Ken's sand-colored, soon-to-be sand-filled hair, and kissed him with everything I had. Trying to massage out that worry with only my lips, tongue, fingertips, and hips, I steadily gyrated into the growing thickness between us. It didn't take long for Ken to respond, grabbing my exposed ass and sliding me up and down his length until we were too stupid from lust to remember where the fuck we were.

When I finally sank down onto him I felt as though I'd been transported to another planet. My senses were being flooded with information that did not compute with what we were doing—the roar of the ocean just feet away, the smell of salt and seaweed, the steady onslaught of exotic wind coming in from somewhere foreign and fabled across the Atlantic. The only familiar sensation I could cling to was the feeling of my body locking into place with that of my other half. I tried to burn that moment into my brain, to hold on to it forever and ever, until a different, much more physical kind of burn grabbed my attention.

The towel Ken had selected to lie on was just a tad too narrow for both his torso and my splayed knees to fit on at once, so while I'd been grinding into him, my knees had been grinding into the sand.

As a kid, I always wondered how it was possible to take sand and make it into glass. Now, I know. It's possible because sand *is* glass. It's just tiny fucking shards of glass that will eat the skin right off your bones if you let it.

At first, I thought I could power through. I'm tough. I've been on the receiving end of more than my fair share of BDSM scenarios. I could take a little pain. It would just enhance the experience.

Fuck that.

I had to stop. If I didn't, I was going to have to explain to Ken's parents why my skeleton was showing when we returned from our little stroll. Pulling the rolled-up towel out from under Ken's head, I hopped off him and spread the terry-cloth strip out sideways under his knees. As I padded our little love nest and made apologies for ruining the mood, Ken's head flopped back with a defeated thud, as did his wilted penis.

Oh no.

No, no, no, no, no!

I couldn't start over from scratch! It was too late! We'd been gone too long.

No!

Ken might crumble under pressure, but not this bitch! I *thrive* under pressure. And I was going to make this happen.

At first, I thought I could just go down on him for a minute to ramp things back up, but while repositioning the towels, I had managed to get sand on not one, but both of my hands. If I went anywhere near Ken's penis with those things, there would be a domino effect of sand contamination that wouldn't end until I had it in my mouth, vag, and probably both eyes.

Maybe it was all the *prana* coming off the ocean, or maybe it was divine intervention, but whatever the source, the solution suddenly made itself known to me. I ripped off Ken's hoodie, followed by my dress, and tossed my bra onto the pile, as if it were the cherry on top. I was completely fucking naked and *sober* (those two glasses of pinot G at dinner were just a distant memory), while outside, in a public place, with my children sleeping mere yards away.

The transcendent feeling I enjoyed earlier? Poof! Gone! Replaced by fear and mortification and the sensation of tiny grains of glass pelting my body in the wind like buckshot.

Happily, my unexpected striptease al fresco sparked an equal and very opposite reaction in Ken. Within two minutes, he was grunting and thrusting his release into me, and although I'd made some muffled noises for his benefit that could have been interpreted as a climax, there seemed to be an unspoken understanding between us that I didn't get mine.

But that was okay, because Ken had given me something far better than any orgasm. He'd given me another shattered fantasy to add to my growing collection.

You see, Journal, every time I find out that something I once salivated over is actually a logistical nightmare and not fun for anybody, I appreciate my comfortable vanilla lifestyle a little more.

From now on, when we go on vacation, I won't be pouting because we're not out there, humping like teenagers on the beach. I'll be *choosing* not to have sex on the beach and *cherishing* the fact that none of my orifices have sand in them.

Maybe for our ten-year anniversary, Ken will finally give me that Mile High Club membership I've always had my eye on! I'm sure that fantasy will turn out to be even more nerve-racking, awkward, and disappointing than this one, especially considering that the only flight we have planned for next summer will be on an overbooked commercial airliner headed to— of all horrors—*Disney World.*

Can't wait!

39

Adieu

BB's Secret Journal

June 12

Well, Journal...

It's been a good run, but this might be good-bye. It's been weeks since I've written a single word in here, and it doesn't look like I'm going to have another opportunity anytime soon.

You see, every time I've reached for my laptop in the last fortnight, I've been immediately intercepted by a gorgeous, square-jawed, cleft-chinned, sexually aggressive man who looks and smells a lot like Ken. We'll call this beautiful stranger the hus-*boner*. I know he cannot possibly be *my* Ken because this man does things the old husbot can't even pronounce.

He has the stamina and control of a seasoned porn star. He pulls hair and spanks and bites and tops me, even from the bottom. Riding the husbot used to feel akin to humping a cadaver, but when I straddle the husboner, I have to white knuckle the headboard with both hands in order to take everything he's giving me. Not that I'm on top much anymore. I've been pummeled into near oblivion in the shower, on the stairs, on the couch, on the closet floor, and bent over the kitchen island on my stomach with my legs wrapped around his waist and crossed at the ankles behind his back.

It never fails. I reach for the computer—I get pounded. I reach for the computer again—I get plowed in four different positions, in three different rooms.

I had to wait for the husboner to fall asleep just so that I could tiptoe away long enough to write this! The sex is incredible, Journal. Incendiary. Dare I say, passionate.

Passionate! I could cry!

For ten long years, I've waited and wished for Ken to grab my hipbones like handlebars and ram himself into me from behind so hard and so fast that the slapping of our two bodies together sounded like a standing ovation.

I went through all five stages of grief and back again as I grappled to accept the fact that my days of being taken like a Viking conquest on the cover of a Harlequin Romance novel were behind me. And now, here I am, my pussy being pulverized on the regular by the very same man who lay motionless beneath me lo these many years.

It doesn't even make sense! I actually came so hard today that I fell into a fuzzy, warm post-orgasmic sleep for a few seconds before realizing, much to my chagrin, that Ken was patiently waiting for me to recover so that he could finish.

I was fucked unconscious, Journal!

I should be thrilled. I should delete you from existence and pretend none of this ever happened. I should spend every waking childfree moment with my ankles around my ears and the chain connecting my nipple clamps between Ken's teeth.

But I can't bring myself to stop. Passionate sex was only one of my objectives. What about my compliments? What about my pet name? My mission isn't even half complete, and as you've probably gathered by now, I don't half-ass anything. I whole-ass it.

And goddamn it, Journal, I still want Ken to get that tattoo!

40

Haiku of Shame

BB's Secret Journal

June 14

Dear Journal,

I wrote a poem today. I'm calling it "Haiku of Shame."
Trigger alert: It's kind of a tearjerker.

When Ken dies, after
A lifetime by my side, his
Arm ... will bear ... her name.

Goddamn Shakespearean tragedy, isn't it?

I wrote it in the car while Ken and I were out running errands, and I decided to recite it for him, beatnik-style, while drumming on the dashboard, as if it were a pair of bongos. Ken just rolled his eyes and said nothing.

Nothing, Journal!

I'd poured my heart and soul out to him through the ancient mystical art of haiku, and he didn't even have the decency to acknowledge my pain!

I should have titled it "Reason Number 2,349 Why Ken Is an Asshole."

I think it's time to bring out the big guns. If Subliminal Spousal Bibliotherapy, ex-boyfriend erotica, direct suggestion, and the majesty of poetry don't inspire Ken to get inked, then he's left me no choice. I'm going to have to employ the oldest and most potent influencer of bad decisions known to man (next to PCP, of course)—the power of peer pressure.

Cue the Alexander brothers.

41

What's Your Beef with Breakfast, Ken?

BB's Secret Journal

June 21

Dear Journal,

Ken has been friends with Devon and Ethan Alexander (the same brothers who were the life of Jason's Super Bowl party) since high school. The three of them have been negatively influencing each other for at least twenty years, so I figured if anyone could get Ken to make a terrible decision, it would be those two.

A few years ago, the Alexanders, who had always been pretty enamored with themselves, moved to California to pursue acting. Ethan, the younger one, morphed into *LA Alexander*. He was fitter, tanner, and owned way more tank tops and plastic-framed non-prescription glasses than ever before. While Devon, who is Ken's age, became the Hollywood version—five foot six and full of shit.

Whenever the Alexanders are around—which isn't much now that they are big shot "producers" (underemployed pyramid scheme–hustlers who live rent-free by always having some teenaged wannabe actress with her own apartment thinking that they are going to make her a star) out in California—Ken tends to let loose a little bit. I mean, he still won't drink or smoke or have fun or anything, but he will stay up *way* past his bedtime.

So, last Wednesday, Ken called me on his way home from work to tell me that the Alexanders were in town for Ethan's thirtieth birthday, so he and the guys were going to meet up at Wild Wing to celebrate and catch up.

"Sure," I said. "You guys have fun," I said.

I'll just stay here and make dinner and do the dishes and bathe your children and put them to bed and drink by myself, I said, in my head.

It was so unfair. Ken is an introverted teetotaler. Why should he get to go when I'm *clearly* the social drinker in this relationship? I wanted to go pound some Jameson shots and talk shit about all the "beat-downs" that Ethan and Devon have been "slaying" in LA.

But, alas, it was too late to find a babysitter, and Ken was almost to the bar when he called. Per my usual, I was marooned on Two Small Children Island without so much as a dinghy.

Then, as soon as I was elbow-deep in dishwater and acrimony, my cell phone chimed.

Ken: I think I'm going to be out pretty late.

Me: K.

Ken: Devon is so wasted. It's pretty funny.

Me: I'm sure it is.

Me: I hope you fuckers choke on your chicken wings (typed, then deleted)

In an attempt to eradicate my envious energy and get back to Zen, I threw the kids in bed, lit a lavender-scented candle, and dived headfirst into one of my favorite Deepak Chopra guided meditations.

Manifesting abundance through the systematic activation of the third-eye chakra? Yes, please!

Most of it was in Sanskrit, so I could have been summoning Lucifer for all I knew, but whatever mantra Deepak had me chanting, that shit worked.

No sooner had my man Deepak said his final "Namaste" than Ken was texting me to announce that the entire party was headed to our house!

Woop, woop! People! Alcohol! Kids asleep! Abundance!

I scurried around, alternating between giddily clapping and trying to machete my way through the plastic jungle that was once my sleek, contemporary adult living room. Once the mountain of toys had been successfully mashed into every available closet, cabinet, corner, and stove I could find, I began pulling vats of alcohol out of the liquor cabinet, hoping to aid in the social lubrication of my guests.

The thing about being married to an accountant who doesn't drink is that, when you ask him to pick up "a tiny little bottle of peppermint schnapps" for your signature holiday candy-cane martini, he will inevitably show up with a two-liter jug of peppermint schnapps because "It was a better price per ounce."

There are bottles of alcohol in this house that will outlive us all, Journal.

As soon as the final gallon of Triple Sec had been removed from the cabinet, my guests arrived. And it...was...glorious. Birthday boy Ethan, true to form, was tan, buff, tank-top clad, and bombed out of his mind. I'd never seen him so drunk, and Ken looked more than a little amused. In fact, he actually seemed to be enjoying himself. Devon, the older brother, followed, plopping himself on the couch where he alternated between contributing his two cents to Ethan's stories and trying to get random girls on Tinder to Snapchat him pictures of their tits.

Bringing up the rear was Ken's best friend, Allen, and his wife, Amy.

Allen and Amy have two kids, but you'd never know it based on the way they party. Just a few weeks ago, they went to an adults-only resort in Jamaica and had a weeklong orgy. I know this because Amy was texting me a blow-by-blow (no pun intended) of the action the entire time.

While they were spreading their ass cheeks for strangers on a nude beach, I was busy scrubbing skid marks out of my son's Batman underwear. I hope whoever wound up blowing them had thrush and beard crabs.

Listening to Ethan and Devon rattle off LA stories while acting out all the characters was like watching a live episode of *Drunk History*. Ethan was bragging about how he'd saved Devon from getting a hand job from a transgender porn star named Tammy Tugwell at the Sundance Film Festival. Devon was telling us about how he'd seen a C-list vampire from *True Blood* fucking a girl doggie-style on their couch in the aftermath of their epic Oscar party.

But as entertaining as the Alexanders' little pissing contest was, something even more interesting was happening on the far side of the room. Ken was smiling. As a matter of fact, he might have even been chuckling softly, like the coo of a dove.

Seeing Ken experience something resembling a good time while listening to the Lifestyles of the Single and Childless simply added fuel to the fire of my brilliant, sinister Gargamelian idea. All I needed to do was figure out a way to get the Alexander brothers and Ken into a tattoo parlor at the same time and let the gentle shove of peer pressure take care of the rest. I could do this. I had the universe and four hundred eighty-seven cubic liters of flavored liqueurs on my side.

I glanced at my bare wrist. "Damn, Ethan. Your birthday's almost over, boo. Is there anything else you want to do before midnight? Like go to Waffle House or get a tattoo?"

Please say tattoo. Please say tattoo. Please—

"Oh, shit!" Ethan slurred as panic forced his eyelids all the way open. "I was *totally* gonna get a tattoo today!"

Fuck yeah! High five, Deepak!

Allen and Amy hopped off the couch and started screaming and doing herkies like Satan's cheerleaders.

Allen grabbed Ethan by the shoulders and started shaking him violently while Amy screamed in his face, "Shit yes, E! Get in the car right now! We're paying!"

I glanced at Devon for any signs of protest, but he was still glued to his phone, willing his Snapchat app to ping.

With the swingers on board and big brother Alexander preoccupied with his quest to score ten seconds' worth of boobies, all I had to do now was convince Ken to go with them and pray that the momentum and camaraderie of a fun night out would be enough to get him to join his good buddy Ethan in a little tat session.

Unfortunately, Ken and his fucking morals didn't share our zest for bonding and making lifelong memories. Instead, he actually insinuated that it was not only *not* a great idea to take our inebriated friend to get a tattoo, but that it was actually "wrong" because he was "blackout drunk" and would probably "regret it in the morning."

Gah! Thanks a lot, Dad!

Ken might have been sober and rational, but I was full of Pucker Sour Apple, hellfire, and tarnation, and I wasn't going down without a fight. Through my liqueur-induced fog, I hoped that maybe, just maybe, if I could prove to Ken that the tattoo Ethan wanted was badass or at least tastefully unassuming, I could get Ken to cave.

"Don't listen to him, honey. Ken just hates fun, that's all. It's your thirtieth birthday! If you want a tattoo, you should let Allen and Amy buy you a tattoo! Do you know what you want?"

Please be something cool. Please be something cool…

Ethan wobbled a little on his feet while he oriented himself to the direction of my voice.

I'm pretty sure he couldn't actually see me through the slits in his eyelids, but he managed to stay upright and enthusiastic as he slurred, "Hell yesss I know what I want! I wan' *brefass*!"

The fuck?

"Did you just say breakfast?" I asked, trying real hard not to cringe.

"Yep. I wan' it to *say brefass*. On my foot."

Oh, for the love of God.

Ethan made an impressively delayed gesture toward one of his bare feet, and the room erupted in laughter. Ken actually snorted. I had to admit, trying to keep my composure as if it were a perfectly natural thing for a grown man to want the name of the most important meal of the day on his foot was no small feat (pun intended), but I persevered.

"Nice choice, Ethan. I like it. Wherever did you come up with such an original idea?"

Ethan was ready with a rock-solid explanation. He had obviously defended this idea before because his retort was immediate and succinct.

Straightening his posture, Ethan declared to the room in a voice that was louder than necessary, "Because iss the firss meal of the day...AND...iss the bess meal." He even threw in a sassy little head wag at the end, as if he'd just thrown down some irrefutable shit, and immediately, he had to catch his balance.

I could practically see my coveted Sailor Jerry–style heart tattoo with the letters *BB* emblazoned across the front slipping through my fingers.

C'mon, Ethan. Give me something I can work with here, buddy. Ken is never going to sign off on this harebrained bullshit.

I glanced across the room at Ken to gauge the situation and found him casually sitting on the floor with his back against the coffee table, necktie undone, top of his collared work shirt unbuttoned, quietly laughing his ass off.

It was not looking good, but I pressed on, determined. "You make some excellent points, E. Have you thought about a font?"

"Normal."

Duh.

"Are we talking Arial? Times New Roman? Helvetica?"

"Caps lock!" Ethan threw one arm up in the air for emphasis while he swayed with his eyes closed.

I bit my lip to suppress the cackle percolating in my throat and managed to summarize through gritted teeth, "So, you want it to say *breakfast*, on your foot, in all caps, in a normal font?"

"Fuck yes ma'am I do!"

My brilliant plan was gasping and flopping like a prized sea bass before my very eyes. At least the swingers were still on board. Allen grabbed Ethan by the shoulder straps of his tank top and spun him around to face Ken.

Jostling Ethan's floppy body like a rag doll, Allen shouted over his shoulder at Ken, "C'mon, dude! This man needs a tat, stat!"

Not even pretending like he was going to get up, Ken turned his attention to Ethan and said, trying like a gentleman to suppress his laughter, "I just think you're gonna regret it, man."

Fuck off, Ken! Who asked you?

In a moment of desperation, and with surprising lucidity, I blurted out, "Ethan, is there anybody you can call who could verify for Ken that you've actually wanted this tattoo for longer than twenty-four hours?"

It was a long shot, but I'll be damned if Ethan didn't produce not one, not two, but three SoCal douche bags on speakerphone who all had the same response when he announced that he was going to get "that tattoo I've always wanted."

Without missing a beat, each one mused in a prototypical stoner drawl, "Duuuude…you're finally gettin' the *breakfast* tattoo on your foot? No way! That is soooo awesome, bro!"

It was divine intervention! Surely, Ken couldn't argue with that kind of evidence! Ethan had clearly been talking about having an ode to the most important meal of the day permanently scrawled along his instep for, like, *weeks*.

Who was Ken to deny Ethan his dream?

I'll tell you who Ken was. Ken was the asshole who was going to deny Ethan his dream.

And mine. As usual.

Once the clock struck twelve and Ethan's big day was over, Ken decided it was time to take the Alexanders and the swingers home. I watched as my final Hail Mary attempt to get Ken to proclaim his love for me through the permanent art of tattoo stumbled out the door and into the night. Sitting alone on my now empty couch, in my now quiet living room, in the wake of yet another defeat, I felt bereft. My psychological tactics arsenal had been depleted.

I was out of ideas, and it was time to face the facts. Ken was *never* going to express his undying love for me—not in words, not in writing, and evidently, not on his skin either.

I'd always believed that those sentiments were in there somewhere. All I had to do was find the right key to unlock them. I mean, of course Ken loves the way I get hiccups every single day and how I always manage to fuck up instant mashed potatoes and how I am perpetually five (ten) minutes late to everything, and the way I get really loud and inappropriate when I'm in uncomfortable social situations, and how I sometimes flip him off when I've been drinking.

Who wouldn't? I'm fucking adorable.

As a self-confident only child, I'd always moved through the world secure in the knowledge that the sun, moon, and stars shone out of my ass.

But there, clinging to my knees in the shadows of my picturesque living room, adrift on my microsuede couch, floating on a current of peach schnapps and desolation, surrounded by my disregarded photography and overlooked paintings, I finally found the courage to ask myself the question I'd been running from since Kenneth motherfucking Easton came into my life.

What if Ken's not expressing his feelings for me because they're just not there?

I clutched my shins for dear life and buried my knees in my eye sockets, trying to both physically protect myself from the implications of that single thought and hold fast against the flood of tears threatening to consume me. I'd spent more than a decade trying to figure out how to get Ken to give me a glimpse into the bottomless well of love he was hiding from me when what I should have been asking myself the whole time was, *What if?*

I knew from experience that the kind of love I was looking for from Ken—the roses-are-red-violets-are-blue kind—was a fickle bitch. It hurt, it betrayed, and it was ultimately unsustainable. This thing with Ken, whatever it was, it was going to go the distance. I knew it in my cells, and I knew it in my soul. I'd already been with him five times longer than any of my other boyfriends, and I could have done it standing on my head. It might not have been carnal or tender. It certainly wasn't emotionally fulfilling. But what we had was surprisingly steady and stable and strong.

Sigh.

The time to give up the ghost of passion past had come. Tears that were eleven years in the making fell in torrents as I tried to choke down my new reality. No man was ever going to tell me *You're so beautiful* again or refer to me as anything other than my full legal fucking name. No man was ever going to feel strongly enough about me to have that name (or preferably the adorable personalized pet name he'd assigned me the moment we first met) gouged into his skin with tiny needles. And it was also time to accept that the lingerie, handcuffs, and bondage gear stashed in my underwear drawer would never again see the light of day.

Fleshy chunks of my hopes and dreams were splattered all over my living room. Sliding down the eggplant-colored walls. Dripping from the custom coffered ceiling. I sat, hugging my knees, in the apex of the crime scene, crying, rocking, and humming a requiem of grief and acceptance.

It's okay. It's okay. It's okay...

I would let those foolish needs go. I would bury them out back, wipe up the mess, and go to bed, taking comfort in the knowledge that, for the rest of my life, I would be uneventfully married to the father of my children, the mower of my grass, the balancer of my checkbook, and the keeper of my heart even if he doesn't have one himself.

Just as I was crawling into bed, carrying on my back the weight of both loss and resignation, I heard the garage door roar to life. Quickly dashing away my tears with the hem of my sheet, I pretended to be asleep as Ken tiptoed in.

Without missing a beat, he asked, "What's wrong?"

"Hmm?" I grumbled, stretching a little. "Nothing. Why?"

"There are wadded-up tissues all over the living room. Have you been crying?"

Way to go, Nancy Drew.

"Maybe."

"Why?"

It was too dark to see him, but I felt the mattress sag next to me, and I heard the quiet concern in his voice.

"Because I'm an asshole."

"You're just now figuring that out?"

Wow, Ken. You're so good with feelings and empathy and stuff. How could I have ever accused you of being a cyborg?

"Actually, I was crying because *you're* an asshole."

Crickets.

"I just told you I've been crying, and all you can do is sit there and stare at me? Jesus, Ken! Just go to bed! It's not like you actually care what's wrong."

I felt Ken's hand gingerly pat my hip. He didn't argue with me or offer any solutions. He simply implied nonverbally that I was right. He did, in fact, just want to go to bed and didn't actually care what was wrong.

Using my legs and free arm, I pushed him off the bed and pointed in the direction of the master bathroom. "Go! Go get ready for bed, asshole!"

Exasperated, Ken's silhouette threw its hands in the air and huffed, "What? What do you want from me? I asked you what was wrong, and you called me an asshole—twice. What am I supposed to do with that?"

Fuck it. Let's do this.

Sitting up in bed, I glared at the backlit black hole where Ken's face should have been and snarled, "You know what you can do, Ken? How about you *don't* ever say anything nice to me, give a shit about my needs or feelings, or get my name tattooed on your body to make up for the initials you have carved into your arm? Okay? How about you *not* do any of that shit? Oh, wait, it's too fucking late!"

Ken's outline looked contrite, and he responded to my out-burst in a small voice, "You were serious about that? You really wanted me to get that tattoo?"

Oh, for fuck's sake!

"Nope. Not anymore. Good night, Ken."

I turned my back on the beautiful shadow and pulled the covers up around my chin, signaling the end of the conversation. After all the cathartic soul-searching I'd just done, I couldn't believe the way I'd lashed out at Ken. Evidently, accepting that he didn't love me as much as I thought was one thing. Pretending to be happy about it was quite another.

42

Take a Picture. It'll Last Longer.

BB's Secret Journal

June 21, continued

With my eyes screwed tightly shut and the comforter pulled up around my ears, I tried to block out the sounds of Ken stomping around the house. I could hear countless cabinet doors and drawers opening and closing in the kitchen—or maybe the office?

What the fuck is he looking for?

It sounded like he was trying to wake the dead, not get ready for bed.

A few minutes later, Ken's heavy footfalls made their way back toward the bedroom. I clutched the comforter and held my breath. When the footsteps stopped just a few feet away from me, the black backs of my eyelids were suddenly bathed in screaming yellow.

Ugh!

I flipped over and squinted through the near blinding rays

of my bedside lamp to see Ken looming over me, a long blunt object in his outstretched hand.

Instinctively, I braced for impact. When it never came, I risked a peek and found, to my utter, unadulterated glee, that Ken was extending to me...a calligraphy pen.

I sat up and stared at him, slack-jawed, searching his face for some indication of what the fuck was going on. He gave nothing away. He didn't speak. He didn't emote. He just stood there, sexily disheveled in his dress shirt and slacks, looking tired yet resolved. His usually bright aqua eyes paled to a steely gray as they bore into me, daring me to take the bait. When I shakily reached out to accept the pen, Ken clung to it for just a moment before relinquishing it to me. He then proffered another object in its place—his right hand.

The Harley entry!

By offering that particular pen and that particular hand Ken was letting me know—in no uncertain terms—that he'd been reading my journal. And he was ending this charade once and for all. Never again would I be able to write whatever my wicked heart desired, leave it out for him to read, and then coquettishly dance around the subject like we both didn't know exactly what was going on. The jig was up.

I thought when this day finally came that I would be elated, but the reality of seeing my constitutionally stubborn, almost pathologically rigid husband standing before me, offering to get a tattoo that I knew he didn't really want because he'd been manipulated into it, made my stomach turn.

My poor Ken. What have I done to you?

I thought back, trying to remember how we got to this point. For as long as I could remember I'd been beating my head against a wall trying to get this man to express his feelings for me. And for years Ken had thwarted every behavior mod tactic I threw at him. So why now? What changed? All I did was tell him *not* to get a tattoo.

Oh my God.

Ken really does have oppositional defiant disorder.

Why didn't I think to use reverse psychology sooner? That shit works every time!

I wanted to honor the breakthrough I had earlier by announcing that I didn't need him to get a tattoo or compliment me or give me a pet name anymore because that's not who he was and I was going to venerate that. I wanted to prove that I really had grown and was no longer seeking validation that I was lovable or attractive from him or anyone else.

But I couldn't do it. Seeing the sexiest, most infuriating man I'd ever laid eyes on standing before me, offering to give me the very thing he'd been withholding all these years—visible permanent proof of his love—was simply too irresistible.

All the progress I'd made during my spell of soul-searching went up in a puff of smoke. The sour, churning acid in my stomach was replaced by delightful little butterflies, and the seal of my tight, angry lips broke open to reveal a stupid shit-eating grin that I could no longer suppress.

I wanted to do the right thing, I really did, but I was so high on the prospect of finally getting my way that I yanked the cap off the calligraphy pen with my teeth and set to work. I didn't glance up at Ken even once, for fear of what I might find, of what I knew was already there—disapproval and obligation.

Instead, I focused solely on the placement and precision of every swoop and halt. Time ceased to exist. It was just me and the ink and the rapture of watching a fantasy eleven years in the making coming true before my very eyes.

An errant tear landed on the back of Ken's hand, missing my masterpiece by a hair's breadth. It was done. It was glorious. It was *everything*.

In my mind, I'd always fantasized about seeing my name broadcast to the world in an old-school heart and banner, but in a moment of inspiration, I'd decided to go with a traditional compass rose, the only tattoo motif Ken had ever admitted to liking. Only, on this compass, instead of the letters *N*, *S*, *E*, and *W*, every direction was labeled with a tiny *B*.

Because wherever Ken goes, that's where I'll be.

It was perfect. It was Ken. But most importantly, it was me *on* Ken, somewhere highly visible and passionately unprofessional.

Peeking up at Ken through my lashes, I held my breath, crossed my fingers, and waited, every muscle tensed, for his reaction. Ken removed his hand from mine just long enough to turn it toward himself and assess the damage.

Oh God, please like it. Please, please like it. Look! I didn't even draw a heart! It's a compass, just like you wanted! See how selfless I am? It's like I was channeling Gandhi!

Ken raised one eyebrow, followed by the opposite corner of his beautifully chiseled mouth. I couldn't tell for sure if he actually liked what he saw or was simply amused by it.

Without saying a word, Ken gently placed his hand back in mine and let his default mask of detachment slide back into place. With his left hand, he picked my phone up from the nightstand and offered it to me, finally looking me in the eyes but giving nothing away.

Hypnotized by Ken's guarded stare, I slowly accepted the phone.

With my heart in my throat I asked, "Wh-what's this for? Do you want me to call the tattoo parlor?"

Ken's face softened a bit, but there was a smart-ass twinkle in his eye that told me I wasn't going to like what came next.

"No. I just thought you might want to take a picture of it before I wash it off. I'm not getting a tattoo on the back of my hand, Crazy. I have a meeting with the CFO in six hours."

43

You Can't Always Get What You Want

BB's Secret Journal

June 21, continued

No.

    No?

I stared at my husband like a moron with my mouth open in disbelief that he'd had the balls to pull a mindfuck like that and also in disbelief that I hadn't erupted into a full-on nuclear meltdown after being told *no*.

Most only children, myself included, are classically conditioned by their parents from birth to pitch a motherfucking fit whenever someone tells them *no*.

All *no* really means is, *I would like to hear you scream and cry and berate and guilt-trip me about whatever it is that you want in a loud, glass-breakingly shrill pitch for approximately five to ten minutes until I am satisfied that you really, really want it. Then, I will I give it to you. Ready? Go!*

So, why wasn't I upset? Or at least pretending to be upset?

I know I heard it. That little *no* bounced around in my skull like a racquetball while I stared, unblinking, into those obstinate aqua eyes, but my brain simply would not or could not process the meaning behind it.

I tried repeating it in my head with different emphases, in different languages.

No?

NO?

Nope?

Nein?

Nyet?

Naheen?

No way?

But still nothing.

Had I actually suffered a full-blown nervous breakdown earlier, and now, I was completely detached from reality? Was I having a stroke? Was this what Wernicke's aphasia felt like?

Perhaps my refusal to comprehend was just a psychological defense mechanism, trying to protect me from the anguish of having my hopes and dreams crushed twice in the same night.

Then, it hit me.

As much as I loathed the word *no*, I had equal and opposite feelings about pet names. My brain wasn't broken. It was simply caught in a tug-of-war between two tiny little words, both fighting to gain control over my next emotional response.

In the red corner, foaming at the mouth and having his shoulders massaged by Satan himself, was the word *No*, the ugliest word ever invented. The word that makes me want to drop to my knees the instant I hear it, only so that my fist will make better contact with the naysayer's genitals.

In the blue corner, flitting around like a drunken humming-bird and laughing at nothing in particular, was the word *Crazy*. Although I'd heard Ken use this pet name to refer to me once before, he had been half-asleep, and I had only been half-paying attention, so I hadn't really gotten the full effect. This time, I had been close enough to see Ken's pupils dilate fractionally, and I'd watched his sculptured lips part as he exhaled the word, *crazy*, like he was blowing me a kiss. If *crazy* won the battle over my emotional response, one of those lips was going to be between my teeth in no time.

Ken and I sustained our silent staring contest for a few seconds, both waiting to see which way my internal struggle was going to go.

When the dust finally settled, I was pleasantly surprised (as was Ken, I'm sure) to find that, instead of being overcome by the desire to head-butt him in the nose, I'd been overtaken by a warm, fuzzy flirtatious little tingle—the kind you got when a cute boy teased you about something he secretly liked.

Maybe my subconscious decided that it had mourned the death of my tattoo dream enough for one night and was ready to celebrate the achievement of another. Kenneth Easton, man of my dreams, had called me something other than Brooke, while fully conscious.

Heart swell!

As soon as my mental master of ceremonies held Crazy's little hand up in victory, I grabbed the front of Ken's dress shirt in both fists and pulled him down with me as I tumbled backward into bed.

There I was treated to another of my recent accomplishments—Ken's newfound libido.

That's when I finally realized just how far Ken had come. I'd been spending so much time focusing on the objectives that I hadn't yet accomplished that I'd failed to fully appreciate the magnitude of Ken's transformation. In ten months, my husband had gone from a frigid old husbot whose idea of a date night involved curling up on his side of the couch and sleeping through the movie we rented, to a confident, insatiable sex panther who surprises me with concert tickets and front-row seats at comedy shows and meals (plural, as in, he no longer insists that we share an entrée to save money) at *non*-chain restaurants before pounding me into oblivion for dessert.

As I lay there, watching the hunky human Ken doll I shared a bed with disappear between my legs, his hand—still bearing my ink—splayed across my stomach, I finally felt accomplished. Like water from a rock, I'd managed to squeeze some seriously passionate sex and a pet name out of Kenneth "Husbot" Easton, using nothing more than my computer, some well-channeled angst, and my ability to function in what medical science refers to as a "chronic sleep-restricted state." Maybe I'm not such a bad psychologist after all.

———

I might not get everything I want out of this motherfucker—mostly because he has oppositional defiant disorder—but on some sick level, I think I like it.

Maybe it stems from being raised by two peace-loving hippies who usually (always) folded under the strength of my will. Or maybe I'm just so spoiled that *not* getting my way simply isn't an option. Whatever the reason, I love nothing more than a good challenge.

Once I've set my mind on something I become obsessed, searching for chinks in its armor and new angles to come at it from until I eventually wear it down and make it my bitch. It doesn't matter how long it takes—weeks, years—or in Ken's case, forfuckingever.

Though my Super Private Journal That Ken Is Never, Never Allowed to Read Ever might be closed for good, if I know me, this is just the first in a series of immoral psychological experiments that I will subject my husband to in the name of trying to get him to express his love for me. And if I know Ken, he will probably continue to ration his affection and approval for the rest of his life just to keep me on the hook.

And as much as I hate to admit it, it will be fun. Ken might even laugh. I will most likely throw things. And we will do this little dance until we're dead. At which point, I will be forced to scour the multiverse over until I find that motherfucker again, just so that we can dance some more.

44

Blue Balls

BB's Secret Journal

July 12

Dear Journal,

I just realized that every man I have ever loved has had blue eyes—starting with my father and ending with my son. Sure, I dated guys with other eye colors along the way, but I only fell in love with the blue-eyed boys. Evidently, I have a type.

If you took all those blue eyeballs and plopped them down on the table, I imagine many of them would look pretty similar. Some would be lighter, some would be darker, some would be bloodshot, overly dilated and/or stained yellow from years of drug use (ahem...Ding-Dong). But Ken's...I could pick Ken's eyeballs out from a *barrelful* of blue-and-white orbs.

They're a sparkling cerulean that feels somehow bright and tranquil at the same time—like those glossy magazine photos of tropical vacation spots where the ocean is that vivid blue-green color. You can see every fish rollicking beneath the waves, every grain of sand at the bottom, and you think, *Pssh. That shit is fake. Nothing in nature is that blue.* Because if something that beautiful really existed and you were missing it, it would be a fucking tragedy.

Well, I'm happy to report that that color does exist. And I don't need a plane ticket and a quart-sized Ziploc baggie full of tiny toiletries to experience it. Whenever I look into Ken's eyes, I can't help but feel as though somebody just thrust a hollowed-out coconut into my hand, filled with rum and love and curly straws and little paper umbrellas. I relax. My cortisol levels go down. My serotonin levels go up. And suddenly, I'm on vacation, content to bury my toes in our sandy-colored frieze carpet and stay a while.

After eleven months of soul-searching and behavior-modification experiments and sleepless wine-soaked nights, I feel like I've finally arrived at my destination, and all that's left to do is exhale, sip something fruity, and enjoy the view. Although my gorgeous Irish Spring–scented sandy-haired husband might still prefer to hang out over on Ken Island, nursing a Gatorade and checking his phone for Braves scores and stock market updates, I now have an open invitation to climb ashore and storm his beaches whenever I want, if you know what I mean (eyebrow waggle, self–high five).

⸻

Listen, Journal, you already know from my breakup history that I'm pretty bad with good-byes, so let's just get this over with. You're the best thing that ever happened to my marriage, okay? And as much as I know that I should just delete you and never look back, I owe you more than that. You deserve to live on, to spend your retirement rubbing elbows with all the other smut I've been stashing in the Cute Stuff I Found on Pinterest folder.

Besides, I'm probably going to need to use you as a reference tool in the future because I'm pretty sure lack of sleep has destroyed my ability to form new memories.

So, until then, Namaste, Little Guy. Your work here is done.

EPILOGUE

Actual Text Conversation with Dr. Sara Snow

Me: Sara motherfucking Snow

Me: Pack your bags bitch!

Me: You've got a date with Matt Lauer!

Sara: Married, middle-aged, and white

Sara: Hmm…

Sara: He does sound like my type

Me: Subliminal Spousal Bibliotherapy is a wrap.

Sara: You're done?

Me: Stick a fork in me.

Me: Ken called my ass OUT last night.

Sara: Oh shit

Sara: Did he hit you?

Me: Oh, he hit it all right. ;)

Sara: Nice

Sara: Hey, speaking of

Sara: Has Ken ever choked you?

Sara: Because if he hasn't, he needs to tonight.

Me: Ha! You're still sleeping with Alex, aren't you?

Sara: Yes
Sara: Didn't one of your exes used to do it?

Me: Not on purpose.

Sara: You need to be choked.

Me: Was it that good??

Sara: No
Sara: At first I thought I'm going to die getting fucked by a guy I met on the Sunset strip on New Year's Eve and then I almost fainted then I came and it was amazing

Me: He pulled it off without a hitch??

Sara: Without
Sara: A
Sara: Hitch

Me: And then you fell in love with him

Sara: He was so sweet afterward

Me: I'm so fucking impressed. That's quite a skill.

Sara: It was
Sara: Sigh
Sara: And that is how Dr. Sara Snow almost got herself a baby daddy with a GED
Sara: I'm slowly getting over it
Sara: I'll eventually forget
Sara: Maybe I should call him

Sara: We could get married

Sara: Then he can choke me for the next 7-10 years

Sara: You realize eventually I'll be intellectually disabled from lack of oxygen

Me: I love that autoerotic asphyxiation is what it takes to finally get Sara Snow to settle down.

Sara: Lol

Me: I'm calling matron of honor. Dibs on that shit.

Sara: If you think there will be a wedding you're the one who's brain injured

Me: Alex wants a wedding!

Sara: That sounds exhausting

Me: Just a little one.

Sara: He may have already had one

Sara: I didn't ask

Me: No he hasn't!

Me: He's been saving himself for you!

Me: Alex wants to write his own vows!

Me: Why do I feel like I know him so well?

Me: Oh, shit

Me: Is it because he's me?

Sara: A clinger who wants to choke his partner?

Sara: He IS you

Me: You guys should make a baby.

Me: That baby would be my favorite person ever.

Sara: Good bc you'll be raising it

Me: I really need to start writing this shit down.

Sara: You're gonna need something new to write about now that SSB is a wrap

Me: Speaking of
Me: On a scale of 1 to 10

Sara: Oh shit

Me: How badly do you think I'll get sued if I write a romance series based on each one of my exes?

Sara: Do it
Sara: You have to
Sara: This is your purpose in life

Me: Like, are we talking lose my house kind of sued?
Me: Or just lose my kids' college funds kind of sued?

Sara: I know
Sara: Just say that they're fiction
Sara: BOOM problem solved

Me: Goddamn, you're brilliant.

Sara: I believe the term is meanius

Me: Are you sure that will that work though?

Sara: Totally
Sara: What's the worst that could happen?

Read on for a sneak peek at *Skin*, the
first Sex/Life novel, available now.

Skin

Chapter One

Positive, positive, positive.

It was my first day of tenth grade, and I was *not* going to be nervous. I was going to think deliriously happy, positive thoughts. I was going to skip down the familiar halls of Peach State High School with a bounce in my steel-toed step and a self-confident smirk on my face because *this* was going to be the year that Lance Hightower finally proclaimed his undying love for me. It just *had* to be.

I wasn't going to beat myself up about the fact that I had been trying and failing to make out with that boy since middle school, *nor* was I going to focus on the fact that I still had zero breasts at the age of fifteen. No, I was going to fantasize about all the wildly spontaneous, highly public ways Lance might choose to propose. After all, I'd just learned—thanks to my dad's unhealthy obsession with watching CNN—that it was totally legal for teenagers to get married in Georgia as long as they had written permission from one of their parents. That wouldn't be a problem for me, seeing as how I'd perfected my mom's signature by the age of twelve.

I was also feeling pretty damn good because I knew I'd

picked out the *perfect* back-to-school outfit. My trademark black combat boots and wingtip eyeliner were firmly in place; I was rocking some kickass black spiderweb fishnets under my favorite pair of too-short-for-school cut-off jeans; my gray midriff T-shirt boasted the logo of an indie band I was absolutely *certain* no one had heard of; and my arms were practically pinned to my sides with the weight of a thousand metal, beaded, and leather bracelets. Also, I'd started smoking over the summer (for real this time), and my shorter, edgier, more angled haircut got tons of compliments, even from Lance (which was the whole point).

Of course, all my positivity went to shit as soon as I made it to the church parking lot for a smoke between classes.

It was no secret at Peach State High School that if you wanted to do something bad, all you had to do was walk out past the rust buckets in the student parking lot, step over a guardrail, and clear the tree line. That was it. On the other side you would find yourself in a magical wooded wonderland called *the church parking lot*, a place where kids could escape the oppression of our overcrowded, underfunded public learning institution to laugh, smoke, and be merry (if only for seven minutes at a time). The church was a long abandoned one-room chapel that was in the process of being reclaimed by the forest, and its parking lot was nothing more than a patch of gravel, but to a band of misfit teenagers it was heaven.

Or so I'd heard. I'd never actually ventured out to the church parking lot during school hours before, but this was my year. I just knew that on the other side of those woods I'd find *my people*. Artsy, quirky free spirits who shared my appreciation for alternative rock, avant garde art, and experimental photography. The group that would embrace me with open arms, invite me to sit with them at lunch, and host raging keggers like the ones I saw on TV.

Instead, what I found was the most intimidating group of human beings I'd ever seen in one place. *Fuck me.* Those kids were cool with a capital *C* and twenty-seven *O*s. They had *multicolored* hair. They had *piercings.* They had expertly painted red lips that I could never pull off with my redheaded complexion. And the accessories—more chokers and studded belts than you could shake a flannel shirt at. One girl was even wearing denim overalls with the legs cut off and one shoulder strap undone. I wasn't punk rock—I was Punky fucking Brewster.

At least my combat boots were vintage and my eyeliner was flawless. That I knew for sure. I'd been perfecting that goddamn cat eye since the age of ten. As long as I kept my grades up my hippie parents never really gave a shit how much makeup I wore, or what I dressed like, or how many F-bombs I dropped at the dinner table. (And by dinner table, I mean my TV tray in the living room.) So I stood on the periphery and tried not to stare, clinging to both my Camel Light and the hope that someone would at least admire my eyeliner art.

I watched the guys all squeezing and kneading and nuzzling their girlfriends, and I watched their girlfriends' giant boobs bounce with every giggle.

I bet they have sex, I thought. *Every one of them.*

My face and neck suddenly felt itchy and hot.

Annnnd, now I'm blushing. Fantastic.

I dropped my head and stared down at my boots, which I could see with no problem at all thanks to my complete and total lack of breasts.

Why can't the heroin chic look still be in? Maybe it'll make a comeback. Please let it make a comeback.

Everyone out there looked like Drew Barrymore and I looked

like somebody drew a smiley face and freckles on one of Drew Barrymore's pinky fingers.

My BFF, Juliet Iha, was supposed to be meeting me out there, but after a few minutes it became pretty clear that she'd flaked out on me yet again.

She's probably out here somewhere fogging up Tony's car windows.

Juliet was dating a grown-ass man who'd dropped out of high school at least a decade prior and never seemed to have anywhere pressing to be. Without fail, that creepy fucker always seemed to be lurking around wherever we were, leaning up against his busted-ass old Corvette like an actor cast to play the part of "Potential Child Molester" in a P.S.A. from 1985. Tony definitely gave me the "no feeling," but Juliet really liked him and he was old enough to buy us cigarettes, so I kept my mouth shut.

Just as I was about to stamp out my Camel Light and drag my sad ass back inside, I felt two solid arms wrap around my body from behind. One snaked around my rib cage and the other hoisted me up from behind my knees. Before I could scream "Rape!" I was flipped completely upside down and plopped, ass up, on the shoulder of a giant. It wasn't until he swatted my backside and laughed in that glorious, soft tone that made my body go all warm and bubbly that I realized I'd been captured by my immortal beloved, Lance Hightower.

Lance Motherfucking Hightower. God, he was perfection. Lance was in my grade, but he was easily half a foot taller than most of the upperclassmen and already filled out like a man. Dude had a permanent five o'clock shadow at the age of fifteen. Despite having the dark, chiseled features of a Disney prince, Lance was a punk rock icon. Every day he sported the same effortlessly badass look: faded black Converse, faded black jeans, and a faded black hoodie covered in patches advertising obscure European underground punk bands and anarchist political statements that he painted on with Wite-Out during class. That hoodie was so well known it probably had its own fanzine.

Topping off all that faded black packaging was an equally faded, slightly grown-out, green Mohawk. It probably would have added another three inches to Lance's already six-foot-three-inch frame if he ever bothered to style it, and the color totally brought out the green flecks in his coppery hazel eyes.

Oh, Lance. I had been obsessing over him since the sixth grade. I admired him from afar until last year when we fatefully wound up sharing a pottery wheel in art class. The flirting that ensued was incendiary. Atomic. The only problem was that I was technically "dating" his best friend, Colton, at the time, so things never really got off the ground.

Then a goddamn miracle happened. Colton up and moved to Las Vegas to live with his dad right in the middle of the spring semester. I pretended to be sad for a few hours, out of respect, then immediately resumed my campaign to become the mother of Lance's children. The only problem was that Lance and I didn't have any classes together, so all of my flirting had to be done in seven-minute increments between periods. But in tenth grade, what I was sure would be the best year ever, Lance and I had been assigned to the same motherfucking lunch period. I was going to be sporting his last name by May. I just knew it.

"Lance! What are you doing?" I giggled. "Put me down! I can't breathe with your shoulder in my stomach!"

Lance chuckled. "That's so sweet. You take my breath away too, girl."

God, his voice. Like fucking angel bells. For such a big dude with such an in-your-face look, Lance's voice was surprisingly soft and flirty. It was a total mindfuck the first few times I heard that sweet sound come out of that ruggedly handsome face. And the pick-up lines. I swear to Jesus he had a new one every time I saw him. I fucking loved Lance Hightower.

I giggled harder, which made my stomach hurt even worse, and swatted at his perfect, patch-covered ass. "Put me down, asshole!"

Before he could comply, we heard a sickening smack from across the parking lot followed by a deep voice shouting, "Say it again, motherfucker!"

Lance held on tight to the backs of my thighs and swung around to face the commotion, making me even dizzier as I grabbed his waist and peeked around his side to see what was going on.

Although I couldn't make out exactly what was happening due to the blood rushing into my eyeballs, I recognized the assailant immediately. I'd never met him, but I'd heard stories. Everybody had. He was "the skinhead," the only one at our entire four-thousand-student suburban high school.

I'd noticed him in ninth grade because he was literally the only person I'd ever seen wear suspenders (skinny ones, called braces) to school. In a world full of studded belts and chain wallets, that motherfucker wore suspenders—the epitome of dorkiness—and made them look as scary as the stripes on a venomous snake.

A snake who was standing about thirty feet away, looming over a little skater boy who was clutching his rapidly swelling jaw and trying not to cry.

When the kid didn't say whatever it was the skinhead wanted to hear, he buried his fist deep in Skater Boy's stomach, causing him to lurch forward and release a noise so guttural I assumed something important must have ruptured. With his left hand, the skinhead yanked the guy's head back by his chin-length brown hair and screamed into his terrified face, "Say that shit again!"

I felt like I might throw up. My heart was racing and my head was pounding from being upside down, but all I could register was a sickening sense of helplessness and humiliation for that poor kid. I'd been raised in a house with pacifist parents and no siblings. I'd never seen anyone get hit before, at least not in real life, and I felt that punch as if it had been dealt directly to me.

In a way, it had. That punch shook me to my core. It showed me that senseless violence and cruelty really do exist, and they come wearing boots and braces.

When Skater Boy remained silent, the skinhead responded by shoving his head so hard that he flew sideways and landed, hands and face first, in the gravel. His body slid a few feet before finally coming to a stop. The kid scrambled to pull himself into a ball and made little screeching sounds as if struggling to suppress a scream.

Instead of attacking again, his assailant began to circle him slowly, like a hawk. I held my breath and gripped Lance's waist tighter, ignoring the throbbing in my eyeballs, and watched upside down as he assessed his victim. I was horrified by how calm he was. He wasn't angry or upset, just…calculating. Cold and calculating.

The skinhead approached the kid, who was now trembling and sobbing quietly, and slowly rolled him onto his side with one very heavy-looking combat boot. Still curled up tightly, Skater Boy choked out what sounded like a muffled, garbled apology. Unimpressed, his attacker bent down toward the kid's face and placed a meaty hand firmly on the side of his head. I didn't know what he was doing at first, but when the brown-haired kid started screaming in pain I realized that the skinhead was pressing his face into the gravel.

"What was that?" he asked calmly, tilting his head to one side as if genuinely interested, the veins in his muscular arm beginning to bulge as he applied more pressure.

"I'm sorry! I'm sorry! I didn't mean it! Please stop! Please!" The scream at the end of his apology got increasingly louder as that heartless, hairless demon crushed his face further into the jagged rocks.

The skinhead released Skater Boy's head and stood up. I exhaled and felt my body relax into Lance's shoulder, then watched in disbelief as he kicked the kid directly in the lower back one, two, three times. By the time my eyes registered the strikes and my ears registered the resulting scream it was over, but my spirit was forever changed.

It said, *These people fuck and they fight and you'd better get used to it, little girl.*

Lance set me down, slowly, and I wrapped myself around him like a tree trunk for stability.

I stared, partially hidden behind Lance's sturdy frame, as the skinhead idly spit on the ground next to his victim, lit a cigarette, and walked with long confident strides...directly toward me. The gravel crunched under the weight of his steel-toed boots, which emerged from the bottom of a tightly rolled pair of blue jeans. Bright red laces wound themselves up the front of his boots, and bright red braces slashed across his muscular chest— a chest which was wrapped in a tight black T-shirt emblazoned with the word *Lonsdale*.

Steeling myself behind Lance's comforting presence, I mustered the courage to peek up at the skinhead's face. It was like looking at a ghost. He resembled a person, but there was no color to help differentiate his features. His skin was white. His

hair and eyelashes were virtually transparent, and his eyes…
His eyes were a ghostly, icy gray-blue. Like a zombie's. And
when they landed on mine, my hair stood up on end so violently
it felt like a million tiny needles were stabbing me at once.

Those zombie eyes flicked from mine to Lance's with a look
of irritation as he approached. I could feel a buzzing electric current of malice radiating off of him well before he reached us, and
I winced as he passed, as if bracing myself for his wrath. When
nothing happened I carefully opened my eyes, relieved by the
change in the atmosphere. The static charge was gone. *He* was
gone. But he left a broken boy, a still-burning Marlboro Red,
and my scattered wits on the ground in his wake.

⚬

As traumatizing as my first smoke break had been, that wasn't
the reason I was having trouble concentrating in my honors eco-
nomics class. It was because as soon as the bell rang I knew I was
going to have lunch with Lance Motherfucking Hightower—
and my best friends, Juliet and August—but mostly *Lance
Motherfucking Hightower.*

I saw the teacher's mouth moving, but all I could hear were
my own racing thoughts. *I'm totally going to sit next to him. But
what if I get there first? Will he sit next to me? Maybe I should hide
and wait for Lance to sit down and then run over and sit next to
him before anyone else has a chance. Yes. Totally. Then I'll find an
excuse to touch him. And I'll laugh at all his jokes. Not that it'll
be hard. He's so funny. And beautiful. And tall. And edgy. And
fucking dreamy.*

When the bell finally rang, I jumped up as if my ass were

on fire and sprinted to the bathroom to touch up my makeup. Then I high-tailed it to the cafeteria to scope out the cool kid table. Every punk, goth, druggie, drama nerd, vegan, hippie, skater, and metal head at our high school wanted a spot at that table, and even though he was only in tenth grade, Lance was the reigning king of them all. Getting a spot next to him was going to be tricky.

When I ran up I realized that not only had Lance already taken his seat—right in the middle of the fifteen-foot-long table—but goddamn Colton Hart was sitting right next to him.

Shit.

Shit fuck damn.

When the hell did he get back?

Colton was going to be a major fucking obstacle in my quest to become Mrs. Hightower. He was the world's biggest cockblocker—that's actually how I wound up dating him in the first place—he just kept inserting himself between Lance and me until I gave in and let him kiss me. Which he did. A lot. Don't get me wrong, making out with Colton Hart was a spectacular way to spend an afternoon. He was super fucking cute. And cocky. And sarcastic. And *bad*. But he just wasn't Lance.

But technically, he *was* still my boyfriend.

Oh my God. What if he thinks we're still a couple? No. There's no way. He never even called me after he left. He probably screwed all kinds of future strippers while he was living with his dad and brother in Las Vegas, and now I'm small potatoes. I'm just the girl he left back in Georgia who wouldn't let him touch her boobs. It's totally fine. No. Big. Deal.

As I walked up, I couldn't help but admit to myself that he did look damn good. Better than I'd remembered. He was like a wicked Peter Pan. Spiky brown hair with blond tips, pointy ears, perfect male model smile. When he left, he had a definite punk rock style, like a mini-Lance, but I guess his skateboarding older brother had worn off on him while he was in Vegas. Colton had traded in his boots for a pair of shell-toed Adidas, his bondage pants for a pair of black cargo shorts, and his studded belt for a chain wallet.

There was a spot open next to both of them, but I made sure to sit next to Lance just to establish whose girl I was. Or at least, whose girl I wanted to be.

As soon as I walked up and set down my backpack Colton cried, "Kitten! Get your ass over here!" I glanced down at Lance, who made no attempt to rescue me, and sighed. Getting up and walking around him, I embraced Colton, who had stood up and was waiting for me with open arms.

Feigning excitement, I said, "Hey Colton! Oh my God! When did you get back?" as he squeezed the shit out of me.

"Last week," he said, rocking me from side to side. "My moms got lonely. What can I say? Living without me is hard." He pulled away and gave me a wink. "Isn't it?"

I rolled my eyes in response, but I couldn't help my traitorous smile. He really was cute. And he smelled squeaky clean. Like a girl. Colton had a thing for products—hair products, skin products—he was vain as hell and proud of it.

After giving me the once-over Colton whistled. "Look at you. You're making me wonder why I left in the first place." I blushed and looked at the ground. "You wanna ride the bus home with me this afternoon? Just like old times? My mom just stocked the fridge with PBR..."

Yes. No. Kinda?

Before I could say something stupid, Juliet swooped in and rescued me. "She's riding home with me, Colton. BB is *my* bitch now."

Juliet set her tray down across from my backpack and glared at Colton. She never liked him. For starters, I kind of forgot she existed after he and I started dating. I just started riding the bus home with him every day instead of her—a dick move, I know, but I was fourteen and he was my first real boyfriend. I'm pretty sure "first real boyfriend" would be accepted as just cause for a temporary insanity plea in a court of law. But Juliet also hated him because I kind of blabbed to her about how hard he'd been pressuring me to do *stuff* with him. I would have given in too, if he hadn't told me he was moving. I was *not* giving it up to somebody who was just going to leave in a few weeks. Besides, I was saving myself for Lance Hightower.

Colton glared back at her for a minute, then smiled and asked, "Can I watch?"

We all laughed, even Lance, who was watching the show with piqued interest. When I sat back down next to him (and away from the pheromone cloud that was Colton Hart) I let out a shaky breath and stared straight ahead at Juliet, thanking her silently. Lance, who had resumed his conversation with Colton, reached under the table and gave my thigh a reassuring squeeze. He left his hand there, and I prayed to every deity I'd ever learned the names of, that he would slide it up a little farther. He didn't, but he did absentmindedly lace his fingers through the holes in my fishnets as he spoke, causing me to stop breathing long enough to almost actually fucking die.

My mind was sufficiently scrambled when August, whom I hadn't even noticed, spoke to me from the spot next to Juliet.

I had been friends with August Embry since I was six, when we wound up in the same first-grade class. Back then he was a shy, pudgy little thing with no friends, and I was a bossy, talkative little thing with no friends, so we just clicked. I loved him like a brother.

August was still a shy, round little thing. He hid his warm, chocolate brown eyes behind a curtain of dyed black hair, and every night he painted his fingernails black to match. Of course, every day he would pick them clean again—leaving little black flecks behind, like a trail of breadcrumbs everywhere he went. August was the sweetest, most sensitive person I'd ever met.

I could tell from his body language that August wasn't exactly happy to see Colton, either. He and Lance had become kind of close since Colton left. They both liked the same terrible music and competed over who had the best, rarest punk records in their collections, so Lance getting his best friend back didn't bode well for August.

"Hey, A!" I cheered, trying way too hard to sound like a girl who *didn't* have a boy's fingers stroking her inner thigh at that exact moment. "I didn't know you had this lunch period too! Are you growing your hair out? I love it!" August just smiled and looked down at the food on his tray, which he suddenly decided needed rearranging.

I turned to ask Juliet if I could ride home with her and Tony, but she was gone. Her stuff was still on the table though, and I thought I could hear the sound of her voice. As much as it killed me, I moved Lance's hand so that I could peek under the table. There she was, sitting cross-legged on the floor talking on her cell phone, which was strictly forbidden at school. There was only one person she could possibly be talking to.

"Juliet," I whispered.

She looked up, annoyed. "What?"

"Ask Tony if he minds giving me a ride this afternoon."

She winked at me and whispered into her brick-sized Nokia, "Hey. BB's gonna ride home with us this afternoon, okay?" She gave me a thumbs-up after hearing his response.

Cool.

Just then, I felt Lance's hand press down on the back of my head and saw his crotch rise up to meet the side of my face. I screamed and tried to sit up, causing my head to smash Lance's hand into the underside of the table. Laughter erupted from the cafeteria as I emerged, red-faced, looking like a girl who'd just eaten a punk rocker's cock for lunch.

I glared at Lance, trying my best to look angry, but his eyes were shut and he was laughing so hard he wasn't even making noise. Just the sight of that giant, Mohawked motherfucker smiling ear to ear had me reduced to a puddle of swoon juice in an instant. I burst out laughing right along with him, and anxiously glanced over at Colton.

He was laughing too, but his smile didn't quite reach his eyes. Guess he didn't appreciate the entire lunchroom thinking *his* girlfriend was giving his best friend a BJ under the table.

In that moment, I knew that Colton wasn't going to be a problem. Lance had just established, with dramatic flair and in front of everyone, that I was his girl.

All the hope and hormones had my insides on the verge of spontaneous combustion, so I barely noticed the loud *slam* that came from somewhere behind me. I hardly felt the resulting shudder that rippled down the length of the lunch table. And I didn't turn to look for the source until the faces of all my friends fell and glanced anxiously over my shoulder. Swiveling around on my stool, I followed everyone's gaze to an empty seat at the end of the table.

Um, anyway. Where was I? Oh, right. Planning my spring wedding…

⸻

That afternoon I fought against the current of teenagers fleeing the building, dragging my swollen backpack behind me by one strap, in search of my new locker. According to my homeroom teacher, my old one had to be torn out over the summer to make room for the new science lab. She had given me a little slip of paper with my new locker number and combination on it, saying only that it was "somewhere over on C Hall." I couldn't wait to find that shit so that I could finally offload a few of the ten-pound textbooks I'd been given that day.

Clutching the piece of paper with my new digits on it, I scanned dozens of identical metal doors until I found the one I'd been assigned. It was almost at the end of the hallway, of course, near the exit doors that led out to the student parking lot. I felt relief wash over me immediately.

My first day of tenth grade was a wrap, and overall it had been a smashing success. I'd smoked with the coolest of the cool kids; wound up with the same lunch period as Lance, Juliet, and August; got a bunch of compliments on my fishnets and new haircut; and now I had a new locker on the same hall as all the seniors. Okay, so maybe it took me a few attempts to get my code to work, but once that shit was open it was glorious.

As I bent over to take the last load of books out of my straining backpack, I stopped short, paralyzed by the sight of two black steel-toed boots with blood-red laces planted just inches away from my face...and pointing directly at me.

Fuck.

Fuck, fuck, fuck.

Not him. Anyone but him.

I took my time gathering my stuff, hoping that ignoring him would make him magically disappear. When I finally stood up, arms full of books, I mustered all the courage I had and looked him in the eye.

Zombie eyes. God, his irises were such a pale, pale gray-blue that his pupils looked like two endless black holes in contrast. Two black holes that were sucking me in.

Speak, dumbass!

"Um, hey," I said in a voice that didn't sound like it belonged to me.

He didn't reply. He simply cocked his head to the side and studied me with those cold, dead eyes. It was the same way he looked at the kid in the parking lot, right before he smashed his face into the ground.

Swallowing hard, I forced myself to break the silence.

"I'm sorry, do you need something?" I squeaked out, trying to sound cute and tiny. I blinked and opened my eyes a little wider, feeling like a woodland creature in danger of being squished by a massive black boot.

"Your shit is in front of my locker," he said. His voice was deep and clear and humorless.

"Oh my God! I'm so sorry!" Tripping over myself, I slid my lightened backpack behind me with my foot. The skinhead immediately grasped the metal latch on the locker beside mine and gave the lower left corner of the door a swift kick, causing the fucker to pop right open, no code necessary. I shuddered involuntarily as my mind conjured images of that same boot landing square in the back of a scared little skater boy just a few hours earlier.

Afraid that he could smell my fear, I quickly hid my face behind the metal door of my own locker, busying myself by arranging my books and notebooks by size, color, the Dewey fucking decimal system, *anything*. Then something occurred to me. Before I knew it, my stupid mouth was moving.

"Shouldn't you be suspended?"

I felt my face blush crimson as the blond with the buzzcut slammed his locker shut and asked, point blank, "Why?"

Was he teasing me? We both knew what the fuck he did.

"That, that fight. Today. In the church parking lot," I said, into my locker.

Thinking about that…*attack* had my blood pumping into my extremities and my mind screaming for me to run. I turned and went back to my organizing, hoping to conceal the terror and embarrassment that I'm sure my big, dumb doe eyes were doing a shit job of concealing. My face always snitched on me, broadcasting my every thought. My every feeling.

My thin metal makeshift shield vibrated as he spoke. "I didn't get suspended for the same reason you're not sitting in detention right now for smoking. That shit happened off-campus."

"Is he okay?"

God! My fucking mouth! Filter, BB. Filter!

"Who? That little pussy wipe from the parking lot? He'll be pissing blood for a week, but he'll live."

Slowly, the door I had been cowering behind began to close. Moving out of the way so that the metal wouldn't graze my face,

I reluctantly turned toward the boy with the cadaverous eyes, who was deliberately pushing my locker shut. Once the door was firmly closed and I had nowhere left to hide, Zombie Eyes leaned toward me and reached around my body with his left hand. I squeezed my eyelids shut and braced myself for something violent and potentially bloody to happen.

With his voice lowered so that only I could hear, he said, "If you hit a fucker in the kidney hard enough…right here…" I suddenly felt a thick finger jam directly into one side of my lower back. "He'll piss blood."

My eyes shot open, and I immediately wished that they hadn't. That gray-blue gaze was way too close, too intense. His finger lingered way too long, and there was a crackle in the air that had my senses on high alert.

Danger! Danger! Skinhead Boy is fucking touching you! He could kill you with that finger, BB! Kill you and eat your brains!

But those zombie eyes wouldn't let me move. Up close they were so clear. Like two crystal balls that I wished would give me a glimpse into this twisted creature's soul. In my curious state of hypnosis, again, words tumbled unbidden from my mouth.

"Why'd you hit him?"

After a pause long enough to let me hope that maybe I hadn't actually asked my question out loud, he answered, "Because he called your little boyfriend a faggot."

About three million follow-up questions slammed into my throat at once:

A) Why would a Neo-Nazi–looking motherfucker beat someone up that he doesn't even know for calling some other dude he doesn't know a faggot?

B) Shouldn't he have given the kid a high five instead?

C) Why would he call Lance my boyfriend? Lance is NOT my boyfriend. I mean, I want him to be my boyfriend. Jesus, I want to ride him like a pony everywhere I go and have all of his babies, but he's not my boyfriend.

D) Why would anyone think Lance was gay in the first place? He's sooo dreamy.

But the only thing I could squeak out was, "You were defending Lance?"

I never knew an eye roll could be so terrifying. *Shit.* I'd done it. I'd finally pissed him off with all my stupid fucking questions. Why did I always have to talk to the scary ones? My mom still loves to tell people about the time I picked up my Happy Meal and sat down with a group of leather-clad bikers at McDonald's when I was three just so that I could ask the gnarliest-looking one why he had a ponytail. According to her my exact words were, "Only girls are 'apposed to have ponytails."

My curiosity was going to get me straight murdered one day.

The skinhead, who now looked positively murderous himself, removed his hand from my back and placed it on my locker, just above my head. Cocking his head to the side again he watched me, as if mulling over the best way to skin me alive, and of course I just stood there blinking up at him like a fucking dumbass.

Basic bodily functions like speaking, breathing, and running were completely out of my grasp. It was as if I'd been cornered by a coiled rattlesnake. A rattlesnake that just so happened to smell like dryer sheets, cigarettes, and a sweet hint of cologne.

"No," he said. "I was defending *you.*"

Too much. It was too intense. I broke eye contact and took a step backward, landing on the backpack I forgot was behind me and almost losing my balance. Turning around to pick it up, I took a deep breath and tried to regroup before facing him again. When I did, his ghostly eyes were crinkled at the corners and his mouth was tipped up just slightly on one side. *Fucker.* He was actually enjoying watching me squirm.

Smirk still in place, he said, "When I was outside I heard that little shit telling his buddy about the hard-on he had for 'the little redhead in the fishnets.' Couldn't argue with him there, Punk. I think you gave every guy in that parking lot a semi."

My face was suddenly on fire. *Oh, God. I'm blushing! Is this really happening?*

He continued, but his smirk had been replaced by something that made my blood run cold. "When he saw that giant mother-fucker's hands on you, he turned into a pissy little bitch." He spat the last word out through gritted teeth. "Told his buddy you must love taking it up the ass to be wasting your time with that queer."

Gulp. Breathe. What??

"S-so, so you punched him?"

The zombie-eyed skinhead leaned down toward my ear and didn't stop until I could feel his hot, venomous breath on my neck. "I. Beat. His. Fucking. Ass."

My limbs were moving of their own accord. Legs stumbling backward. Hands fumbling with backpack straps. "Um, thanks?" I mumbled, eyes darting everywhere but his. "I, uh, have to go…I'm gonna miss my…Thanks again…"

"Knight," he announced, as I turned and sprinted for the double doors. "Thanks, *Knight.*"

Fuck me.

ACKNOWLEDGMENTS

I suppose I should probably start by thanking my parents for resisting the urge to ship me off to a convent or have me fitted with a chastity belt when I was sixteen. The men I brought home—well, you know, they were pretty spectacular. I don't think Confucius himself could have watched with my parents' level of Zen-like stoicism while his only daughter gave it up to not only the village skinhead, but also a grown-ass man with no car, education, future, or hair covering his tattooed cranium, all before she even got her braces off.

Then again, maybe *they* should be thanking *me* for all the sainthood they've got coming when they die. I mean, by the time I graduated high school, my mom was already guaranteed an eternity spent smoking Bob Marley's ganja and having three-ways with John Lennon and Jimi Hendrix.

So, you're welcome, Mom and Dad.

I'd also like to thank my editor, Jovana Shirley, and literary agent, Flavia Viotti, for making it all the way through this mess without ripping up my contract even once. You two ladies are sharp and thorough, and I apologize for sullying your good names and refined minds with my filthy book.

And to my beta readers and proofreaders, April, Stefani, Lezlie, Ellie McLove, and, of course, Dr. Sara Snow—The fact that you ladies took my project seriously, devoted your time and brilliance to helping make it better, and mustered up enough enthusiasm to make me believe you weren't just bullshitting me means more than you will ever know. I feel like I owe you all baby showers or something.

To Larry Robins, Jay Fragus, and, of course, J. Miles Dale—I still can't believe what you've done for me. Thank you for opening the door to a future I never dared to dream for myself. You guys are my heroes. Netflix, baby!

To Elias George, a copyright attorney Sara met at a party once, who gave me, like, two phone calls' and three emails' worth of free legal advice—You, sir, are a class act. Thank you.

And finally, I want to thank the women who have inspired me. These bitches go forth day after day in a blaze of brilliantly funny, flawed, fierce glory, giving zero fucks about the haters and leaving nothing but stereotypes and expectations in their wake. It is because of them that I found my own voice.

Oprah—For obvious reasons. Your face appears on my vision board at least three times.

Kelly Ripa—You are a true badass. Every time you dye your hair pink or flash a new tattoo or drop an F-bomb on daytime TV, you embolden me to fly my freak flag a little higher. Every time you waltz onstage, looking confident and radiant and sexy as hell, without a dollop of silicone or drop of saline, you remind me that my femininity, my *worth*, is not determined by my cup size. And every time you gush about your beautiful family, you give me hope that maybe we really can have it all.

Lena Dunham—You brilliant, honest, humble, hilarious writer/producer/actor/director/artist/feminist/activist, you. Way to make the rest of us feel like slobbering slack-jawed underachievers. I would say I want to be you when I grow up, but you're fucking younger than me, too. Bitch.

Amy Schumer—Thanks a lot. I *was* going to write an entire book about Sara Snow, call it *Trainwreck*, and get Judd Apatow to turn it into a movie, but you went and beat me to it. It's okay. I forgive you. Let's be best friends.

Which brings me to you, Judd Apatow—Sorry to out you, but you, sir, are a big, fat feminist. You're like a modern-day Gloria Steinem, only hairier and with a Y chromosome. And you're much, much subtler. Every time someone cracks up over Maya Rudolph shitting in the street in a wedding dress or cringes at the sight of Katherine Heigl soberly trying to figure out how sex with Seth Rogen is supposed to work with her massive pregnant belly, they are being taught to see women as *human beings* rather than archetypes. Through your rom-coms and sitcoms, America is subconsciously learning that women can be sexy and gross and intelligent and maternal and successful and hilarious and flawed all at the same time. Don't worry. Your secret agenda is safe with me.

To Colleen Hoover—I feel like I owe you my firstborn. I know you already have three boys, so that's kind of a shitty gift, but he's really cute. He looks like a Mini-Ken and is even quiet and good at math, too. You'll love him. (Almost as much as I love you.)

To Jenny Lawson and Allie Brosh—Thank you for baring your souls and sharing your comedic genius with the world. Your books and blogs are the funniest things ever published. Jenny, I don't even know how many of your jokes I referenced in this book because my brain just vomits up your punch lines whenever I'm searching for something clever to say. Just send me a bill. I'm sure I owe you something beyond just my undying admiration.

To Jay Crownover—Thank you for writing the men who inspired me to write about my own men, for always answering my questions, for greeting me with a genuine smile and an appreciative hug every time I came to one of your events even though you had no idea who I was, and for using your platform to promote other authors. You're the real deal.

To E L James, Olivia Cunning, T.M. Frazier, Abbi Glines, Tillie Cole, Katy Evans, Jamie Shaw, and the countless other romance writers whose books ignited something in me, something feral, something forgotten, that simply would not be denied.

And to my growing social media community of book bloggers, authors, and readers—You ladies are my greatest support system. You are the first ones to wish me a good morning every day and often the last ones to bid me a good night. Considering that most people in my real life don't know this book exists, your enthusiasm, exuberance, and encouragement have meant more to me than you can imagine. To those of you who read my words—Thank you for your time. To those of you who made teasers—Thank you for your talent. To those of you who tagged me on your posts, whether they were dick pics or kittens riding unicorns—Thank you for your friendship. I love you beautiful book whores to the ends of the universe and back.

ABOUT THE AUTHOR

BB Easton lives in the suburbs of Atlanta, Georgia, with her long-suffering husband, Ken, and two adorable children. She recently quit her job as a school psychologist to write books about her punk rock past and deviant sexual history full-time. Ken is suuuper excited about that.

BB's memoir, *Sex/Life: 44 Chapters About 4 Men*, and the spin-off Sex/Life novels are the inspiration for Netflix's steamy, female-centered dramedy series of the same name.

The Rain Trilogy is her first work of fiction. Or at least, that's what she thought when she wrote it in 2019. Then 2020 hit and all of her dystopian plot points started coming true. If you need her, she'll be busy writing a feel-good utopian rom-com to see if that fixes everything.

You can find her procrastinating at all of the following places:

Email: authorbbeaston@gmail.com

Website: www.authorbbeaston.com

Facebook: www.facebook.com/bbeaston

Instagram: www.instagram.com/author.bb.easton

Twitter: www.twitter.com/bb_easton

Pinterest: www.pinterest.com/artbyeaston

Goodreads: https://goo.gl/4hiwiR

BookBub: https://www.bookbub.com/authors/bb-easton

Spotify: https://open.spotify.com/user/bbeaston

Etsy: www.etsy.com/shop/artbyeaston

#TeamBB Facebook group: www.facebook.com/groups/BBEaston

And giving away a free e-book from one of her author friends each month in her newsletter: www.authorbbeaston.com/subscribe